THE ORIGIN

OF

LANGUAGE

THE ORIGIN OF LANGUAGE

A Formal Theory of Representation

ERIC GANS

UNIVERSITY OF CALIFORNIA PRESS
Berkeley, Los Angeles, London

University of California Press
Berkeley and Los Angeles, California

University of California Press, Ltd.
London, England

Library of Congress Cataloging in Publication Data

Gans, Eric Lawrence, 1941–
    The origin of language.

    Bibliography
    1. Language and languages—Origin.
    2. Representation (Philosophy) I. Title.
P116.G36   401   80-19653
ISBN 0-520-04202-6

Printed in the United States of America

1 2 3 4 5 6 7 8 9

For Monique

Richard
Mark
Jean-Pierre
Danielle
Jean-Louis
Gisèle
and
Georges

Contents

Preface

The origin of language, favored topic of the *siècle des lumières*, has in the past decade begun to reemerge from a century and a half of neglect and even of interdiction.[1] To examine the reasons for this fluctuation would be to go beyond the scope of the present work, although not beyond that of the historical reevaluation it suggests. Let it suffice to say that the anthropological naiveté of the *philosophes'* constructions instilled in the minds of linguists and others a skepticism that still casts its shadow over recent discussions of the subject. This would be all for the best, of course, if the rigor of these discussions effected a genuine "sublation" of this not unjustified skepticism. Such has not however been the case. Jacques Derrida's extremely influential *De la grammatologie* (Paris: Minuit, 1967; English translation, Johns Hopkins University Press, 1976) makes this skepticism a sine qua non of philosophical lucidity; past philosophy ("metaphysics") has done nothing but seek to fix a point of origin, an endeavor condemned to endless repetition because the "origin" is "always already" inhabited by the search for itself. At the empirical end of the spectrum, the recent anthropologically oriented speculations on the subject[2] shy away from anything resembling the recreation of a "primal scene." These social scientists, modestly emboldened by recent successes in teaching language to apes, are content to suggest how, over many thousands of years, the present complexities of human language might have evolved in such a manner that the violence of the change involved would have remained invisible to its perpetrators. In this view (linguistic) consciousness emerges from (prelinguistic) unconsciousness at so microscopic a rate that it emerges . . . unconsciously. The paradox that underlies Derrida's agnosticism is blissfully ignored in the precritical context of American (and not only American) social science.

The present work takes this paradox itself as its anthropological foundation; it affirms that violence and origin are one, and indeed that the fear of intellectual violence so characteristic of contemporary social science is one and the same with the motivating force behind the creation of language and of culture in general. We thus find Derrida, whose "deconstruction" of the origin respects its paradoxical unity to the extent that its evenemential nature may be "metaphysically" translated into the structures of signification-in-general, of far more use to our own linguistic anthropology than the linguists and anthropologists themselves. But the chief inspiration for this work is to be found in the writings of a thinker who, although alone in insisting on the violent reality of a human cultural origin, has scarcely a word to say on language.

With the impressive success of his *magnum opus Des choses cachées depuis la foundation du monde* (Grasset, 1978), René Girard is today obtaining in France a recognition that in our eyes has been long overdue.[3] It remains, however, a fact that, particularly in the United States where Girard is known only as a literary critic, appeals to his authority are likely rather to intensify than to allay the skepticism of the reader. In the interest of avoiding misunderstanding, a few words of preparatory explanation are therefore in order.

It may be claimed that because philosophers from time immemorial have formulated hypothetical "scenes" of the birth of language, neither Girard's original hypothesis nor that to be developed here have anything particularly new to offer. This facile generality is simply false. No doubt there have been earlier theories of the origin of language, too numerous even to mention in a work not specifically devoted to the history of the question. But even on superficial examination it will be found that none of these works presents an original "scene" of language—or indeed of any cultural phenomenon—that is both *collective* and *evenemential*.

Writers who describe collective origins either presuppose *prior* deferral of action, that is, of event—this is true of all forms of social contract theories—or depict the establishment of language and/or other institutions as the result of nonspecific evolutionary processes. Conversely, those writers who, like Condillac, or, more ambiguously, Rousseau, actually depict *scenes* of the birth of language, limit themselves to abstractly individual encounters between "men" who are somehow supposed to have previously lived in perfect isolation from one another, or even (like Herder, or, in recent times, Trân Duc Thao) between a lone human and a significant object.

Our hypothesis is alone in being both collective and evenemential. What is the particular importance of this double imperative?

That human culture is a collective phenomenon is not a mere empirical proposition, although it has been the advances of the empirical sciences of ethology and ethnology that have put this proposition beyond the possibility of doubt. By placing the prevention of anarchic "mimetic" violence at the origin of all cultural forms, Girard permits us to define the otherwise amorphous notion of "collectivity" as the group formed from the breakdown, in times of crisis, of instinctual restraints, a breakdown that presupposes the exercise or at least the felt danger of violence—it being clear from ethological studies that animal "rituals," hierarchies, and so on are above all instinctively evolved means of avoiding intraspecific violence. This notion of collectivity, understood in its most radical sense, already implies that the violence of the internal disorder could only be arrested by an originary event: the imposition by the group on itself of a noninstinctive restraint that defers further violence and constitutes thereby the origin of all cultural "deferrals."

For Girard this event is the "arbitrary" designation of an emissary victim to whom is attributed a posteriori the "blame" for the original crisis. We have here accepted the substance of Girard's hypothesis, but not as complete in itself. Girard's event ends with the collectivity, in the first moment of "non-instinctual attention," silently contemplating their victim, marveling at the peace the murder has brought about, and storing up the memory of the process so as to repeat it more readily in the event of future "mimetic crises." In the alternative version of the hypothesis presented here, the collective murder—which could indeed be replaced by the hunting of an animal, for our theory requires no prior crisis—is only the prelude to the originary event that is the *designation* of the victim by an abortive gesture of appropriation, an appropriatory movement toward the body checked in each individual by his fear of the potential violence of the others.

We need not elaborate further here on a subject that will be dealt with extensively in the text. It is, however, necessary to insist that the differences between our "formal" hypothesis and the "institutional" one of Girard (the terms are ours, not his) are less by a full degree of magnitude than those that separate both hypotheses from those either of the Enlightenment or of contemporary (linguistic) anthropology, none of which embody the necessity that the "presence" all cultures posit at their beginning be derived from an originary communal event—albeit one that is "always already" inhabited by absence. Our hypothesis is alone in providing a *functional* setting for the paradox of presence that Derrida has elucidated in the text of Western philosophy.

The reader should note that the title of this work is circular: The origin of language is "at the same time" the language of the origin, a language that both belongs to it and designates it as what language can only express the desire to return to. The circularity of language as elaborated here is by no means that of the Hegelian spirit nor indeed that of "Western metaphysics" in general. Posited at the outset it constitutes an anthropological rather than a philosophical point of departure. The justification for such a beginning is not that the origin of language is a "merely" anthropological question, but rather that only by grounding the formalism of language—and by extension, all other formalisms—in a hypothesis of reference, however inadequately formulated, can the relevancy of language and its origin to our own experience be maintained. We thus do not need to quarrel with the metaphysicians' assumption that language exists only to justify itself; for between language and itself, the world of *significant* human experience, in all the ambiguity of the term, has from the beginning been inserted.

E. G.
Los Angeles
January 1980

Mysteries should not be multiplied beyond necessity. Thus although the entities of nature may not be knowable directly, but only phenomenologically, it is hardly acceptable for us to content ourselves with this same attitude toward the products of our minds. Referents may remain mysteries, but surely not our representations of them. Thus no theory should be more lucid than the theory of representation. If this is not indeed the case, the source of the difficulty may be sought in two directions. Either the representation cannot be sufficiently separated from its referent, or the meta-representation of theory cannot sufficiently separate itself from the representations to which it refers. A moment's reflection shows that the two cases are identical. But on further reflection one wonders how such problems could arise at all were "representation" indeed a self-substantial category. If signs and their referents were independent entities, then surely no difficulties would arise in creating meta-signs to represent the former. But if they are not independent, then one may indeed wonder how thought itself is possible. That representation is something of a mystery is itself the greatest mystery.

To begin to talk about any subject we have recourse to language, with the faith that in thus representing the subject we will become able to grasp it, operate on it through the intermediary of signs with which we are already familiar. That the process of understanding does not merely consist in the reduction of worldly objects to manipulable symbols is apparent from its application to language itself. Nor is this

1

latter case merely a matter of finding patterns—syntactic, phonetic, morphological—in our normally non-reflective use of these symbols. This last is the subject matter of grammar and of linguistics as it has traditionally been conceived. But now we are referring not to the question of patterns, but to that of representation itself, and of language in its most general terms as an example of a system of representation. Understanding language then means being able to talk about, that is, to represent, the act of representation itself.

Now it is my contention that this cannot be done fruitfully from within the confines of a *pure* theory of representation, which would take as its exclusive object representations themselves. For such a pure theory, in the sense of a set of meta-representations, could contain no meaningful epistemology. That is to say, it could say nothing of the relationship between signs and their referents because the only example of this relationship it could discuss would be that which it has itself established with its own object-representations; and the very possibility of this establishment, that is, of the theory's existing at all, could only depend on the prior existence of such a relationship between first-order representations and their own (nonlinguistic) objects. The theory's own possibility of doubling its representational object requires a representation-object distinction not merely as an internal postulate but as a "transcendental" given from without. Failing this, the distinction, if posited a priori, could be developed logically (without taking into account the paradoxes involved) but not genetically, because it would appear as an irrational element. Logic can no doubt do without the genetic, at the sacrifice of the ontological. But in any case the alternative is between logic and a genetic epistemological-ontological theory of representation.

Before abandoning the subject of logic we might do well to remark on the peculiarity of the notion of representation that is there employed. The destiny of logic is to express itself entirely in metalanguage, because it considers concepts only in relation to other concepts and not to empirical referents. It thus tends to merge with mathematics. The notion of representation (which alone distinguishes logic from mathematics) remains only residually. In an equation a letter "stands for" a constant or variable as a mere locus within a structure; in logic the elements represent in any case assertions about an object-world the truth or falsity of which stands outside logic. The logical definition of truth (due to Tarski) as the correspondence between a proposition and the "state of affairs" in an undefined object-universe makes explicit the incompatibility between ontological rigor and the purely combinatorial necessities of logic. On the one hand, the definition ' "P" is true'≡'P is the case' can only have meaning if "P is the case" refers to an object-world ontologically prior to that of the propositions themselves. On the other hand, no formalization of the (representative) relationship between the words of "P" and their referents is possible, or even conceivable—because the very point of the definition is to presuppose the "adequacy" of this relationship. The object-world where things "are the case" thus acts as a *transcendental signified* (*signifié transcendantal*) for the system of representations, which can then be in their turn referred to by a metalanguage. As we shall see, the existence of a transcendental signified is not a defining characteristic of logics. The distinction to be made is rather that whereas logics merely posit such a signified, ontological thought defines its manner of subsistence as being prior to its representation, and epistemology studies its manner of appearance either as or prior to representation.

All such approaches are by nature genetic, although not necessarily in the strong, historical sense. But the inadequacy of any nonhistorical ontology can be demonstrated from the nature of the representation-relationship itself. The temporal coexistence in the world of representations and their objects is not only in general a prerequisite for the use of language, but in particular a sine qua non of the appearance of theories of language. The historical birth of the theory alongside its object is inconceivable other than as a repetition of the birth of the representations themselves alongside their objects. Whatever the differences between our "free" elaboration of scientific metalanguages and the creation of the first signifiers, if the latter was not a historical event then the former remains a mystery: How can we create new signs, or even new meanings for old ones, unless the old ones, too, were created in the course of "human events," by which we mean history as it not merely is but also as it appears to its participants.

Every theory of representation has need of a transcendental signified by which it posits an object for the representations it purports to study. This is because reference to an ontologically prior other is inherent in representation not merely in, but for, itself, as the word indeed implies. Now the only scientific, that is, potentially verifiable form in which such a signified can be postulated, is as a *hypothesis* concerning the historical origin of representation itself. Because representation as such (as we will shortly define it) is essentially a human phenomenon, this hypothesis will be of an anthropological nature. Before presenting it, however, some methodological discussion is appropriate.

The Transcendental Hypothesis

We owe to René Girard the insight that only the construction of what I shall here call a "transcendental hypothesis" can provide a meaningful ontology—which is at the same time a meaningful epistemology—for the social sciences.[1] The revolutionary methodological implications of this insight have only just begun to be developed by Girard himself. The social or "human" sciences have the peculiarity of dealing with material that is of the same representational form as the discourse of the sciences themselves. Here we are of course simplifying the domain of the social sciences in what may appear to be a radical manner; such phenomena as political institutions, systems of exchange, or even works of art, architecture, and so on are not ostensibly equivalent to "discourses." But all such phenomena are essentially systems of representations. To the extent that the representational element may be neglected, as in certain areas of economics, geography, phonology (and even in the linguistic study of syntax which confines itself to the generation of syntactic structures from more elementary structures the genesis of which is not considered), the traditional empirical methods remain operative, although, as we shall see, at the cost of cutting off these phenomena from their roots in human representa-

tion—a serious matter in linguistics, although of less consequence in phonology than in syntactics. But the most
remarkable feature of the social sciences up to the present
has been their neglect, not to say their deliberate ignorance,
of the epistemological problems posed by the representational nature of their subject matter. The choice of an empirical methodology, more effective in some areas than others,
was not made *en connaissance de cause* but rather in emulation of the natural sciences. "Laws" of human behavior were
sought that would rival the Newtonian system in objectivity.
The enormous impetus toward genetic studies of culture
given by Darwin's *Origin of Species* led to the widespread
adoption of evolutionary models in ethnology and general
anthropology which, although suitable for the gathering of
significant data, were inferior to Hegel's metaphysical schemata as means for investigating the intentional, self-reflective
specificity of cultural phenomena. Metaphysics with its presupposition of the equivalence between cognition and desire
and consequent restriction of epistemology to the elaboration of the (individual) subject-object relation was replaced
by appetitive schemata of desire oriented to irrationally
privileged objects rather than by genuinely intersubjective
models. The ultimate source of the epistemological weakness
of the human sciences over the past century has been their
reluctance to come to grips with the question, falsely rejected
as metaphysical, of the ontology of representation.

But if it be recognized that the social sciences are in
essence theories of representation which, being themselves
representations, can invoke no essential epistemological
superiority to their subject matter, then it becomes clear that
it is necessary to posit an ultimate guarantee of the correspondence between representations and the reality they purport to represent. Philosophy has always done this through
what we have called the "metaphysical" affirmation of the
unity of the mind and its objects. This unity, whether
immediate or mediated immanently or transcendentally, is
evidently incompatible with scientific discourse, because it is
not subject to verification within the realm of the discourse
itself. A *scientific* theory of representation can only posit the
unity of "mind" and "matter," or more precisely, of repre-

sentations and reality, as a verifiable *hypothesis* concerning the historical origin of representation. Only on the basis of such a hypothesis can the theory claim any right truly to represent anthropological reality. The hypothesis as such must remain in a transcendental relation with the body of the theory, because its verification can never become an established fact, but only a heuristic probability. Its role is that of a transcendental signified to which the representations studied are made to refer through more or less complex sets of mediations. The theory can then be shown to itself refer back to the hypothetical origin, to constitute, in other words, merely the latest and presumably the most truthful of the representations that fall under its purview. But then the earlier representations are seen to have not merely the same (ultimate) object but the same (ultimate) goal as the theory itself.

It might be objected that even if a transcendental element of some sort be necessary, it need not take the form we have given it. But if we refer all representations ultimately to some event other than a historical origin, then the origin of representation becomes a reference to this event, and the theory of representation is obliged to furnish an explanation of this reference. By an "explanation" we mean the constitution of a (hypothetical) model of the passage from the event itself to the first representation of it. Then either this latter followed immediately on the presence of the former, or a delay occurred during which this presence was preserved by means other than representation (e.g., visual memory). In either case we note that the preservation of the presence of the event is continuous with the first representation of it, so that no generality is lost in considering such an event as the historical origin of representation; if the delay (or more precisely, deferral, *différance* [Derrida]) be taken as a significant element, it becomes a part of the total model, with its counterpart in the temporality of representation in general. It thus becomes clear that the necessity of a transcendental hypothesis is independent of empirical considerations, although not of course of the empirical nature of the data that concern us. For the reference to a historical origin of representation is at the same time a point of departure for the theory and for its object, which *both* have as their goal the "explanation" of this origin. Or in other words, the object of the hypothesis is identical to that of the original representation. This does not imply a vicious circle in which the first representation would appear to be the representation of itself; on the contrary, it precludes it. To speak of a *historical* origin of representation is to conceive the event of the first representation as encompassing at the same time the object, or as Girard's hypothesis makes plausible, the event represented, so that the intention to represent had an object necessarily other than itself. This dichotomic nature of the (hypothetical) origin must of course be reproduced in the theory itself, which as we shall see leads to constructions of no small complexity. But the unitary nature of the origin of representation can only be hypothesized in this manner, and this is an inescapable problem of any theory. The methodological insight of Girard is nevertheless fundamentally a simplifying one because it provides a heuristic temporal model to which all combinatorial problems can be referred. The real complexities of human institutions can thus be reduced and ultimately rendered accessible in this method, whereas empirical "techniques" merely simplify such complexities by limiting the nature of the acceptable data.

The other chief objection to this method will come from those who, relatively indifferent to heuristic values or to "results," will reject the necessity of a transcendental hypothesis on the basis of its exteriority to thought itself, which by the fact of recognizing its own limits reveals the futility of any attempt to go beyond them. In this view the end of representation is silence, which is the only alternative to metaphysics. But this nihilistic epistemology fails to acknowledge that the unity of human institutions, and consequently of the social sciences, comes from their participation in representations of transcendental objects, and that both the sudden discovery of the nonimmanence of these objects and the consequent pessimism are only secondary phenomena. It should become clear from our discussion that the entire conceptual vocabulary of "postmetaphysical" philosophy from Nietzsche to Derrida can be given concrete historical meaning within the context of a transcendental hypothesis. It will then appear that the specificity of this vocabulary may be defined by its reference to the central problematic of representation, which earlier metaphysics had maintained separate from the historical, but which must henceforth be dealt with as a historical reality.

The Nature of the Hypothesis

Those who are familiar with Girard's statement of his hypothesis may be surprised that no reference has yet been made to the sacred, which is its explicit object. The question might indeed be raised whether this does not constitute the very reduction of the sacred to the (merely) representational against which Girard reacted in formulating his hypothesis. For the empiricism of the social sciences is particularly characterized by the inadequacy of its theory of the sacred. Durkheim was willing to accept the primacy of the sacred/ profane opposition over other semantic categories, but lacking any adequate theory of its origins he had no means of constructing a general theory of representation that could attempt to justify its own existence.[2] On the contrary, the intuition of the essential nature of this distinction even for the understanding of modern social institutions was coupled with a sense that the mission of the social sciences was to release if not man in general then at the very least the scientists themselves from any dependence on such a distinction. For even the radicalism of situating the sacred/profane opposition at the origin of human representation is insufficient, because it presupposes at the moment of origin a dichotomous structure independent of its contents. The first content may then indeed be constituted as the sacred, but a more "rational" choice of content would have no effect on the form itself. Girard's radicalism goes beyond such content-form distinctions. For him the sacred is not merely the first object of representation, the "marked" term in an original, constitutive opposition; it is the origin of the very form of representation, and of all cultural forms. How then can we discuss his hypothesis as an origin of representation without prior reference to the sacred?

The answer to this question can only emerge from the notion of the sacred itself. Now it is significant that although

Girard *determines* the sacred, he never defines it but accepts it as an a priori. We hesitate to qualify this attitude as empirical because the sacred is not merely explained phenomenologically but constituted (hypothetically) from its elements. The very crux of the hypothesis appears to be precisely this: The sacred is an irreducible primitive category, and any attempt to subordinate it to that of representation-in-general will make it impossible to explain the genesis of the latter in other than metaphysical terms. The question then arises whether a still more radical view cannot be maintained: that because in their origin the sacred and the representable were one and the same, the two categories may be treated as essentially identical. This means that the *original* category of the sacred is simply the significant as such, so the sacred/profane opposition can only be thought of as the result of a posterior reflection in which the nonsignificant becomes representable, but in an inferior or mediate mode.

Now by the choice of the word "representation" rather than "sacred" as our primitive category we imply that this "secondary" mode is really fundamental; that is, we *criticize* the original conception of the significant-as-sacred by revealing the arbitrary nature of the primitive choice of the object of representation. But this critique is precisely that performed by the hypothesis itself in proposing an immanent or "worldly" event as the original transcendental signified. In other words, the very existence of the hypothesis, by de-sacralizing the sacred, in effect reduces the latter not to a form but to a *name* of representation—to representation's original reflection on itself: hence the essentially atheistic nature of Girard's theory of the sacred.[3]

We have dealt elsewhere with the significance of the centrality of the sacred in Girard's own conceptual universe, a matter that is not germane to the present discussion.[4] The implications of the primacy of representation will be developed in the course of our own exposition. It should suffice at this point to note that this approach leads to an "open" or progressive view of the history of representations as opposed to the "closed," apocalyptic vision of Girard which is implicit in his fidelity to the category of the sacred. Thus a theory of representation, unlike a theory of the sacred, can serve as a foundation not only of an anthropology but of a *sociology*, by which we mean the study of the historical evolution of the society within which the theory itself has been elaborated. This is not to deny the sociological insights permitted by the anthropology of the sacred. But if this latter remains the primitive category, any development of "profane" representations being necessarily referred to it, then the evolution of these representations can only be understood as a movement away from their essence, subject only to the apocalyptic return of the sacred from without. In such a perspective sociology can only be a temporary mask worn by anthropology, and the discovery of the necessity of a transcendental hypothesis cannot be distinguished in its essence from the revelation of a transcendental truth (hypostasis). In contrast, an anthropology of representation naturally evolves its own sociology and ultimately its own auto-justification. The advantages as well as the pitfalls of this approach will become evident from the subsequent discussion.

The Origin of (Sacred) Representation

It is necessary at this point to outline briefly the transcendental hypothesis of Girard as a prelude to further discussion. For it must never be forgotten that even if the necessity for such a hypothesis can be deduced a priori, the hypothesis itself must be concrete, that is, an extrapolation from available data (i.e., representations) subject to heuristic verification by means of these data. If a concrete hypothesis could not be formulated, the "deduction" would indeed be empty because our argument was merely that the social sciences can only be founded on such a hypothesis, lacking which they would presumably continue to emulate the (inappropriate) model of the natural sciences. We should further remark that the concreteness of the hypothesis must be both historical and structural (diachronic and synchronic); that is, it must refer to an *event* or series of events, not necessarily unique, but able to be situated at least in principle in historic time, and at the same time to a causal mechanism capable of producing such an event. By "event" we mean an occurrence perceptible as such to its participants. An event can thus only exist if it becomes *present*, and as we shall shortly see, the notion of presence itself implies the existence of representation. This apparent circularity is not however a contradiction, but rather a confirmation of the (as yet undefined) hypothesis: The existence and the representation/perpetuation of the event being one, the event represented is at the same time the birth of representation. In contrast, a nonevenemential hypothesis that would posit the historical origin of representation as an essentially continuous process would have no way of defining the object from which the first representation had presumably separated itself. (Epistemologically this *aporia* would be equivalent to that posed by the "emergence" of the theory itself from among the representations it would take as its object.)

Girard's hypothesis may be outlined as follows:

1. *Emergence of a quantitative difference.* All higher animals have a tendency to imitate the gestures of their own (and sometimes other) species. Early man, as a result of various factors, acquired greater gifts for and inclination toward such imitation than any other species.[5]

2. *Transcendence of nonsignificant ("animal") mechanisms for maintaining the collectivity.* The imitation of appropriative behavior leads to potential rivalry among members of the same group, which among animals is controlled by the mechanism of stable dominance relationships. This mechanism functions in the absence of any "event," i.e., of any occasion in which the entire group is present to itself, through dual relations of dominance and submission. Beyond a certain threshold of mimetism (Girard uses the term "*puissance mimétique*") this mechanism can no longer function: Disagreements over specific objects lead to mimetic conflict between rivals in which the object is forgotten and which spreads beyond the dual relation to contaminate the other members of the group.

3. *The event: Choice of an "emissary" victim.* The crisis produced by mimetic rivalry will tend to polarize the violence of the group as a whole against an individual arbitrarily designated as the cause of the crisis. The victim will presumably be a marginal figure—diseased, crippled, of strange appearance or origin—apt to arouse the suspicions of the group. With the collective murder of this victim the group

discharges its aggression and at the same time creates the conditions for the coincidental emergence of the sacred and of representation.

4. *The victim's body as the first signifier of the sacred*. The discharge of aggressive energy, the sudden passage from paroxystic violence to quietude, leaves the murdered victim the object of the "first non-instinctive attention" of the group as a whole.[6] Because the victim appears to the group as both the cause of the crisis and the source of its resolution, he signifies to the community the totality of the process, and thereby the significant-in-general. His sacredness consists precisely in this transcendental signification.

5. *The reproduction of the sign*. Because the appearance and murder of the victim not only resolve a specific crisis but produce a communal peace not otherwise accessible, the group will tend to reproduce the original event by the murder of new victims now designated in advance. Thus ritual sacrifice arises as a re-presentation of the original event. It is in this context as well that Girard situates his brief remarks on the origin of language, which he sees as emerging from ritual reproduction of the cries accompanying the crisis and murder.

The nature of the "original" event, as is already clear from this outline and as Girard takes pains to insist upon in his discussion of "hominization," is that it should not be considered as unique, but as subject to *cumulative* repetition. Within the same community a second "emissary" murder need not be considered as an explicit representation of the first, but as a reproduction of the same mechanism provoked by similar critical circumstances. It suffices that such reproductions leave what we might call a "sediment" of representation, that their degree of reference to earlier events be in Girard's words *"faiblement cumulatif."* This in no way contradicts our earlier a priori assertion of the necessarily evenemential nature of the hypothesis: The origin of representation involves necessarily an original presence of the community to itself, even if the reproduction of this presence evolves only gradually into explicitly representational forms (e.g., language or even ritual). This is not to say that these hypothesized events are historical in the sense that they can be distinguished or even enumerated. But the category of the historical in the sense of the representable—and at the origin, the sacred—can only emerge in this manner.

The "sediment," the representative accumulation, however "feeble," already distinguishes these events qua events from all previous temporal experiences. But although the techniques of reproduction of the event develop only slowly, its status as an event is from the beginning absolute. The particular "attention" involved in the community's mediated presence to itself—before which it would have been impossible to speak of a community—does not "evolve" from the background of generalized violence which the Hobbesian imagination of some ethologists seems to see as the original human condition. Generalized violence can only be experienced as crisis—a crisis practically unknown to the animal world—and the sudden end of this crisis, as an event, the reproduction of which in ensuing crises could not be other than a sedimentary form of representation because this reproduction involves at the very least the renewal of the presence of the community to itself. In the event that this presence has been utterly forgotten, it would have to be rediscovered; but in this case we could simply say that the *event* of this presence never occurred, that we too can afford to forget it. For it is not our burden to demonstrate that culture exists, but merely to explain it, which means in this case to reconstruct the sedimentary layers that must lie at the base of the observed forms of representation.[7]

Commentary on the Hypothesis

The present commentary can make no attempt to deal with the mythographical and ethnological evidence on which the hypothesis is grounded nor with its explicative merits in the various specific areas of social science (which we have already defined as the study of human representations). We will only draw a few preliminary conclusions relevant to the notion of representation-in-general.

The most surprising aspect of the hypothesis is what we might call its "anesthetic" character: However convincing the linkage of the specific ideas, however persuasive the applications, there is felt to be a disparity between the totality of culture, religion, representation on the one side and violence on the other. The question then arises as to how this disparity is dealt with by the theory itself. It is in the first place an intuitive reflection of the necessarily concrete nature of the hypothesis. The latter is antiintuitive for the simple reason that it is concrete and evenemential: No *historical* event can appear intuitively as the origin of representation. For the hypothesis is, as we have seen, a transcendental signified, and although the scientific form taken by the latter is certainly not the product of a refusal of representation, it does presuppose rejection of the sacralization of its object, the original process of which it cannot describe without rendering it anesthetic to the reader. But more fundamentally, the violence that the theory evokes at the origin is simply identical with that which it provokes at the moment of its publication. This equivalency is of course present in exemplary fashion in the evangelical model so central to Girard's own epistemology. The "scandalous" nature of the hypothesis is part and parcel of the de-sacralization it performs; its polemical de-mystification of previous theories demonstrates that representation has always done violence to its object, at the same time as its potential for self-reflection is derived from the merely metaphorical nature of the violence exercised within it. Ultimately, we do not deal with signs because they are more convenient than their referents, nor even because their reproducibility prevents conflict, but because they reproduce mimetic conflict in a domain of diminished violence. Thus the first object of representiation is precisely the passage from the greatest possible violence to total nonviolence. But this "object" is not in fact a well-defined entity for which a sign has been found ex post facto, but a totality of signification attributed to the original sign which is, according to the hypothesis, the body of the first victim. This is the crucial point of the hypothesis as a theory of representation and it therefore merits our particular attention.

Let us examine Girard's own discussion of this point:

Grâce à la victime, en tant qu'elle paraît sortir de la communauté et que la communauté paraît sortir d'elle, il peut exister, pour la première fois, quelque chose comme un dedans et un dehors, un avant et un après, une communauté et un sacré. Nous avons déjà dit que cette victime se présente à la fois comme mauvaise et bonne, pacifique et violente, vie qui fait mourir et mort qui assure la vie. *Il n'y a pas de signification qui ne s'ébauche avec elle et qui ne paraisse en même temps transcendée par elle. Elle paraît bien se constituer en signifiant universel* [emphasis added].

Jean-Michel Oughourlian: N'est-ce pas là l'idée d'un signifiant transcendantal, qui est énergiquement repoussée par toute la pensée actuelle?

Girard: Je ne dis pas que nous avons trouvé le *vrai* signifiant transcendantal. Nous n'avons trouvé encore que ce qui sert aux hommes de signifiant transcendantal.

J.-M.O.: Vous parlez de signifiant transcendantal, ne faudrait-il pas plutôt parler de signifié?

R.G.: Le signifiant, c'est la victime. Le signifié, c'est tout le sens actuel et potentiel que la communauté confère à cette victime et, par son intermédiaire, à toutes choses.

Le signe, c'est la victime réconciliatrice. Parce que nous comprenons sans peine que les hommes veuillent rester réconciliés, au sortir de la crise, nous comprenons aussi que les hommes s'attachent à reproduire le signe; c'est-à-dire à pratiquer le langage du sacré, en substituant à la victime originaire, dans les rites, des victimes nouvelles pour assurer le maintien de cette paix miraculeuse. L'impératif rituel, donc, ne fait qu'un avec la manipulation et, constamment, s'offrent alors de nouvelles possibilités de différenciation et d'enrichissement culturel.[8]

[Thanks to the victim, to the extent that it appears to emerge from the community and that the community appears to emerge from it, there can exist for the first time something like an inside and an outside, a before and an after, a community and a sacred. We have already said that this victim presents itself as all at once bad and good, peaceful and violent, life that kills and death that guarantees life. *There is no meaning that is not inchoate in the victim and which at the same time does not appear to be transcended by it. It appears truly to constitute itself as a universal signifier* [emphasis added].

J.-M. Oughourlian: Isn't that the idea of a transcendental signifier that is energetically rejected by all contemporary thought?

Girard: I don't say we have found the *true* transcendental signifier. We have only found so far what serves men as a transcendental signifier.

J.-M.O: You speak of a transcendental signifier, shouldn't we rather speak of a signified?

R.G.: The signifier, that is the victim. The signified is all of the real and potential meaning that the community confers on that victim, and through its mediation, on all things.

The sign is the reconciling victim. Because we understand without difficulty that men wish to remain reconciled once the crisis is over, we can also understand that they desire to reproduce the sign; that is, to employ the language of the sacred, substituting for the original victim in ritual, new victims in order to insure the maintenance of this miraculous peace. The ritual imperative thus is one with the manipulation of the signs, with their multiplication, and thus new possibilities of differentiation and cultural enrichment constantly present themselves.]

We see from this passage that the victim, insofar as he is the first object of the attention of the community, becomes the signifier of the entire process of crisis and resolution. Girard is careful to insist that it is not the signified but the *signifier* that is transcendental. Indeed the Saussurian dichotomy, inexplicable on its own terms and thus paradigmatic of "structuralist" oppositions in general, is powerless to explain the origin of signification, which rather explains *it*. The victim-sign does not so much signify as be *significant*—a word which, like "meaningful," makes it evident that the primary characteristic of the sign is not its transitive relationship to an object but its position at the center of interest, or more specifically, at the center of the event in which the passage from the extreme of violence to the extreme of peace was effected at his/its expense. This spatiotemporal center will subsequently provide a point of reference for all future signs; but at its inception it is not signified, but itself possesses all signification, which at this stage we might better call "significance." By the "reproduction of the sign" Girard refers to the killing of further victims to produce the desired communal reconciliation. The original victim cannot of course be reproduced as such; but insofar as he has become a sign, subsequent victims will appear as tokens of the same sign, and their significance will be guaranteed a posteriori by the same "miraculous" results. The gradual elaboration of the *"langage du sacré"* is in this perspective the equivalent of the process of "sedimentation" discussed earlier. Each successive ritual murder is less a reproduction of the original mechanism and more a re-presentation of the original victim-sign. At the same time the organization of ritual leads to the creation of other signs, presumably through the metonymic differentiation of the original—members of the body, tools employed in the sacrifice, roles of the participants, and so on.

We may take this brief elaboration of the hypothesis, which merely develops points already present in Girard's text, as an expression of the elements of a theory of representation. It is true that Girard never develops the subject as such, but that fact does not in itself constitute proof of the inadequacy of the theory. It does demonstrate, however, that an explicit theory of representation-in-general is not the foundation of Girard's anthropology; that the elaboration of the latter can be accomplished in the absence of the former. We will now attempt to show that this is no accidental product of Girard's own "interests," a lacuna presumably to be filled in by interested disciples, but an inevitable feature of the hypothesis as he has presented it. This demonstration will serve as a preliminary stage in the presentation of an alternative version of the hypothesis from which a fully developed theory of representation can be derived.

Representation of the Sacred

Although in the course of Girard's exposition the notion of the victim-as-sign appears before the term "sacred" is attached to it, the association of the two categories is dominated by the latter, which alone possesses an independent dynamic. Thus the "language of the sacred" evolves as a function of the sacred and not by virtue of its dynamism as language. The apparent primacy of the significant is simply "strategic"; it serves as a point of departure, but no more. The victim, before he can appear as sacred, must *appear*, that is, be present, and this presence is already equivalent to significance. Only once his significance is established can he be sacralized, that is, made the object of ritual reproduction. This observation points up the ontological difference between the sacred and the representational, a difference that must be considered as neither originally constitutive nor merely empirical, but as arising directly from the hypothesis itself. Stated in simple terms, the sacred is an *institutional* whereas the representational is a *formal* category. This distinction is not, however, a simple opposition between the a priori and the a posteriori, between the logical and the empirical, as it would be in metaphysical thought. The hypothesis postulates the original unity of all such oppositions. But it does not obviate the need to reestablish them on the basis of this unity, and before this can be done, the unity

itself must be more precisely characterized. Just as the metaphysical always asserts the priority of the formal over the
institutional so that the specificity of the institution can only
be understood as an allegory of form, a theory based on
a concrete hypothesis might appear to simply invert this
priority: What has a historical beginning is a fortiori institutional. But a hypothetical empiricism would be an absurdity.
To affirm the historical orign of human representation is not
to explain what follows as the continuation of an arbitrarily
begun narrative, but to extrapolate from all the arbitrary
details of mythological and ritual narrative a fundamental
mechanism that must have functioned historically. Thus the
hypothesis as such does not place the sacred, as an "irrational" institution, in a more dominant role than the representa-
tional-as-such. It simply posits a beginning to which the
dynamism of all categories of representation can be traced.
The sacred is not, of course, merely a "category" among
others. That is why we have preferred in this context to refer
to the relevant dichotomy as institutional/formal. The real
question is not after all whether the "sacred" is prior to the
representational (a more rigorous statement of the problem
would show that this formulation is meaningless), but
whether human representations should be conceived of essentially as commemorations of a concrete event or as the forms
of communal presence. Because what we have called the
"institutional" aspect of the original event is directly linked
to ritual and religious practice, and thereby to cultural institutions in general—to those aspects of human history which
must be referred to specific historical origins—this aspect can
be traced to the commemoration of the *specificity* of the
event, which is to say, in the terms of the hypothesis, to the
body of the victim and to the concrete circumstances surrounding the murder, all of which can be said to be signified
metonymically by it. This aspect of representation defines
the perspective taken by Girard, which as we have seen tends
to organize itself around the notion of the sacred. What we
have called the formal pole of representation, from which
develops scientific and logical discourse, and in general those
cultural elements that involve the creation of models of
reality-in-general rather than the preservation of historical

memory, derives from the presence of the community to itself as mediated by the victim-sign. For this presence, although the product of a specific event, is in itself a pure "space" of signification, an awaiting of the sign-in-general. The specific character of the first signs to fill this space do not determine its possible future contents, once it is accepted that the presence is independent of these contents, which can therefore evolve in directions that will tend to reflect this formal independence (e.g., logic).

The question of the primacy of the institutional or the formal is one that should merely be posed but not answered. Of course one can divide up the human sciences into those that emphasize one or the other, but such a division merely replaces the investigation of the foundations of these sciences with an intellectual empiricism isomorphic to the divisions existing between university departments. This divided emphasis, which a more detailed version of the hypothesis would place within the original event itself, can certainly not be foreclosed by an arbitrary choice.

Let us assume with Girard that the community contemplates the body of its victim as a "transcendental signifier" of the whole process of crisis and resolution. Now during the murder, as a collective act, a virtual community already existed among its perpetrators. This collectivity could only become conscious of its existence when, the deed accomplished, action ceases, and the remains of the victim, no longer an object of aggression, become to all a sign of their solidarity. But in effect this "sign" could only have a collective significance within the presence of the community to itself. That is, not only would each member contemplate the victim, he would be aware of his fellows as participants in the same act of contemplation. Awareness of presence and awareness of the cadaver are two elements of the same moment. Now certainly the peace thus brought about could be sought again by a reproduction of the murder, later regularized in ritual sacrifice. But in that case this peace would be a mere *state* of collective experience, whereas, as we have seen, it is in fact the occasion for the creation of a presence of the community to itself. This presence is not itself a simple state, but a moment in the process of signification. That is to say, on the one hand there is the positive experience of solidarity, but on the other there is the formal presence within which the victim-sign appears. Now we may assume that the vision of *disjecta membra* is such as to imprint itself in the memories of the participants as a sign of the whole. But such a "sign" is not in itself a *representation*. As the object of a deed, it can be said loosely to "signify" the deed and its consequences; but the reproduction of such a "sign" can only be accomplished through the repetition of the deed. In this model no collective decision for such reproduction could be made because the collectivity would have no way of reestablishing its presence, its space of communication, outside of the context of the act itself. We can of course assume that such a situation may well have recurred many times within the same group. But in this case we can at best speak of prerepresentation, whereas the "sedimentation" process mentioned earlier presupposes at least a rudimentary form of representation in which the "sediment" could accumulate.

If the body of the victim is indeed a "transcendental" or "universal" signifier, a "sign" created by the collectivity that at the same time creates it as a community, its signification can only be present to the group at the very moment of the murder. In order for this meaning to be present beyond this single moment, it must be designated by a *linguistic* sign (gesture or word). A hypothesis for the evolution of such signs will be presented in the next chapter. It suffices here to note that these signs, like the victim-as-sign, can only exist within the context of the presence established at the moment of the murder among the members of the community. But because this presence has never existed separately from the original situation, it has no separate reality for the community. Although in our analysis we have considered it as the formal ground or "space" in which the sign manifests itself, it is also a part of the original signified, indeed its fundamental or generating element, because this presence is both the result of the collective murder and the primordial manifestation of communal peace.

The question of the reality of presence as such to the community does not at this point require us to consider whether it is ever, or indeed can ever be *represented* separately from the original event. But if in the terms of our theory this presence is the origin of the *form* of representation, which will eventually find its objects in domains far removed from the sacred, then even at the origin it must be considered as already other than the signified ("meaning") of the victim-as-sign. For an institutional theory like that developed by Girard, the (sacred) sign carries with it its own presence, which indeed is at the root of its meaning. A formal theory must consider rather that the presence precedes the specific sign, just as in the original event the silence that follows the murder is a prerequisite of the new "non-instinctual attention" directed by the murderers at the former object of their frenzy. The original sign signifies the ground of its own existence, and hence its future evolution can be discussed without further explicit reference to this ground. But, by the same token, the evolution of representations can be discussed without reference to the specific filiation of concrete signs, simply in terms of the different forms evolved from this original auto-referentiality.

Thus the primitive development of syntax culminating in the creation of the declarative sentence can only be conceived as a progressive integration into the linguistic object of its auto-referential element, so that this object evolves into a self-sufficient model of lived experience. Such an evolution cannot be described as a ramification of an original privileged object; it can only be understood as the realization of a *formal* self-sufficiency originally present in the sign, which is to say, its reference to the communal presence outside of which it cannot exist.

The Future of Representation

The institutional/formal polarity would appear to lead to two possible sciences of human representation. The first would take for its object the sacred and the forms derived from it, in particular the esthetic, all of which would be conceived as taking as the basis of their content the communal solidarity inherent in the original presence. The second would deal rather with language and logic, and in general with those forms that reproduce in their structures (and, in the case of logic, in their explicit content) the pure abstraction of this presence. Girard's work would of course fall within the first category, and the present volume, to all appearances, in the second. It is evident, however, that in the modern world this distinction cannot maintain itself—"modern" being defined here simply as the period in which the theory itself is formulated. For in the terms of the formal theory the existence of an institutional theory contradicts its very basis, because a theory being by definition a scientific discourse based on logical rather than institutional filiation, the institutional theory cannot explain its own existence without providing a counter-example to its universality. The institutional theory, if it is not to deny its status as science (which, in the terms of our definition of the human sciences, means in particular being able to justify its existence) must situate itself apocalyptically at the end of the history of the sacred, and must further explain its role in this history as an auto-destruction of sacred (institutional) representations. But this explanation is a theoretical act that at the same time demonstrates the potential of (sacred) representations for revealing the truth of their origin, an origin that they were originally elaborated in order to conceal. The formal theory is in this view at best a derivative doctrine, suitable for the study of the forms, but not the content of representation.

Yet according to the apocalyptic perspective of the institutional theory, the sacred is no longer a privileged content, and thus representation is henceforth a mere formalism—an ideal object, that is, for a formal theory but one that is no longer of primary interest because it has become pure signification without significance. It is thus equivalent to formal theory as such, which simply becomes the sphere of "modern" representation itself. Against this background of mere formalism, the institutional theory views itself as truly scientific because it alone is concerned with the significance of its content. For the formal theory, on the contrary, the triumph of form in the modern era is a victory of human representation over the violence of its origins, a victory in which the theory has a central role to play because for the first time this violence can be fully revealed—which is to say, formalized in the corpus of the theory.

Up to this point the oppositions we have described remain on the level of polemics traceable to differences of emphasis within the same theoretical basis, which is, as we have seen, the presence of the original event. At the moment of greatest divergence the institutional theory asserts its own importance as the last heir of sacred representation, whereas the formal theory sees itself as the final liberation of formal representation from all specificity of content. Because both conceive of themselves as scientific doctrines based on the same original hypothesis, these are indeed merely differences of emphasis. The vision of the future, although only an extrapolation of the theories in question, produces a more radical division that can then be shown to reflect a more fundamental divergence in the theories, a divergence that cannot yet be demonstrated empirically and which therefore remains latent in their concrete analyses.

For the institutional theory the present is a time of apocalypse in which the violent foundations of culture are revealed and at the same time rendered powerless to support the edifice. Representation is not an issue, but rather man's ability to retain the solidarity that was the original fruit of the *meurtre émissaire* in an era when sacrifice is no longer possible. Because representation as such is not envisioned as a substitute for the sacred, this solidarity can only be conceived of in ethical terms, as the result of a free choice the only alternative to which is the return of a violence no longer controllable through the mechanisms of the sacred. This choice, although it may be temporarily deferred, is a matter of historical urgency because only continued ignorance of the truth revealed by the theory can provide time for delay. It is worth noting that in Girard's version of this theory the progress of formal representation is visible particularly in the sphere of the means of violence, nuclear bombs being in this view the primary product of scientific and technical progress.

Thus the choice presented is that between war and peace, destruction and reconciliation; but the symmetry of the alternatives makes this a choice between absolutes in which no time or space remains for mediations. Warfare bringing henceforth absolute destruction, its opposite can only be absolute reconciliation, the establishment for all eternity of

the presence first made possible by the original lynching.
Because this presence has never been conceived of as a space
of representation, but as a communion in the sacred, the
removal of this latter can only leave behind a universal
immediacy. And because such an immediacy is not concretely conceivable, Girard can only guarantee it by reference
to a *truly divine* transcendence, a "true" sacred that takes the
place of the old, as the kingdom of God is to succeed to that
of this world. Without this ultimate faith, which is in his
terms simply the ultimate corollary of the hypothesis, Girard
would indeed be unable to sustain his institutional perspective.

From the standpoint of the formal theory, the future,
although presenting the danger of annihilation, need not be
conceived of as apocalyptic, but as determined by the progress of representation. The existence of the theory is itself a
revelation, but one that signifies rather the maturation of
representation, the final detachment of formal presence from
its institutional-historical origins, a detachment that has
remained until now incomplete in the absence of a satisfactory hypothesis of this origin. In this view the salient feature
of our epoch is the expansion of the means (or "media") of
communication, and the general tendency of economic goods
to themselves become representations. In this context the
decline of the sacred and its final unveiling does not leave
mankind faced with a simple existential choice, but with a
system of representations which has gradually usurped the
purgative function of the sacred in effectuating the transcendence of desire. The gradualness of this decline, which will
certainly not reach its conclusion with the publication of the
present theory, is due to the concrete, specific nature of this
transfer of functions, the completion of which we have no
means of anticipating. In any event the formal theory has no
reason to hypothesize that these functions will disappear, for
desire is a necessary product of representation. But once it is
realized that the presence of the community to itself, and of
one human being to another, is itself only possible in a
context provided by representation, a universe increasingly
dominated by the latter can no longer be seen as a hell in
which mediation destroys all "human values." The ethical

dimension need not be abandoned to the institutional theory. The choice of universal love and peace, even supposing that it could somehow be made by humanity as a whole, can only be maintained by means of systems of representation; and this is as true of a family or a couple of lovers as it is of humanity in general. The utopia of immediacy is by no means a necessary consequence of even the institutional theory, although this theory can only avoid it through the invocation of a transcendent agency.

We shall return to these questions in our concluding chapter. At this point they have only a programmatic significance. Our purpose is not to insist on the somewhat artificial dichotomy between what we have called the institutional and the formal theories of representation, but rather to emphasize the strength of the transcendental hypothesis as a basis for the human sciences in general, including domains, such as in particular that of linguistics, that cannot be understood simply as outgrowths of the sacred. We require only one further preliminary clarification of this hypothesis before turning to the elaboration of our theory; this concerns the place of transcendence as an element of the form of representation in general. This clarification belongs in our introduction in that it suggests a possible divergence of views concerning the nature of the hypothesis.

Transcendental Signification

We have spoken earlier of a transcendental signified, Girard of a transcendental signifier. In both cases reference is made to signs that stand outside the approximate one-to-one relationship between *signifiant* and *signifié* that we find in Saussure's original conception: in the one case a "sign" that refers to the totality of the significant, in the other, a significance to which all signs (indirectly) refer. The two conceptions not only do not contradict one another but they are easily transformed one into the other: It suffices to posit a second sign referring in turn to the transcendental signifier to transform the latter into a transcendental signified, because however many such signs are created to refer in detail or in totality to the signifier, the totality of their signification (or "meaning") remains contained within that attributed to the latter as signifier. Thus all signs refer to the same sign, which becomes a transcendental signified.

Yet despite this ease of transformation, the two concepts function in very different ways. Girard's transcendental signifier is internal to the hypothesis as a moment of unity previous to the establishment of representation as such. To say that the body of the first victim is the source of all signification, has at the origin "all" possible meanings, is to oppose such signification to the scientific language of the theory, and to representation-in-general insofar as it consists in the designation of its object. To the extent that the emissary mechanism is understood, its reproduction will break down the simple signifier into a plurality of more specific signs. The real importance of the "transcendental signifier" for Girard is elsewhere; it is the divinity conceived as an active principle, as a being-that-signifies. Hence his otherwise obscure reply (quoted above) that the hypothesis does not let us discover the "true" *signifiant transcendantal*, but only what men have considered as such, which is to say, the gods of violence rather than the God of peace.

Signification is thus subordinated to incarnation; the signifier is not an arbitrary sign but a being, formerly alive, whose central role in the crisis and its resolution is partly real and exemplary, partly mythical and as such ultimately inadequate. This conception of the transcendental lies at the foundation of the "institutional" subordination of representation to the sacred, by which the formal relations that constitute the former cannot exist in the absence of the guarantee provided by the latter. The existence of the notion of divinity is of course easily accounted for in this theory. In contrast, a rigorous concept of signification becomes all but impossible to elaborate. The original moment of presence in which the community and its mediating "sign" first confronted each other never appears as a formal space of representation but as an epiphany that is an end in itself. This is of course the mode of appearance of this presence for its participants. But representation, however directly inspired by the intention to reproduce (and not "merely" represent) the original event, could not exist unless presence had already become a permanent virtuality tantamount to the existence of the community as such. This virtuality is no doubt ultimately a reference to the sacred, but it can only function oblivious of this fact, as a mere *ground* of communication. The notion of a transcendental signifier implies that in view of the unbroken filiation that connects all signs (e.g., those of language) to the original sign, the question of "pure" formal presence need never arise.

The functioning of the transcendental signifier is never metatheoretical; not so that of the signified. By situating the transcendent in the realm of content, the formal theory identifies its own construction with that of its subject matter: The hypothesis is a transcendental signified. For a signified, as opposed to a signifier, is referred to without itself appearing; every act of signification is to some extent hypothetical. And if the body of the original victim is indeed a transcendental signifier, then the first act of signification, by which the community would do no more than signify to itself its presence, would be an act of pure hypothesis, each supposing the sign to possess the same significance for his fellows as for himself. The signifier remains "transcendental" only insofar as it is a specific object outside the immediate power of any individual to reproduce it—insofar, finally, as it is a sacred object. But the act of signification, which designates a signified not present in the sign itself, is transcendental by its very nature. The postulation of the hypothesis only makes explicit what is inherent in the process of representation in general, and in particular what was hypothetically present at its origin. Thus the formal theory carries the hypothesis to an additional level of specification at which the origin of representation requires the presence not merely of an (original) sign but of an *act of designation*. This aspect of the hypothesis will be developed further in the following chapters.

What then precisely is denoted by the adjective "transcendental," which for Kant referred to the domain, inaccessible to the understanding, where mind and reality, which is already to say representation and its object, were reconciled? The Saussurian "signifié" is, much like the Platonic Idea, an a posteriori reflection of the signifier is an "ideal" world constructed from words. In the history of representation such constructions could only arise from a reflection on meaning posterior to the signs themselves and to their designation of their referent. Now it might appear mere verbal sleight-of-hand to speak of a "transcendental" relationship between a sign and a concrete, present object to which it refers. But the otherness of the object is more than its status as a "horizon" of perceptions. The sign exists only in a presence and refers to an object potentially accessible to this presence, yet at the same time existing previously to it and independently of it. The body of the victim as the first significant object is at the same time the source of this presence and the first object to occupy it, and thereby the prototype of all transcendence. For on the one hand, as a unique object, it alone can signify the reconciliation of the conflict, but on the other, as itself the designatum of the signs of the collectivity, it is in the act of signification both made present and revealed as absent.

The first transcendence, that of the "signifier," is in reality not that of signification at all, nor even originally that of sacralization, which involves in addition a shrinking back from the object from which we will attempt to derive the first linguistic signs. It is that of collective presence, the empty form of representation, which is revealed from the beginning as something given from without. The (second) transcendence of the object-as-designated is the source of representional form, which is at the same time a critique of the very transcendence it posits. For the object is unalterably other; and yet the sign purports to make it present. But were it not for this otherness, the sign would have no function— just as our hypothesis would be useless were the origins of human culture not in the same way inaccessible and yet presentifiable through representation.

Chapter **2** The Origin of
Representation

Our introductory remarks have suggested a foundation for
the social sciences, conceived fundamentally as specialized branches of the study of representations. But it does
not suffice merely to propose a methodology in general
terms as a model for the "reform" of already established
disciplines. If indeed the human sciences have lacked a foundation, this has not prevented their elaboration of highly
complex and varied methodologies of their own, and it would
be folly to attempt to impose on them a new intellectual
context. The social sciences will no doubt remain for a long
time what they are at present; if we would improve on them,
we would do better to create new ones. In particular, if we
claim that these sciences are branches of the study of representations, then our first task is to create a general theory of
representation.

Language and Representation

Representation is by no means limited to language, and yet
no systematic theory of representation can begin otherwise
than with language. The most obvious reason for this is
heuristic: Language alone of the forms of representation
constitutes an explicit model of its object the internal structures of which are subject to codification. Another way of
making this point is to evoke the strength of linguistic norms.
Whereas other forms are generally evaluated judgmentally
according to the "esthetic" criteria of good or bad, appropriate or inappropriate, language possesses in addition the crite-

rion of *correctness*, which applies in particular to the sentence, or minimal utterance. The comparison between language and ritual on this point is suggestive: A ritual act, like a sentence, is subject to a strong norm of correctness. But there is no general, abstract form of ritual. What is "correct" or "incorrect" is the content of the gestures, not the structure that links them.

In these two versions of correctness we find once again the dichotomy between the institutional and the formal theories of representation; the "heuristic" problem of finding a theoretical point of departure is seen to be merely another version of the fundamental question of the nature of hypothesis. But whereas the connection between ritual and the institutional theory is explicit—because the reproduction of the original event is the very definition of ritual—it is not immediately evident why the formal theory must have its starting point in language. And this is precisely because language, unlike ritual, has no obvious definition, which is merely to say that there is no way to reduce it to something more fundamental. This is a sign of its fundamental nature which our formulation of the hypothesis should not neglect. It is simple to define ritual in terms of the hypothesis because the hypothesis is the product of inductive reasoning from ritual data, the historical concreteness of which it reflects. This reasoning makes use of language, but only as a supplementary source of understanding not requiring justification in its own right. Thus ritual is deemed the source of language at the same time as language is being used to explain ritual.

This last observation is so obvious as to appear banal, and as a result the contradiction it reveals risks not being taken seriously. But the hypothesis cannot possibly explain its own being as language, or the more general fact that scientific understanding is inconceivable without language, unless it posits the existence of language at the origin. For the hypothesis must not only justify its own existence but demonstrate that this existence is predicated on the ultimate identity of all representations. Such an identity could no doubt be established independently of any specific form of representation, but its very establishment implies that only through language could representation reflect on itself and thus become an object of study. Only by situating language at the origin of representation can the theory remain an application of its own doctrine. Were language merely a derivative of ritual, nothing could explain its privileged role as vehicle of the (hypothetical) truth.

Such reflections would appear to make the task of defining "natural" language simply impossible. Within the opposition between the institutional and the formal, it would be a grave error to oppose language to ritual by simply placing it on the formal side of the barrier. Such a classification would be rather appropriate to the institutional theory because it in effect subordinates language—and the formal in general—to ritual by making it a mere reflection of the latter. For the formal theory, on the contrary, language is as institutional as ritual, and as such must be present at the origin. The quarrel between the two theories is in effect defined most precisely by the relative generality they give to the categories of language and ritual, one of which must precede the other. If this definition remains lacking in precision, in particular as regards its specific terms, this is not a "defect" but a necessary consequence of the fundamental nature of the theories in question. To define the question in terms sufficiently precise so as to permit its restatement in a neutral theoretical language would simply be to create a new more general theory that would invalidate a priori the two others. Whether this may conceivably be possible is from our present standpoint an idle question.

We will assume, therefore, that representation begins with language, so that at the origin, where the formal and the institutional are indistinguishable, the first representative act is envisaged as creating a reproducible formal structure. The only defining characteristic of language at this stage, as opposed to ritual, is economy of reproducibility. Ritual, in this perspective, appears as a de-formalization of language, explicable by the collective intention to reproduce rather than designate the original crisis and its resolution. Thus in order to situate the origin of language in the hypothesis we must locate the moment of the hypothetical event at which the (linguistic) sign defines itself as a reproducible designation of its object.

Having begun from a definition of man as simply the "most mimetic" animal, Girard deduced the inevitability of crises provoked by mimetic rivalry. The generating mechanism of these crises is the imitation of *appropriative* behavior. A human, or an animal, can imitate another's gestures without conflict so long as these gestures do not require for their accomplishment an object that is functionally unique, that is, a duplicate of which cannot be found in the context of the imitation. The imitation, for example, of feeding behaviors may be essential for the apprenticeship of young animals of certain species, but the behavior of the imitating animal is not directed at the same object as its model. Where objects are functionally unique and thereby potential sources of conflict, various mechanisms of domination/submission eliminate conflict by clearly attributing the object (e.g., a sexual partner) to the dominant animal.

The explanation of conflict-avoidance by instinctual mechanisms is a *deus ex machina* unless the evolution of these mechanisms is explained. The conversion of rivalry into submission, or at the very most into a limited conflict seldom if ever leading to the death of one of the participants, and above all never spreading beyond the limited circle of the original rivals (e.g., two stags fighting over a female), can only have evolved selectively as a more efficient means of assuring the reproduction of the species in question. Animals inclined to fight to the death would simply destroy each other, and no doubt such intraspecific conflicts did occur throughout the evolutionary history of the animal kingdom. The mechanisms of conflict-avoidance, different among different species and subspecies, and dependent on habitat, food supply, and above all on the killing power of their natural weaponry, could not be derived from a single source but must constantly have been revised. Man would then constitute an exception not because he was the first to kill one of his fellows, but because he managed to survive intraspecific violence without having evolved an instinctive mechanism for dealing with it. This lack cannot be explained as a product of the increased violence that the use of stone tools or simply the greater intensity of mimesis would bring to human conflicts. On the contrary, these would make the advantage of an instinctual solution all the greater. Instead of viewing human representation, as it is presumed to have originated in the hypothetical event, as the necessarily nonbiological solution provoked by an excess of violence—we have just seen the unsoundness of the reasoning behind such an explanation—we should rather understand the absence of a biological solution as resulting from its *preemption* by representation, in both its profane and sacred, or more precisely, linguistic and ritual forms. The excessive human tendency to mimesis, which may simply be another way of describing our species' superior intelligence, need not then be understood primarily as the source of an increased potential for violence, but as that of a capacity for representation. This interpretation is in fact plausible even given Girard's version of the hypothesis, which we have followed here.

Appropriative mimesis, then, is the source of the original mimetic conflict. The gesture of appropriation of one individual cannot be imitated by another in the absence of a duplicate object; and the very choice of the first party insures the uniqueness of its object. Now if we return to the hypothetical murder scene, the members of the community are gathered round their collective victim, their aggressive energies discharged. A silence falls, and the body of he (or she) who has brought about this sudden reconciliation receives a new, "non-instinctual" attention, which makes him, or rather it, the sign of this reconciliation, and of the crisis that led to it. Without questioning the plausibility of the murder scene itself, if only because of the impressiveness of the evidence marshalled in its favor, we can nevertheless question the specific mediations that lead from the murder to its status as event, which is to say, as representation.

The dubiousness of a "discharge" of aggressive energy need not detain us because the murder is not merely an act of destruction but at the same time an act of solidarity. This solidarity is, however, only implicit in the course of the act; only its completion can permit it to become present to the murderers. We have referred in the introduction to the *presence* that the community would have to itself in its contemplation of the body of the victim. Now this presence has been up to this point guaranteed only by collective simultaneity, the reproduction—but not the perpetuation—of which is only possible through the renewal of the violence by which such bodies are produced. This explanation is, indeed, faithful to the assumption of the institutional theory that the "sacred" object is itself the origin of representation. But what is not explained in this version is precisely how the presence is *realized* at all by the collectivity as the ground of (the first) noninstinctual *communication*.

If the ultimate cause of the "mimetic crisis" was a gesture of appropriation, then the end of the crisis should be marked by a limitation on such gestures. Now in the hypothetical murder described by Girard the victim should be thought of as the object of the most violent form of appropriative gesture, that of *sparagmos*, in which he is literally torn limb from limb. It is thus difficult indeed to picture the chastened community of murderers surrounding the still-intact body of their victim. The moment of silent attention that is essential to the hypothesis can have at best fragmentary remains as its object; nor is it implausible that the missing parts have not merely been "appropriated" but ingested as well. What then could bring about such a moment of silence? If we assume the collectivity now temporarily united against the victim, we must account for the fact that this alliance, which expresses itself in appropriative gestures of the most violent sort, does not itself break down in the rivalry the potential for which is always latent in such gestures. If the community forges itself by tearing a victim to pieces, then it risks destroying itself at the very outset by fighting over the pieces. How many times such breakdowns actually occurred, and whether or not they were ultimately reparable, is unimportant. But for the moment of silent attention to occur, it is necessary that at some point the gestures of violent appropriation cease before degenerating into rivalry. It is useless to assume that this moment arrives on the "satiation" or "purgation" of aggressive energies which the central postulate of a mimetic anthropology would define as virtually unlimited. For such satiation, even were it to come about, would scarcely give rise to a moment of collective consciousness; rather it would provoke a turning away from the no longer desirable appropriative activity. Only if the gestures of appropriation were voluntarily

terminated could their cessation be at the same time the institution of a collective presence, which is by definition already
the locus of communication. Thus the ending of appropriative gestures and the beginning of communication must be
one and the same. But to put an end to such gestures, they
must be begun and not completed. We can therefore reformulate the hypothesis in the following terms: *The first linguistic
act is constituted by a collective abortive gesture of appropriation.* The first representation is already language, and the
hypothetical origin of the human is at the same time the
origin of human language.

The crisis can only come to an end upon the designation of
a unique (or quasi-unique) victim if the aggressive acts of the
collectivity toward this victim do not lead to the internal
division of the collectivity itself. These acts are, as we have
seen, themselves acts of appropriation which would naturally
lead to the sparagmos of the body. But at some point further
gestures of this sort by the members of the group would
become mutually incompatible. The hypothesis we are proposing is this: At a moment when all are about to carry out
such a gesture, the fear of conflict is such that the gesture is
aborted. This abortive gesture, which *designates* its object
without attempting to possess it, is then the first *linguistic*
act. But before we can even begin to justify this thesis, we
must make plausible the collective existence of the abortive
gesture.

To explain the termination of the crisis by the fear of
conflict may appear equivalent to evoking as above the "purgation" of aggressive energies. But the crucial difference is
that the concentration of the violence of the collectivity
against a single victim would qualitatively increase each individual's fear of coming into conflict with the collectivity,
that is, of becoming the new victim. Nor is it implausible to
suppose that some particularly belligerent members of the
original group of murderers may have met with such a fate.
This fear that makes each member of the collectivity draw
back from further appropriative action and thereupon recognize the same hesitation in the others, possesses an ethical
dimension not without significance in the opposition between the institutional and the formal theories of representa-

tion. In this avoidance of conflict the need for solidarity with the group is chosen in preference to individual gratification. Thus it is not quite sufficient to speak of the solidarity that comes from the common persecution of a more or less arbitrarily chosen victim. For this solidarity must remain unrealized, and hence liable to break down at any moment, until such time as it has expressed itself not merely in acts of aggression toward the victim, but in an act of nonaggression toward the remainder of the group. The reconciliation of the collectivity may appear to it to be a grace bestowed by the victim, but we should not make the collective murder alone responsible for the passage from a state of violence to a state of peace. The benefits conferred by the murder are not immediate and "magical," but mediated by a collective decision, or rather by the conjunction of individual decisions that constitutes the collectivity as a community by giving it a "language." The fact that this solidarity is a positive rather than a negative phenomenon, that it depends on a representative structure rather than on an object (the body) external to it merely confirms that the community and its representations can at least in principle survive the demise of the institutionalized sacred. The renunciation—"sacrifice"—of potential appropriative satisfaction is thus present at the outset as an ethical, "altruistic" act that creates a pure form—language—independent of the particular content that happens to fill it. Although the victim will get the credit for the reconciliation that follows, and the murder/sacrifice be indefinitely repeated, the possibility is thus left open that this form will emerge in its own right as the only *necessary* element of the origin.

The "attention" spoken of by Girard as particularly directed toward the victim could not indeed arise without the intervention of some form of designation. But the abortive gesture of appropriation is already a form of designation before becoming a sign. This is demonstrated in the very fact of appropriative mimesis. The appropriative gesture not merely inspires imitation as a gesture, but designates its object specifically to its imitators. At this stage designation is not an independent phenomenon, however, but an accidental byproduct of appropriation—and a dangerous one as well because it is precisely its (involuntary) component of designation which turns appropriative mimesis into rivalry. Now in the selection of the emissary victim the element of designation becomes, from rivalry-producing, creative of mimetic unity among the murderers, because the sparagmos permits the concentration of aggression on a single victim for a time without rivalry. No aggressive gesture has so far been separable into component parts of appropriation and designation. These gestures designate in the temporal process of appropriating, because they necessarily involve some form of movement toward their object. But in an abortive gesture of appropriation this movement is checked before the object is attained and precisely at the moment when the gesture would be perceived as designating it. The attention of the group is called to the object at the same time as all fear to attempt to appropriate it. In this manner the attention focused on the remains of the victim is a first moment of *intentional* nonviolence which "sacralizes" its object as inappropriable. The sacred consists precisely in the attribution to the object of this inappropriability which results, as we have seen, from the concentration of the collectivity's desire on a single victim-object. To reproduce the sacred object, repetitions of the original murder will be organized. But at the same time the abortive gesture remains as the *sign* of the sacred object, and from this sign can evolve the various formal structures of language.[1]

We can already refer to the abortive gesture of appropriation as a *linguistic* sign. The etymology of this word, which refers to the tongue, should not present difficulty, particularly if we keep in mind that gestures of appropriation are intimately associated with eating, and thereby with oral gestures as well. But in any event a point we will insist on as preliminary to the exposition that follows is that the physiological (phonetic, gestural) elements of language are only secondary with respect to the question of signification. Once given the *form* of language, in which a reproducible gesture— manual or oral—designates an object not itself equally reproducible (assuming, of course, the precedence of concrete worldly designata over abstract ones, the existence of which presupposes and indeed refers to this concrete vocabulary),

the fact that one type of gesture comes to be preferred over
the other is of minor interest. The linguistic sign can function
only within a communicative context defined by the *presence* of the interlocutors one to the other.

The fundamental importance of presence can be gauged
from the fact that the whole point of the hypothesis is to
provide a plausible context for its origin. The beginning of
specifically human culture coincides with the institution of
the presence required for human communication. The original conditions of this presence are, of course, reproduced in a
painstaking manner in ritual, where its birth is revived, but
even the most trivial use of language depends on its continuous virtual existence, able to be activated at any given
moment among members of the community. Designation and
presence are thus the fundamental concepts of language.
Their "fetichisation," that is, their detachment from the
historical context of their origin and assimilation to—what
comes in the end to the same thing—divine or "natural"
phenomena, defines the "metaphysical" basis of classical
philosophy and of all the forms of thought which even today
fail to respect their anthropological origin. This is not to
affirm the invalidity of the studies (logic, cybernetics, etc.)
founded on "metaphysical" principles. The question of
whether these sciences can or should be integrated into a
comprehensive anthropology cannot be answered a priori.
Our only certitude at this point is that the study of human
society and its culture as an enterprise of self-comprehension
must at the very least recognize the hypothetical rather than
absolute nature of its fundamental concepts, and this even if
in some domains a nonhistorical, "metaphysical" hypothesis
may prove more economical than a truly anthropological
one.

Before elaborating our hypothesis of the evolution of elementary linguistic structures a few additional words should
be said, chiefly as a caution, concerning the fundamental
concepts of presence and designation. In describing the origin
of the latter, it has been impossible to avoid altogether the
implication that designation was already implicit in gestures
of appropriation and was merely "detached" from them by
their noncompletion in the circumstances we have described.

The whole point of the hypothesis would be lost if a poste-riori teleological notions were permitted to obscure the criti-cal nature of the historical context we have hypothesized. Designation is not born as a single "arbitrary" association of a sign with an object. The pacific nature of the designative act is not simply inherent in it, as the symmetry of the Saussurian terminology would lead one to think, but rather the result of an equilibrium, at first precarious in the extreme, between the violence of the act of appropriation of the object and that anticipated from the remainder of the community if the former be carried out. The "otherness" of the designatum, which we take for granted, is an effect of this equilibrium, for the fear that holds each individual back from carrying out the act of appropriation he has begun is precisely the fear that he will become in his turn the object of a similar act. The setting apart of the sacred, or we may simply say, the *significant* object, is at first the others' means of protecting themselves from suffering its fate. Designation thus creates its own otherness, which is originally of a sub-stantial rather than a formal character: The designated object is not "simply" referred to, but by that referral is shown to be universally desirable,[2] and for that very reason universally untouchable. The first designation takes place, as we have seen, by coincidence. But if the sign is to survive, as we must assume it does, its purpose can only be to designate-as-desirable-and-untouchable, in a word, to *sacralize*. The neutral hypothetical mode of designation characteristic of scientific discourse ("let G be a group," etc.) can only occur at the end of the linguistic evolution we have just begun to describe.

We have already similarly commented on the concept of *presence*, which Jacques Derrida has shown to be the presid-ing divinity of the metaphysical theory of language.[3] Here again the hypothesis returns anthropological tension to a concept that has simply been taken for granted or, in post-Cartesian thought, internalized as the self-reflection of the subject. Presence as we have defined it is originally that of potential violence averted by fear for the future based on memory of the immediate past. The community becomes present to itself not simply in an act of silent contemplation of its collective victim, but as a result of mutually designating it. The noncompletion of the act of appropriation can be said to be founded on an implicit intuition of this presence in the members of the collectivity because what prevents them from carrying it through to its conclusion is precisely the fear generated by the presence of the (rest of the) group, conceived of not merely as a collection of individuals but as a potential united adversary. But this intuition grasps merely the presence of rivals in a battle for supremacy. The abortive gesture is in this context nothing more than an *effect*; it only becomes a sign when each man grasps that the others, like himself, fear to appropriate the object and thus are merely gesturing toward it without attempting to possess it. These gestures, which we may imagine as being repeated by all in order to give further assurance of the absence of aggressive intent, convert the presence of rivalry into a presence of communication, in which action is deferred until the gesture-sign is communicated and interpreted. Presence and designation are the inseparable foundations of the communication situation: the relation between interlocutors, mediated by the sign and its referent, and the relation between sign and referent which is mediated in its turn by the presence of the interlocutors. The lexicalization of signs can occur only once all members of the (linguistic) community stand in a virtual relation of presence to one another.

At the origin the presence of the members of the community to one another arises concurrently with their common designation of the sacred object. Each member's spontaneous gesture of nonappropriation designates the object, but at the same time reinforces the peaceful symmetry of the community by contributing to the certitude of all that no individual will attempt to secure the object for himself. It is this symmetry, which is nothing else than presence itself, that is in Girard's sense "signified" by the sacred object. This form of signification is not, however, linguistic: It does not involve reproducible signs, but privileged objects that are felt to influence the community by association. Such objects, the archetypes of the institutional theory of signification, cannot, however, function, as we have seen, without having first been signified linguistically, or in other terms made *present* to the community. Conversely, the analysis of linguistic structures ignores at its peril the *significance* of the designatum. To designate linguistically is originally to sacralize, because to designate is originally to designate as something too generally desirable to appropriate; and in the same way, the presence of the partners in linguistic communication is only made possible by the fearsome fascination exercised by the object.

To sum up the origin of linguistic signification:

1. The abortive gesture of appropriation designates its object in the presence of the collectivity of the interlocutors.

2. The object thus designated is by this very fact sacralized, rendered *significant* to all, and for that reason inaccessible.

3. The significance of the object consists specifically in that it has made possible the nonviolent presence of (1).

Before tracing the evolution of the linguistic structures elaborated on the original form of designation, we should note in particular the closed, "circular" nature of this schema which is precisely the structure of formal creation. The original moment separates itself into components that, like the differentiated organs of a fetus, will then develop in relative mutual independence.

The first or *formal* moment is that elaborated on by linguistics generally and in particular referred to by the Saussurian Sa/Sé relation, which is oblivious of the *significance* of the referent to the point of replacing it with an ideal, purely linguistic object. This act founds the empirical science of linguistics independently from the anthropological considerations that inhere in the schema as a whole, and which are explicitly present in the moments that follow. We will have further occasion to deal with the problems posed by the metaphysical conception of "arbitrary" signification.

The second or *institutional* moment is that seized on, as we have observed, by Girard in his elaboration of an anthropology of the sacred. The category of the significant which it constitutes is also central to esthetics, but the arts even more than religion can only be understood with reference to the schema as a whole.

The third or *reflective* moment of the schema, in which it becomes an instrument of self-consciousness, or more simply, an auto-representation, has also been noted by Girard, who, however, sees it as a consequence of (2) rather than as circularly dependent on (1). This moment is of particular concern to the "transcendental anthropology" grounded on the hypothesis, for it furnishes the model of its epistemology: Like the sacred object providing the preconditions for its own appearance, the theory must justify its own emergence. We have already dealt with some aspects of this problem in the introduction.

The schema as a whole is "circular," but not paradoxical, because its internal temporality is not in contradiction with chronological time. This "noncontradiction" is guaranteed by the historical nature of the hypothesis, and indeed this guarantee is, from the standpoint of the theory of representations, the fundamental utility of the hypothesis. (In this regard, the relative priority of language and the sacred is unimportant, the point being that the hypothesis proposes a historical origin for both, whereas in its absence the attempt to describe the origin of either leads to a contradiction.) The circularity of the schema does give rise, however, to a paradoxical situation as soon as one abandons the detachment procured by the hypothesis, which is to say, for the participant in the linguistic act itself. We speak here of a paradox not logical but pragmatic.[4] A logical paradox is no doubt converted into a pragmatic one by being "posed" to a new victim; but it is in the first place a problem of theory, an inconsistency in a theoretical construction specifically devised to be without contradictions. The pragmatic paradoxes with which we will deal henceforth cannot be "resolved," like the logical ones, by the simple expedient of sacrificing, in whole or in part, the guilty construction, for the construction in question is not a theoretical one, created by definition, but the structure of signification as present to the imaginary contemplation of the subject, whose experience may be more precisely defined as *esthetic*. Nor are these paradoxes of a merely epistemological nature, so that the creation of the hypothesis might be said to "resolve" them. Nevertheless, the epistemological paradoxes that can be

derived from them, and which have tended to express themselves as "mysteries" or as simple confusions of thought
rather than in a logical semantic form, have no doubt reinforced their pragmatic origins, and thereby contributed to
the good conscience in which we experience them. Pragmatic
paradox arises in the first instance not from the attempt to
create a rigorous theory of signification, but from the very
experience of signification. Thus it arises at the birth of
language, although it is not limited to linguistic experience
and indeed comes more noticeably to the fore in the experience of "iconic" or pictorial signs. (Thus "esthetics" has
always dealt preferentially with painting rather than literature.) But we must first be concerned with the elementary
forms taken by "esthetic" paradox before any attempt is
made to capture it within the limited and specific communication-situation provoked by the promulgation of the
artwork.

Pragmatic paradox exists by degrees because the temporal
situation that arouses it can always be abandoned at some
cost, even if this be the death of the party involved. Thus it
may be negligible in certain situations, central in others, for
reasons dependent more on external circumstance than on
the structure of the experience. Conversely, this structure
must itself be "paradoxical" for pragmatic paradox to occur
under any circumstances. The difficulty of analyzing such
situations is to separate the "circumstances" from the experience, and because all pragmatic paradoxes arise from experiences of representation, this difficulty boils down to the
problem of defining such experience. The more clearly we
can delimit this experience within its worldly or "referential"
context, the more clearly our esthetic can be defined.

Let us then consider the situation of a member of the
community at the hypothetical moment of the first linguistic
sign, conceived not as a propagator but simply as a receiver of
this sign. He observes the others' abortive gesture of appropriation as designating, let us say, the remains of the victim's
body. He is relieved to learn that the others are content to
designate the object without daring to appropriate it. At the
same time he is aware of the presence of the others and of
their (apparent) intention to attract his attention to the

object, presumably as something which he should not attempt to appropriate. Were the process of signification to end here, however, neither the sacred nor the esthetic could exist. For it is not enough to establish the category of the sacred for the object to be designated as inaccessible to appropriation; were this the final step the members of the group would simply turn away from it. This inaccessibility, by the fact of its being designated, has become the essential mediating element of the nonviolent presence of the others to the individual member, a presence he wishes to prolong.

Thus presence and signification appear as causes each of the other. If the presence exists as the locus of the communication of a signification, then its function is fulfilled with the achievement of this communication; but here what is communicated by the signifying gesture is that the designated object is the necessary mediator of this presence. This circular appearance of mutual causality is in itself euphoric, involving no sense of internal contradiction, and thus apparently no pragmatic paradox. And this is because the illogicality of the situation has thus far been made visible only to us, but not to the participants. Could such euphoria perpetuate itself, we would have no need to pursue our analysis any farther; or rather such analysis could never have arisen in the first place within the realm of signification. But this analysis is not indeed complete. The discovery of the mutual causality of signification and peaceful presence, what Girard calls "reconciliation," cannot be the final moment of the process. Although it does indeed complete the circle of the three moments we have described, it is not itself complete; for these moments were described from without as elements of the hypothesis, whereas the participants in the event experience them from within. Such schemata as these indicate the logical framework of the pragmatic paradox but not the mode in which it is experienced. In order to grasp the nature of this experience we must introduce at this point the concept of *desire*.

Desire and Signification

A few words of caution must first be given. The concept of desire is the chief battleground of modern thought because it defines, or appears to define, man's essential relation to the world. Philosophy, or in other terms metaphysical thought, made cognition the fundamental relation; the forms of "post-philosophical" thought which have dominated the modern world and which in particular are embodied in the human or social sciences have all had as their starting point the substitution for cognition of a more fundamental, precognitive relation that can most simply be understood as falling under the rubric of desire, whether or not the term itself plays an important role in the thought in question. Psychoanalysis of course bases its entire conceptual structure overtly on a concept of desire—which is not to say that this concept does not vary throughout Freud's work, nor that its elaboration does not lead him to contradictions. But all the other "human sciences" which propose to explain the various aspects of man's conduct are equally founded on a conception, explicit or implicit, of an appetitive relation to the world, one that leads men to the appropriation and assimilation of certain objects, ultimately for biologically useful ends.

The social sciences, having rejected the explanations formulated in sacred myths, sought in the "objectivity" of biological imperatives the point of departure for a scientific analysis of human conduct. Thus the primary thrust of these sciences can be said to be *functionalist* in nature. But in addition the social sciences are, as we have seen, by choice or in spite of themselves, theories of representation. And this not simply because man obstinately surrounds all "natural" facts with a cloak of representations, but because in the absence of such representations there is no distinctive mark of the human. "Structuralism" was the explicit expression of the representational subject matter of the social sciences, and structuralism at least in its classical (Lévi-Strauss) mode has no theory of desire.

A most instructive history of the growth of structuralism from Durkheim to Lévi-Strauss could be written in which the crucial de-functionalization would be seen to be that of the sacred, which is still for Durkheim a functional guarantee of the significance of *all* social representations, whereas for Lévi-Strauss it has become merely the prototype for a non-functional conception of representation. The reason why the

association in Durkheim of the sacred with a functional
theory of representation did not lead directly to the formulation of an adequate hypothesis concerning their origin, but
instead to the explicit agnosticism of Lévi-Strauss, can be
expressed very simply: Although Durkheim saw the sacred as
functional, and therefore ultimately as "desirable" because it
was the basis of all representation, he failed to perceive the
necessity of a common origin of desire and representation
with the sacred. Thus the sacred became for him a mediating
force, an ultimately mysterious means of transforming desire
into knowledge, and from this position it was but a short step
to the structuralist one, which jettisons desire altogether and
merely registers the dichotomies of representation, the non-
functionality of which appears to vitiate all interest in their
status with regard to the sacred. The original sin of Durkheim
can be expressed as a misconception of the sacred; but from
the present standpoint it is more useful to see it as a misconception of desire. For if desire were understood to be internal
to representation in general, then it would a fortiori be
internal to the sacred, which is at the origin nothing other
than the quality of the representable.

The simplest notion of desire is that it is a precognitive
object-relation, for it is surely something other than knowledge, and, to the modern mind, at least, which is to say a
mind familiar with the ever-expanding system of exchange
that characterizes Western civilization since around 1800, it
just as surely cannot even ideally take knowledge as its point
of departure.[5] But once desire has been categorized as precognitive, its inevitable connection with representation can
no longer be understood. To make the latter an external
influence on desire is as unsatisfactory as to make desire an
external influence on representation. Nor is it useful to
attach desire to a "natural" form of representation, as in
Jacques Lacan's *stade du miroir*, the mythical character of
which is at once evident if it be transposed to a phylogenetic
rather than an ontogenetic context, where the "mirror" of
each individual is plainly the presence of the others. The only
viable solution is to postulate a common origin for desire and
representation, in which, however, they are not considered as
equivalent but rather as coexisting within the same formal
framework.

We have just observed that the circularity of the signification process, if viewed from "without," that is, in cognitive
(theoretical) terms, could appear to present no pragmatic
paradox. The introduction of the concept of desire establishes the paradox. One might object, however, to the apparently unverifiable supposition that a pragmatic paradox is
indeed present in the experience of representations-in-
general. The preliminary reply to this objection is that circularity without paradox cannot end, so that the extension of
the individual's experience to the entire community would
bring about a permanent collective euphoria neither necessi-
tating nor even permitting any further representation of
itself, representation being dependent on the esthetic and
only thereby memorable nature of its object. Or to put it
more briefly, although the forms of representation are composed of reversible relations, human representation could not
exist in the absence of (irreversible) desire. We will later
touch on the means employed for circumventing this necessity in the "detemporalized" forms of scientific or logical
discourse.

Let us then return to our schema of representation
(p. 41), considered from the standpoint of the individual's
relation to the (sacred) object. The abortive gesture of
appropriation expresses a tension between the conflicting
forces of attraction and repulsion. The individual wishes to
appropriate the object (thereby perpetuating the violence of
the crisis), but at the same time fears to do so. So long as this
tension remains present in the gesture, we cannot truly speak
of representation; the gesture itself is nothing but a compromise between opposing forces, and indeed can have at this
stage no definitive form, consisting as it must in an ill-defined
set of movements toward and away from its object. It is only
when the individual becomes aware of similar gestures on the
part of the other members of the group that he can conceive
of them, and consequently of his own, as *designating* the
object. At this point the gesture can acquire a form, become
the object of a specific intention. Once this has occurred, and
the gesture has become a sign designating the object, which
by the very fact of its collective designation is recognized as
inaccessible to further attempts at appropriation, the tension
originally expressed in the gesture (a tension we can assume

to have been literally present in the muscles of the gesturing subject) is abolished.

But the conflicting forces of attraction and repulsion have not been, as a result, simply eliminated, nor have they annihilated each other in the "compromise" reached by the gesture-as-sign. The object has not indeed become less attractive because it is now no longer attainable—on the contrary. But this attractiveness can no longer express itself directly in an act of appropriation; and this because the presence of the others forbids it—the very same presence which has just been established through the act of communication. The act of representation, in its *public* reality, is as we have said not paradoxical but circular and self-perpetuating, because by designating the object around which all have become reconciled it only reinforces the certitude of reconciliation. But within the individual the act of representation opens a separation between his participation in the collective nonviolence (from which he of course benefits) and his now inexpressible attraction to the object. This attraction was, in its origin, indiscernably both appetitive and mimetic, the similarly directed aggression of the others serving to reinforce that of each individual. But now the similar attraction of the others, rather than reinforcing his own appropriative conduct, has become a bar to it. The more each individual imitates his fellows in designating rather than appropriating the object, the more he is compelled to remain attracted to it.

Thus the collective representation of the sacred object indefinitely prolongs what we might call the *time of attraction*, the period that lies between the original perception of a potential object of appropriation and the act of appropriation itself, which whether or not successful can normally be expected to stabilize the situation at least temporarily, either through the appropriation of the object or through its disappearance, on its own or on another's power, from the field of perception. Now the object remains in the presence of all, but the presence of each to the other removes all possibility of appropriation.

This prolonged "time of attraction" is the time of the "non-instinctual attention" that sacralizes the object. If indeed the remains of the victim can acquire in the eyes of the community the extraordinary powers of a sacred object, it is as a direct result of this prolonged attraction. At the same time the source of the universality of this attraction is precisely the designation of the object by the community, and its source for each member of the group is its designation by the others. It is this association of attraction with representation which permits us to refer to this attraction as *desire*: The object of attention becomes at once both sacred and desirable.

This is not, however, to say that the sacred and the desirable are simply two names for the same concept; for the separation of the two is already present in the situation of their origin. The remains of the victim are sacred because they are the object of the attention and designation of the entire community, and are therefore perceived as infinitely attractive and infinitely dangerous, the cause of the crisis as well as the source of the reconciliation that ends it. These associations are not "meanings," and there is no need to assume that they must exist as "thoughts," which would indeed imply the necessary preexistence of language. Obviously what we have called the "sedimentary" nature of the hypothetical event(s) will enrich the language in which such thoughts can be formulated. But prior to any form of representation other than the original sign of designation, the sacred object can assimilate these powers in the eyes of the community because it has indeed demonstrated them by the role it has played in the events just concluded. The sacred is founded on "illusion" only in the sense that the powers attributed to the victim were not his before the event but were, as it were, forced on him, or rather on his corpse, as a result of his chance selection by his fellows as the object of communal aggression. But once the choice has been made and the murder and reconciliation accomplished, these powers are truly his, because his remains have become the indispensable mediator of the presence of the entire community.

At the same time these remains have become for each member of the community something infinitely desirable, that is, something that each individual wishes he could appropriate for himself. The two perceptions of the object as sacred and desirable are both determined by its collective designation, but they depend on the two different roles in which the individual finds himself in the process of designation. On the one hand he *participates* in the collective act of designation; his own gesture, whatever its original motivation, has become one with that of the community. In this act of participation the object appears as sacred, and *functions* as such, in uniting by its inaccessibility the members of the group. But on the other hand the individual's act of designation is something other than a mere participation in a collective act: It is an "expression" of his own desire for the object in opposition to the desires he perceives as being expressed by the designations of the others. Representation, *faute de mieux*, is in this sense a form of possession of its object in which the representers act as rivals, but without this rivalry ever appearing openly, which is to say, entering into the meaning of the sign.

The separation thus defined between the sacred and the desirable, or more precisely between the experience of the sacred and the experience of desire is constitutive of the individuality of the particular member of the collectivity, of his *ego*, which we can define as an awareness of self mediated by representation, or more simply, a self which desires. It is worth noting that the word "sacred" is originally an adjective attached to its object, whereas "desire" is, even more than a verb, a verbal noun independent both of the desirer and the object. Desire, although directed toward its object, must at the same time involve awareness of the self in the act of representing the object, representation being here understood as necessarily intentional in nature. Now the sign by which the object is designated is never for the individual a private, personal one. Even if at the origin each member of the collectivity spontaneously "invented" the first linguistic sign, the abortive gesture could not become a true sign until its communicability to others had been demonstrated, or in other words until the presence of the members of the community each to the other had been established.

Thus the individual's use of the sign to express *his own* desire in opposition to those of his fellows not only is in itself but is perceived by the user as the manifestation of a "token" of a sign-type rather than as an idiosyncratic act. The individual becomes aware of himself in the performance of an act not only functionally but formally identical with that of his fellows. His desire is defined by the common sign at the same time as the sign itself designates the object independently of the individual who manifests it. This inadequacy of the sign to express the *specific* significance of the designated object for the employer of the sign is characteristic of the desire-relation, and in fact defines it. It is important to clarify what we mean by "express" in this context. Precisely because the sign merely designates "objectively," the question of the individual's intention to communicate his desire to the others cannot even be raised. Nor are we simply speaking of a "cathartic" discharge of energy, although of course the energy expended in producing the sign had originally been destined for the appropriation of the object. The sense of "expression" here is rather the evocation of the object by means of the sign, so that the frustrated attraction felt for the object in the world of action is compensated for by its possession in a personal universe of representation, in which the sign or "word" is a model of the object. The individual use of the sign—which is not simply the knowledge of the code or language of which the sign is a part, but an *act* of signification—in intentionally designating (denoting) the object, nonintentionally communicates (connotes) at the same time this possession to the others.

This form of possession, which we may call "sublimated" because it obviously permits of no temporal modification (e.g., assimilation) of its object, is of course not the equivalent of real possession. But for him to whom the sign is communicated, and who in the situation at hand does not possess the object either, the manifestation of even this form of possession can only appear as an advantage to be contested by the manifestation of the same sign.

Originally the remains of the victim were attractive as an object of (perhaps cannibalistic) aggression. But the situation of its designation-sacralization demonstrates that it has the power to halt the aggressive activities of the community as a whole. (The fact that this power is really conferred on the object in the act of designation itself is not merely incomprehensible to the participants, but simply irrelevant.) The desire for the designated object is no longer simply an impulse toward aggressive appropriation, but a desire to possess this power over one's fellows. It must be stressed that this transfiguration of the object of desire is not a mere byproduct of the circumstances of the original event that might disappear under a variant formulation of the hypothesis, but a direct consequence of the relationship between desire and representation. Thus the fact of designation does not simply make the object more attractive in an appetitive sense by demonstrating its attractiveness to the others of the group; it makes the object desirable specifically for the power it confers on (but appears merely to reveal in) it to become the mediator of communal presence and hence to put an end to mimetic rivalry. The effect of desire would indeed be indiscernible were it to consist merely in the intensification of natural appetites under the mimetic influence of a single or collective model; desire would be in fact indistinguishable from mimesis itself.

The schema of representation we have outlined (p. 41) is circular rather than paradoxical because it is merely self-reinforcing. And indeed for the community as a whole the reconciliation of the original presence is euphoric rather than paradoxical. But let us now reconsider this schema in terms of the individual. In the first moment the abortive gesture of appropriation designates the sacred object in the presence of the others: The attraction of the object at this point remains that of the sparagmos provoked by mimetic rivalry. In the second moment this designation sacralizes the object and thus renders it both inaccessible and desirable in the rigorous sense of the word. But the desirability as opposed to the sacrality of the object is not made present to the community. It remains, so to speak, the secret of each individual, who, although designating the object as inaccessible to appropriation, at the same time and by the very fact of this *act* of designation (which we have noted to be the emission of an individual "token" of the sign-type just defined by the group as a whole) is implicitly affirming the possession of the object within his own linguistic universe.

Thus the third moment, in which the object thus designated is understood to be the cause of the nonviolent presence in which its designation has been effected, is experienced divergently by the individual and the group as a whole, or more precisely, by the individual qua ego and by the same individual qua member of the community. For insofar as he is a member of the group, he experiences this presence as a universal equality and reciprocity in which he participates through his designation of the object. But insofar as his act of designation is his own, it expresses his desire to appropriate the object, no longer in the context of the mimetic rivalry of the sparagmos, but precisely for its power to prevent the others from pursuing this rivalry, which is to say, for the power that it has manifested in giving rise to the communal presence.

This desire is indeed paradoxical, because what is desired to be appropriated is precisely the power that manifests itself in the object's nonappropriability. Were its appropriation to be attempted by any individual, the result would be not his possession of that power, but its dissolution in a return to the condition of crisis which the nonappropriation of the object had just put an end to. But the paradoxicality of this desire, which is that of desire in general in its most radical form, in no way implies its logical impossibility. This impossibility attaches, certainly, to the *fulfillment* of desire; but the impossibility does not make the desire itself any less potent. Desire is paradoxical because its content is self-contradictory: The possession of the desired object would despoil it of the very qualities for which it is desired, and this because the very designation of the object denotes it as inaccessible. The existence of the desire depends on the designation that alone gives it form, because desire, even if logically unfulfillable, must be able to define its aim. Or conversely, the designation of the sacred object by a given individual defines a desire and thus gives rise to a paradox. Which is to say that if the "word" of this designation contains no contradictions, its use inevitably is attended by one. This is a radical statement, and therefore a stronger one than might appear to correspond to the everyday use of language. But this is because the linguistic situation has not stood still since the original event. We refer here not to the *deus ex machina* of "history" but to the dynamic factor contained in the original situation itself. This dynamism is the source of all cultural form, including in particular the forms of the sacred. The institutional theory of representation, which derives these forms on a collective basis, as though the original presence remained at least functionally intact, able as it were to resummon itself into existence in ritual, in fact takes this dynamism for granted, and in doing so foregoes the possibility of evolving a theory of human communication, that is, of language.[6]

In order to understand the dynamism generated by the paradox of desire we must examine in greater detail the conditions of its temporal existence. The self-contradictory nature of desire, in expressing itself through the agency of representation, will tend to generate new forms in which the contradiction is resolved. These new forms in their turn will generate new desires, and from these desires still newer forms will emerge. The process thus abstractly described is without end, and indeed the whole of human history can be located within this dialectic, which the Hegelian dialectic reproduces in an "idealized" form. But if the forms of representation have their history, the manner of their genesis makes them at the same time defenses against history, forms of de-temporalization which transcend desire and which desire must struggle increasingly hard to transcend in their turn.

The whole point of the hypothesis is to give a historical basis for the first such transcendence that is constitutive of the specifically human, of representation, the sacred, and of desire itself. Thus we begin with mimetic rivalry and end with the establishment of the most primitive form of human culture. The transcendence cannot take place without violence; and we may assume that the later moments of the dialectic will not be exempt from it either, although we should expect the "higher" forms of violence to be both more subtle and more deadly than the first lynchings.

With these considerations in mind we can now return to our analysis of the original situation of the desiring subject. We have been speaking for some time of the sacralization of the victim's remains, which we have already referred to as a "sacred" object. But these references to the sacred in the mode of the institutional theory anticipate from our own standpoint the dialectic that we have only now begun to develop. This procedure is defensible heuristically, but only

so long as the incomplete nature of the preliminary exposition is not forgotten. Thus the circularity of our preliminary
schema of representation, which in effect implies that the
communal presence is permanent and all-absorbing, so that
individuality ceases before it is even called into being, should
merely serve as an indication that an atemporal schema
having been laid down, its temporal limitations will follow.
The error that we wish to avoid is to suppose from the
original absence of limits that the schema is not simply
atemporal but transtemporal, eternal—this being an ambiguity not resolved by the institutional theory.

Thus before introducing the notion of desire it is inaccurate to speak of the sacred, because all the preconditions of
the sacred have not yet been realized. The object is, at the
point at which we have left our analysis, still present to the
entire community that has formed around it. This situation,
the conclusion of the original event, is in our hypothesis the
origin of all forms of signification, and in particular of the
sacred. But these forms cannot yet be said to exist, to the
extent that the original presence in which they have been, as
it were, preconstituted, has not yet come to an end. To call
the object "sacred" is to affirm that it plays a role in the life
of the community; but to the extent that the community has
only just come into being around the object, its "life" has
not yet begun.

This is not a mere quibble but an essential departure from
the institutional theory, which derives the permanence of
(sacred) signification merely from the impact of the event,
which is assumed to remain fixed in the memory of the
community. But, at least outside Jungian mythology,
memory is not collective but individual, and it is not sufficient to evoke the communal significance of the "sacred"
object to explain why this significance is retained by the
individuals of whom the community is composed. We have
already taken this consideration into account in our insis-
tence on the *linguistic* element of the original situation: the
abortive gesture of appropriation which designates the object
in question. But we see now that this designation does not
function collectively but individually. It is only once ritual
has come into being that we can truly speak of a *collective*

representation in which the roles have been allotted in advance, in principle, at least, irrespective of the desires of the individual participants. At this point such is not yet the case. The presence of the entire community, necessary in order that the gesture acquire a significance and become a linguistic sign, at the same time prevents this sign from operating in a truly linguistic context in which its function would be to convey information. Designating the object in the original event conveys no information, because it can only direct the attention of the others to what they are already contemplating. Or rather the "message" conveyed to the others by each individual member of the group is simply the fact of designation. This might be called the "zero degree" of linguistic communication: The message conveyed is entirely that of the fact of enunciation, not at all that of the content. Here the linguistic form—the "word" that is the gesture—does not provide in any sense a model of the entire message. As we shall see, this separation between linguistic form and message conveyed is never altogether abolished even at the highest levels of linguistic communication, although it is progressively reduced at each successive step in the formal dialectic. This reduction is in fact equivalent from the hearer's viewpoint to the very telos of the dialectic, which we have just stated from the perspective of the speaker as the resolution of the paradoxes posed by desire.

In the original situation we take note of the structural symmetry between the "zero degree" of linguistic communication (to the addressee or "locutee") and what we may call with equal justification the "zero degree" of signification (for the speaker or "locutor"). For the enunciation of the "word" designating the object implies the same division within the intention of the speaker that we found in the reception of the message by the hearer. The linguistic content of the message is nil, the intent behind the enunciation being not to convey information about the world but to assure the group of the individual's lack of appropriative intention toward the object. This formulation of the symmetry of the communication-situation is lacking, however, in any internal dynamic, each communicating to the others, through an act of signification empty of linguistic content, his participation in the nonviolent communal presence. But just as each individual as speaker, in the very act by which he affirms this participation, at the same time "secretly" expresses his desire to possess the object, so each individual as hearer understands the others' acts as demonstrating a communal possession from which he fears to be excluded. And just as the desire is paradoxical, incapable of realization without destroying the meaning it attaches to its object, so is the fear; for if indeed the others could appropriate the object in any concrete sense that would exclude a given individual, then the object, no longer inaccessible, would become anew a source of mimetic conflict.

It is in response to the desires and fears of the individual members of the group that the object can truly be sacralized. That is, it can acquire the powers attributed to it in the original situation on a permanent basis, as attributes independent of communal presence. In the same manner the abortive gesture designating the object can only truly become a word once its signification of the object—which we still assume to require the presence of the object or of some "monument" of it (which might simply be the place of the murder), but not of the community—can itself serve to reestablish this presence, in which alone communication is possible. In order for the word to carry with it this presence, it must revive the memory of the power attributed to the object. But this memory is, for each individual, the product of his desire.

The object has, of course, no powers in itself; its "sacred" attributes in the original situation depended entirely on that situation, and could not be preserved by the community after the dissipation of the presence outside of which, we should recall, the "community" has no concrete existence. The memory of this presence can only be preserved by individuals. We must however be careful at this point to distinguish between each individual's particular memories of the event, which we can call his "souvenirs," and *significant* memory that, although individual in each case, can be evoked by one individual in another through communication, i.e., through enunciation of the linguistic sign. Now the content of significant memory, in order to be evoked by the linguistic sign, must have already been not simply "associated" with but

actually expressed by this sign in the original situation. Here
again we use the much-abused word "express" in a specific
sense to denote the effect of the act of signification by which
the linguistic content of the act (the *énoncé*) becomes a
model of the real world and thereby a *form* of desire. The
original act of designation was, as we have seen, a possession
of the object within what we have called the "linguistic
universe" of the subject, which is simply to say, within the
model created by the act itself. And as we have also seen,
possession within this imaginary model gives rise to a desire
for possession in the real world, and to the paradox entailed
by such (imaginary) fulfillment.

The construction of such imaginary models is not a distinctive feature of desire as we have defined it; they can be
assumed to exist wherever we find evidence of telic behavior,
in the higher animals as well as man. The distinguishing mark
of desire is that its imaginary models of fulfillment are
mediated by signification and, as a consequence, paradoxical.
Thus the simple imagination of possessing the "sacred" object, or any object for that matter, however irrealizable in
practice, is not paradoxical because it involves no inherent
contradiction. Only when the object becomes the bearer of a
signification is a paradox generated, because the possession
of the object itself modifies the original signification that was
dependent on its not being possessed. In the case at hand,
where the signification is unpossessibility itself, desire for the
"sacred" object creates the most fundamental, most radical
form of paradox. It is this desire that is evoked by the repetition of the sign designating the object, along with the corresponding fear of the possession of the object by another.

Now the imaginary possession of the object as such is not,
as we have just noted, paradoxical in itself, but only insofar
as the object is conceived to be the source of the presence
within which its designation can be communicated. In the
course of the original event the designation of the object and
the communal presence were inseparable and could not
indeed be conceived of separately. But once the crisis is
terminated, the repetition of the sign designating the object is
no longer a spontaneous product of the collective fear of
rekindling the crisis but an intentional act on the part of one

or more individuals. We may well assume that the fear of precipitating mimetic rivalry of some kind remains the motivation for the renewal of this designation, and that the emergence of the linguistic nature of the gesture designating the object was the "sedimentary" product of a series of crises extending over a period of indefinite duration. Such repetitions of the crisis situation are no sign of the anteriority of ritual to language, because the repetition will only be ritual to the precise extent that the gesture of designation is linguistic, that is, that it can be intentionally reproduced and communicated within a *virtual* presence already established among the members of the community.

But the repetition of the gesture, to the extent that it is experienced not as a spontaneous act of renouncement but a linguistic act of designation, makes increasingly evident the distinction between the act of designation on the one hand, and on the other, the communal presence within which this designation is communicated. Now we shall show, in the first place, that this distinction is a product of desire, and, in the second, that its actualization leads to two symmetrically opposed resolutions of the original paradox of desire. One is constitutive of the sacred *proprement dit*, and the other, of linguistic form in general. In the first case the object itself is sacralized by the attribution to it qua object of the powers it originally possessed as a result of its central role in the resolution of the crisis; in the second, the form of designation, shorn of its causal relationship to communal presence, and with it, of the desirability aroused by its power to create this presence by imposing its peace on a collectivity in crisis, becomes that of "secular" signification indifferent to its object, so that any object may henceforth be designated by a linguistic sign. This division marks the parallel emergence of the two fundamental forms of human representation: sacred ritual and secular language.

The Emergence of Cultural Forms

If in the preceding section we referred to an "original" event that gave rise to a spontaneous act of renunciation, an abortive gesture of appropriation designating the remains of the murder victim, we shall now refer to a second historical moment in which this gesture has become an intentional act of signification. The number of repetitions of the "original" event that may have been required to reach this second stage is both unknowable and immaterial—immaterial because unknowable, because no hypothesis of the origin of representation can consider any other than reproducible events. Our fundamental epistemological principle is simply that both the form and the content of the representations of which we have concrete knowledge must have originated in events, which implies that the (formal) reproducibility of representations must have been preceded by the (in-formal) reproducibility of events. It is sufficient for our purposes that the sedimentation of representation must occur, as we have attempted to show, through the agency of individual significant memory in which the sign evokes the desire to possess the object and sets in motion the paradox thus created.

We shall now examine the mechanism of memory and repetition more closely. The desire to possess the object is paradoxical when conceived atemporally, that is, under the supposition that significations are invariable; but the pragmatic paradox thus set up is not of the sort that is productive of paralysis. From the standpoint of practical action, the subject is only "paralyzed," incapable of acting, so long as the presence of the community maintains the tension between attraction and fear that characterizes the original situation. The original abortive gesture of appropriation expressed the paradox at the first moment of signification: To possess the object and to ignore it are equally impossible. But once this paradox is internalized as signification and desire, the possession of the object itself becomes self-contradictory, whereas at the same time the removal of the communal presence, or we might better say its *bracketing* within the process of signification, permits this self-contradiction, if not to "resolve itself" in the realm of signification, at least to work itself out, that is, to reveal itself in practice.

Thus the object, or some fragment or token of it, could conceivably be possessed by an individual, whose experience would then constitute a "resolution" of the original paradox of desire in the sense that the irreversible modification of the original signification as a result of this experience would remove the contradiction that had attached to possession: Presumably either the object would revive mimetic conflict or it would truly give him power over others. The first case would merely return the community to the original situation of crisis; the second would on the contrary truly constitute the object as sacred, because now its power to arrest aggressive action would appear as unambiguously vested in it alone rather than bound up inextricably with the original situation.

But we must stress that this last "scenario" (which might be considered to depict the origin of shamanism) is not a necessary element of the hypothesis. For the same concentration of power in the object itself might as easily result from its simply remaining untouched. The "practice" that brings the original paradox of designation to a resolution need consist of nothing more than the absence of action in time. In either case the dynamic is the same: The individual's desire for the object, active outside the original communal presence that the object evoked, calls up the image of the possession of the object separately from this presence and henceforth capable of evoking it, no longer as the presence within which the designation was communicated, but rather as that presence virtually imposed by the interdiction of violence under the "power" of the object, and which makes it effectively or "functionally" sacred.

This division of the original presence is a product, not of practice (although the successful appropriation of the object would certainly provide a striking demonstration of it) but of significant memory, which, in preserving the significance of the original sign of designation, preserves at the same time this presence within the linguistic universe of the individual subject, in what we have called a "bracketed" state, not as an *image* or a concrete *souvenir* but as the ground of signification. The gesture of designation could not continue to refer to the object were this presence not implicit in it—were it not, in other words, remembered less as a private expression of desire than as a communicable sign, one that would remain capable of again designating the object to the others and again summoning up for this purpose the nonviolent context of the original communal presence. (We should note that this does not imply that the gesture in the absence of the object would be understood as a sign of it; this form of signification will only appear at a later stage. The physically designative nature of the gesture pointing toward the object already implies this.)

Here the sign might be said to take on, in the significant memory, reinforced, we may assume, by practice, the "power" of the object to compel nonviolent attention. But the power of the sign and that of the object are in fact differentiated by the process we have just described: On the one hand, the object acquires for itself the power to forbid under any circumstances acts of appropriation directed toward it, whereas on the other hand, the sign, which by referring to the object serves to remind its locutees of this power, derives from it the independent power of compelling the nonviolent attention, which is to say the *presence*, of the others.

This differentiation definitively constitutes the sacred character of the object, and is therefore the true point of departure of the sacred. The original paradox of desire has now been resolved by the permanent attribution to the object of power over the members of the community. Whether or not the "scenario" described above has occurred the important point is that henceforth, for each member of the community, either the sacred object could conceivably be appropriated, thereby conferring on its possessor "absolute" power over the others, or its appropriation, inconceivable given the power of the object to interdict such behavior, can no longer even be desired. At this point the tension present in the original gesture disappears, or more precisely is converted from an equilibrium between the alternatives of attraction and fear into a unified attention to the object which we may call the attitude of representation.

But the term must here be understood to refer to the general form from which both sacred and secular forms— ritual and language—may be derived. For although our exposition has up to this point concentrated on the constitution of the sacred nature of the object, this constitution contains a latent ambivalence that it would not be accurate to attribute to the sacred alone as we have just defined it. For the constitution of the *sacred* object is at the same time that of the sacred *object*, which is to say of the object of representation in general. The attitude of representation, as expressed by the gesture of designation now purged of its internal contradictions, is still not a simple one because it stands in a double relationship to communal presence, which is on the one hand the ground, always virtually existent, of communication with the locutee(s), and on the other, an attribute of the designated (sacred) object, and consequently a component of the reference of the gesture of designation. There is no contradiction, but merely an ambiguity in this double relationship which will lead to its evolution along two different paths, the one that of reverence and ritual, the other that of reference and language.

The necessity of such an evolution will become clearer if the situation is examined from the standpoint of the sacred object, which is now perceived by the community as endowed with the power to interdict its own appropriation by recreating around it the same nonviolent presence of the members of the community to one another that characterized the original situation. As we have just seen from the standpoint of the individual act of signification, the presence of the community is no longer necessary a priori for the object's significance to be perceived. This significance, however—that which is signified by the designating sign—is precisely its power to impose this presence. The sacred object has now taken into itself the whole circular schema of representation that in the original situation required the prior presence of the entire community, this presence being now perceived as implicit in the object. But the relation of presence to the designation of the object by a given individual is ambiguous. What was originally a temporal progression of events having become an atemporal attribute of the sacred object, the act of designation, which was originally sandwiched between (1) the prior (violent) presence of the community reconciled in the common direction of their aggressions toward the victim; and (2) the victim-object designated as the mediator of the (nonviolent) presence that follows the interdiction of all further appropriative activity, now refers to the object as the source of presence in general.

The act of designation in the original event was intentional, and appeared as such to the participants. For the act was not an automatic consequence of the presence of (1), which is a necessary but not sufficient cause for it, because the very specificity of the abortive gesture of appropriation is precisely its noninstinctual character in which it appears as subject to a higher level of intentionality that can reflect the "drive" toward appropriation. But with regard to the presence of (2), the gesture of designation is dictated by the situation it has itself established; the object having become the mediator of presence, the designation of the object by each member of the community is the necessary sign of his participation in that presence. The presence of the victim-object to the community thus compels its own designation: What in relation to (1) was "language" has become "ritual."

This dichotomy could pass unnoticed in the primary moment of the hypothesis because it took place in an irreversible temporal sequence, the function of the same designative gesture varying with the progression of events. But in the secondary moment the two relations, "linguistic" and "ritual," of the sign to its object are expressed simultaneously. And this implies that the sign will evolve according to the context of its use, emphasizing one or the other of its functions. What is of primary concern to us will not, however, be the specific appearance that the sign may take on in this process of differentiation, but the differentiation within representational form.

The individual designating the sacred object stands, as we have seen, in a double relationship to communal presence. On the one hand, the power of the object to call this presence into being as the ground of communication obliges him to participate in this presence by designating the object; this form of designation conveys no information about the object, but is rather a sign of his own participation. This form of representation is thus a ritual demonstration of reverence, and from it will tend to evolve gestures of increasing complexity, or more precisely it will tend to assimilate to itself elements of the gestures of crisis and resolution that had originally been spontaneous expressions of mimetic conflict. This evolution is the aspect of representational "sedimentation" explicable on the basis of the institutional theory. From crisis to crisis, an increasingly large proportion of acts become formalized as representation, with the result that mimetic violence is replaced by its ritual representation: The symmetrical gestures of battle become those of dance, war cries take on the regular rhythms of song, and the at-first arbitrarily chosen victims are regularized into classes of sacrificial beings, animals and even plants being eventually substituted for humans.[7] Once the gesture of designation thus becomes an affirmation of the power of the sacred object to create and maintain communal presence, the ease of reproduction characteristic of linguistic acts, which was present as a potentiality of its original form, becomes rather a handicap than an advantage, and will therefore be lost as the participatory ritual element takes precedence over the function of signification.

But on the other hand the ambiguity of the relationship of sign to presence also makes possible its evolution in a direction opposite to that of ritual. For the existence of a virtual presence, mediated by the sacred object, within which significant communication between members of the group can be accomplished outside the crisis situation of the original event, serves to liberate the intention to signify from any situational restrictions. Indeed, once the power of presence has been localized in the sacred object, that object can freely be designated outside of any prearranged ritual context for the simple reason that the designation of the sacred object will always attract the nonviolent attention of others, or, in other words, establish presence between the speaker and his intended audience. Now that the sacred object has taken into itself, in the eyes of the group, the interdictive power exercised by the group in the original event, designation of the object can become the occasion for the reenactment of the event considered as the origin of communal reconciliation and, indeed, of the community itself.

But by the same token, the event and its benefits now being graspable in the object as an atemporal whole no longer subject to the irreversibility of a temporal sequence, this totality can, in the object, be designated from without, disregarding the circularity of signification in the original

situation. It may be objected at this point that such designation generally falls under a taboo, such as the one that
prevents Jews from uttering the name of God even in prayer.
But the existence of these taboos is, here as elsewhere, simply
the best indication that the forbidden phenomenon is at the
very least a dangerously real possibility. The taboo also
implies that the further development of the forms of representation cannot simply be derived from the internal differentiation of the sacred object. Precisely insofar as it plays for
the community the role of a "transcendental signifier" of the
nonviolent presence established in the original event, its
designation outside the ritual context must remain a forbidden virtuality, the free actualization of which would lead to
the loss of its powers, which in the context of nonritual
signification would be unable to manifest themselves.

The resolution of the original paradox of desire by the
sacralization of the object has produced not a final stability,
which indeed could only be realized at the "end of history,"
but a state of semistable equilibrium. For the power of the
sacred object is not truly its own, but that of the community,
and its evocation in the absence of the community would be
inefficacious. The interdiction on designating the sacred
object by name nevertheless depends on this same power,
inherent in the object and thus in its name (at the present
stage, in the gesture of designation); the representation of the
sacred object in significant memory is what prohibits the
actualization of the representation in an act of signification.
This prohibition, insofar as it is not merely a fear of punishment by the community but a fear internalized in the representation, exemplifies what we can already call a first stage of
moral consciousness or "conscience," which here functions
to maintain the necessary communal fiction of the "sacred
object" rather than, as in its higher forms, directly to promote concern for others.

This example, which we could not enlarge on here without
vastly exceeding the limits of our subject, can at least serve as
an indication of the intimate relation between the ethical and
the cognitive, a relation the context of which we have shown
to be *esthetic*, the "beautiful" being thus seen to be anterior
to the "good" and the "true." Higher forms of morality are

based on forms of signification that are nearer the truth, the fragility of the primitive forms requiring for their maintenance cruder restraints on the free use of the forms of signification. And as we may observe from this discussion, these restrictions are not in the first instance imposed through laws decided on by the group, but through the need to avoid the emergence of new paradoxes which would destroy the efficacy of their sacred representations and return the group to chaos. The evolution of language, to which we shall now turn, thus depends on the distancing of its referents from the domain of the sacred.[8]

3 The Elementary Linguistic Forms

Part I

The Emergence of Linguistic Form: The Ostensive

Our exposition of the origins of representation in the preceding chapter has led us to the threshold of the emergence of representational form from its dependence on the sacred object which has up to this point provided its sole content. The constitution of this object independently from the original presence of the community to itself in the crisis situation can be located in a second moment of the hypothesis, in which the repetition of the mechanism of crisis and resolution has produced sufficient "sediment" in the significant memory for the sign of designation to retain its meaning in a *virtual* presence, the maintenance of which is attributed to the "power" of the object. At this moment, as we have seen, the splitting of the original presence into two components creates for the sign two divergent paths of evolution which we may call by the names we have given to the theories of representation in which they are respectively given priority, the formal and the institutional.

We have dealt briefly in the preceding chapter with the institutional path, in which the sacred object's power of presence becomes the content of the representation, which loses its proto-linguistic character to become collective participation in the evocation of this power: religious ritual. We shall now turn to the formal path—that of language. The priority we have given to the institutional in our exposition is that of the history of theory rather than of our own theory, Girard's original formulation of the hypothesis being in what we are calling "institutional" terms. This concession to the heuristic should not, however, be taken as an abandonment of our ontological commitment to the formal. The reader should recall that in our version of the original event, the designation of the remains of the victim—its *representation*—preceded its sacralization. The formal theory differs from the institutional in the priority thus given to representation in the establishment of the original presence, which in Girard's exposition is attached immediately to the object. More than this, however, the formal theory does not claim; to affirm the anteriority of language to ritual and of the profane to the sacred would be to regress beyond structuralism, which has at least the good sense to avoid granting a privileged role to either member of the dichotomy. The original designation is no more and no less a sacral act than a linguistic one. That the formal theory does not, however, maintain its original neutrality between language and ritual is amply demonstrated by the contents of the present work, which will from this point on be devoted almost exclusively to the forms of language.

The historical advantage of language over ritual is, after all, a reality of our era of "de-ritualization"; the forms of language or, in other terms, of *signification*, which are essentially unaffected by social transformations, are far more stable than those in which the *significant* presents itself. Within this opposition the task of the theory of representation is not to reduce one pole to the other but to account for all phenomena. Yet the priority given to signification over significance is not merely a heuristic one but a necessity of theory as such, which can only become significant through the signification it contains. The first duty of theory, before it can attempt to understand the practice of the significant, is to understand itself. We must therefore accept the greater vulnerability of linguistic structures to formal analysis as a valid sign of their greater historical compatibility with it. If language structures desire more neatly than ritual, we may draw the historical conclusion that the structures of the significant will tend, as theory increases man's control over his practice, to approach those of language, within which structures are included those developed in the theory. Thus the ultimate reason for giving preference to language over ritual, to the signifying over the significant, lies in the fact that language alone can express the truth of its object, and in so doing reduce its object, for all practical purposes, to language. The formal theory of representation thus pays homage to the ultimately superior significance, over and above all sacralized objects and significant images, of theory—of formal representation—itself.

The Emergence of Signification-in-General

In the preceding chapter we described a presumably gradual transition from the gestural designation of the victim-object at the original moment of crisis to the use of the gesture as an intentional sign in a nonconflictive context guaranteed by the virtual presence of the community embodied in the object. Now the motivation for this sign has been shown to be double: on the one hand, the designation of the power of the object to enforce communal presence and thereby to evoke its own designation, on the other, the simple designation of the object as such, made possible by the virtual presence it embodies. In this second form of designation the sacred power of the object is not the point of the gesture but merely an a priori guarantee of its success as an act of communication. But once this is the case the same gesture can be used, under the same guarantee, to designate other objects, those, for example, in the vicinity of the sacred object. Indeed, once the virtual presence of the members of the community to each other has been established, the various forms of instinctual communication—gestures and cries—used by animals as well as man to indicate danger, the presence of food, and so on, can begin to be used intentionally, maintaining their function as signals but at the same time calling into being qua communication the virtual presence of the members of the community to one another guaranteed by the sacred object. It is in this context that we can understand the existence of a plurality of linguistic signs which, whatever their specific origin, have now become forms of signification existing within presence as their "space" of communication.

In discussing instinctual forms of communication the notion of intention is gratuitous because the relations involved can all be explained by means of simple causality. Perception of a certain situation produces an instinctive cry that when heard by others provokes an instinctive reaction. Our attribution of intentionality to human communication is of course at the present stage only hypothetical, the only possible proof of it being supplied by higher linguistic forms. Our justification is simply this: The development of these higher forms, nonexistent among animals, can only be explained on this basis. The dialectic of representation, in our hypothesis, is driven by desire, and desire in our definition is not an instinctual force, but an effect of the intentionality of representation, which is itself born from the renouncement of the instinctual object. The validity of these hypothetical affirmations cannot of course be demonstrated apodictically but only made greater or less by the explicative (and ultimately predictive) power of our theory of representation as a whole.

The clarification of the relationships between intention, representation, and desire can at least serve to de-mystify the first and most maligned of these concepts. Intention can be felt intuitively, but not verified directly in practice—whence the possibility of the Skinnerian theory of language as "behavior." Discussions of intention have always suffered from the apparently unbridgeable gap between the richness of its "subjective" process and the relative poverty of its "objective" expression, which even when it claims to bear witness to the former can never give proof of its assertions, the subtlest responses being, for example, programmable on a computer. It would appear that if intention as a noninstinctual phenomenon is inconceivable in the absence of a system of signification, i.e., language, in which it can express itself, this very system cannot but betray the inner world it was to reveal.

The hypothesis is really nothing other than a plausible historical scenario for the origin of the intentional. For to abstract from its model of the origin of representation the specifically intentional nature of the representations whose origin it describes is to reduce it to the uncritical level of etiological myth. Now the signs of the intentional within the hypothetical event—tension between atraction and fear in the presence of the others, "non-instinctual attention"—have been postulated as intentional because only thus can the subsequent evolution of the representation of the event, which in our version of the hypothesis is already the central moment of the event, be explained. But so long as the explanation remains limited to vague notions of "development," "elaboration," "forgetting," and so on, the conception of intention as the motive force for this evolution cannot demonstrate its advantages over the oversimplified behavioral model.

The dialectic of desire and representation, of which we have described up to this point only the preliminary stages, can be said to offer an implicit definition of the intentional that avoids the traditional subjective-objective dichotomy. Instead of opposing futilely an intuitive sense of intentionality to the cold neutrality of the behavioral scientist's grasp of the data, this dialectic simply defines the intention at each stage in terms of the intersubjective relationship between speaker and hearer formalized in the linguistic model. Thus intentionality is not a mysterious quality of representations in themselves, but a dimension of the total communication situation. The intention of an act of representation, defined in the most general terms, is the correspondence it establishes between the moment of presence in which the act takes place and the temporality of the real world. The forms of this correspondence range over many degrees of complexity, each successive level of the dialectic within which they can be supposed to have evolved constituting a resolution of the pragmatic paradox aroused by the instability of the correspondence on the preceding level, by which we refer to the interference in this correspondence of the moment of *presence* of representation experienced as at the same time a *present* moment of real time. So long as the structures of this correspondence are made explicit—sufficiently explicit, that is, so that their latent paradoxality can be observed—it is a matter of total indifference whether they be expressed in "behavioral" terms. Thus in this conception it is behaviorism, not the doctrine of intentionality, which appears as a functionally irrelevant dogma vulnerable to Ockham's razor.

Nor need we trouble ourselves with the problem of the "intentionality" of, say, animal communication, in which, whatever its complexity, we have no reason to assume that the presence in which the communication takes place has ever itself become an object of representation. In contrast, human communication, according to our hypothesis, makes this presence not only the condition but the content of its first distinctive sign. But it must be stressed that the essential quality that separates human representation as such from animal forms, even where the external features of these are retained by humans, is independent of any specific formulation of the hypothesis. For it is sufficient to note the empirical fact that human culture does indeed represent this presence thematically in ritual—a fact that is already a sufficient explanation of the chronological priority of the institutional theory of representation that takes its conception of the hypothesis directly from this fact, over the formal theory that postulates the existence of representation as prior to ritual. Whatever hypothesis may be devised to explain the origin of human culture, it cannot avoid explaining this unique reflexivity of human representation with respect to its intersubjective ground. The only alternative is to ignore or reject the need for such a hypothesis, in which case the notion of a ground ceases to have any meaning.

Derrida indeed attacks the "metaphysical" ground of original presence as a myth, that is, as *content*, while opposing it with his own critically de-conceptualized mechanism of "différance" or deferral as the true ground of communication. This critique fails to remark that presence and deferral, far from opposing each other as (spurious) plenitude and (real) absence, are merely different terms for the same phenomenon, the original presence being precisely a deferral of appropriative action. The difference is merely one of emphasis in which, indeed, we can find a suggestion of our own distinction between presence-as-ground and presence-as-content, and consequently of the opposition between the formal and institutional theories of representation. But the opposition cannot be developed rigorously so long as presence is understood—and rejected—as an illusion of metaphysics, traceable ultimately to ritual (see *De la grammatologie*, and "La Pharmacie de Platon" in *La Dissémination* [Editions Du Seuil, 1972]), whereas "différance" is opposed to it as the nonconceptual truth behind the illusion of the concept. No doubt "deferral" could stand as a synonym for what we have just defined as intention, viewed now from the standpoint of the hearer rather than the speaker in the intersubjective communication situation (the asymmetry of intentionality from the perspectives of the two interlocutors, being constitutive of desire, is essential to our definition). This equivalence could only be realized, however, within the "space" provided by intersubjective presence, in the absence of which the "deferral" through representation could never take place.

The prior existence of presence as the ground of communication does not turn signals as such into intentional signs. Human beings have not ceased to employ instinctual cries and gestures simply because they possess articulate language. We may take lexicalization as the touchstone of intentionality: those cries of pain, surprise, and so on, which have been lexicalized ("Ouch!," "Aha!" etc.), must be considered, however "primitive" their content, as words, and therefore as intentional signs; those which have not remain on the level of the instinctual and can be assimilated to animal cries. The very ease with which we can make this distinction demonstrates its pertinence: Certainly the speaker's intention in the most general sense must be different according to his "choice" of "Ouch!" or an unarticulated scream. Or, more precisely, the use of "Ouch!" *connotes* such a choice, whereas that of the scream does not, even though the latter, like instinctual actions of all kinds, may be "performed" deliberately, in which case we would tend to call it "feigned."' The signal does not then disappear. But the possibility arises of a sign that, although fulfilling *grosso modo* the same function as the signal, depends implicitly on an already-established presence, or more precisely, on the activation of the virtual presence guaranteed by the sacred object. Such a sign—or rather such a plurality of signs, because this plurality follows a fortiori from the preexistent plurality of signals—may be considered as the beginning of articulated language and the ancestor of all more complex linguistic phenomena. The original sign was meaningful only in the presence of its referent, and such must remain the case at the most primitive phase of linguistic evolution. It is notable, of course, that instinctual signals, too, are necessarily associated with the presence of their referent. But, indeed, this should not surprise us because the original sign was derived directly from the instinctual gesture toward an object of potential appropriation, a gesture that already served as a signal on far lower levels of the animal kingdom. Because these first linguistic signs designate their referent as present we shall call them *ostensives*. With this definition we enter into our discussion of the evolution of linguistic structures *proprement dit*.

This discussion will not be, like the analyses of the preceding chapter, purely hypothetical, but will seek confirmation in our current use of linguistic forms. This evidently advantageous shift in methodology is only made possible, however, if we may postulate the permanence of these forms, or more precisely of their intentional structure, and this postulation is itself an element of the hypothesis, a corollary of the assumption fundamental to the formal theory that the accessibility of linguistic forms to analysis is an indication of their ontological priority. To whatever extent modern languages may differ from the primitive stage now under discussion, we may assume that the structures present in these primitive stages are preserved, as indeed prelinguistic signals are preserved, because they retain their original function, albeit in a "dead" or fixed form no longer subject to evolution, which is to say, no longer productive of the analogical extensions that characterize the "living" forms at the forefront of the evolutionary process.[2] And this function remains fixed, despite the explicitation and transcendence of internal contradictions characteristic of the dialectic of desire. For, as our definition of intention implies, language is essentially a means of creating, within the sphere of intersubjective presence, models of real situations that, because they occur and recur in time according to material and not representational necessity, do not simply "evolve" out of existence. The preservation in modern languages of the most primitive linguistic structures may, conversely, be taken as further justification of the priority given to language by our theory. The argument is, of course, formally circular because only the hypothesis absolutely guarantees the term "primitive structure." But in this domain the plausibility of the evolution proposed by the hypothesis can be confirmed by its conformity to the gradient of complexity of linguistic structure—the existence of this gradient being the "heuristic" reason for the exemplary status of language within our theory of representation.

The Ostensive: Beginnings of Lexical Differentiation

We may define ostensives as intentional acts of signification which call attention to the presence, in principle verifiable, of their referent. The verifiability of this presence by the interlocutor is not a minor point, for it is the essential *functional* distinction between ostensives and mere signals. The signal, in the assumption at least that all members of the group are equally capable of emitting and receiving it, is also therefore implicitly verifiable. This verifiability is not, however, an explicit feature of the act of communication, and the condition of *intentional* correspondence between the representation and the real world is not met. If in hurting myself in the presence of another I say "Ouch!" I am not merely expressing pain but encouraging my interlocutor to observe the source of my pain—say, for example, having struck my thumb with a hammer. A mere cry of pain would not have this effect—and we might note that "Ouch!" is not used unless the source of pain is clearly external. On the contrary, "Ouch!" is particularly appropriate when the addressee is in some sense the cause of my pain, for example, through the act of stepping on my toe. In such cases, indeed, "pain" becomes a purely conventional attribute of a situation supposed a priori to be pain-causing: Thus I say "Ouch!" when my toe is stepped on, or even when I hit my finger with a hammer, more to express the violation of a norm than my own physical suffering. The use of the ostensive in the mutual presence of the interlocutors and the referent establishes, as the examples show, the same relationships as in the original event, where the presence of the "sacred" object to the community-as-locutees was as essential as its presence to the community-as-locutors. In the example we have given, however, and in the ostensive in general, the presence of the referent to the locutee is not created spontaneously with the designative sign, but is intended as its result. The ostensive, generally speaking, conveys from speaker to hearer the information that the referent is present.

This information-bearing character is not new, of course—it is the common characteristic of signals. What is new is its association with presence. The first sign, as we saw, carried no information about its object, nor in general do ritual signs.[3] Information-bearing intentional signs, in particular, ostensives, can only exist on the preexisting ground of virtual presence within which new relations to objects other than the original object can develop. The placing of a new object at the center of attention attributes to it a situational equivalent of the "power" of the sacred object to compel the attention of the interlocutor. It is this analogous attribution of "power" to the object that differentiates the ostensive from the mere signal expressing instinctual interest. The verifiability of the ostensive covers not only the presence of the object but this power, which is to say, its significance. Because we may assume that instinctive signals have a predetermined physiological threshold of activation, the obvious point of insertion of ostensives is just below this threshold, where the referent is perceived and judged to be potentially significant. Evocation of the presence of the community in the absence of a sufficiently "powerful" object being in effect the equivalent of a return to a state of unreconciled mimetic crisis, with the locutor in the asymmetric and therefore vulnerable role of the victim, we must assume that the instinctual threshold was lowered only very gradually. But the judgment that led to this lowering, and which is indeed the first example of judgment as such—not judgment as falling under a specific concept, but *judgment as significant*—could not have been made at all unless the speaker had reason to expect that the reconciliatory effect of the original act of signification would be likewise produced by his own, so that his message would at least be heard in peace. It is thus that we speak of a "virtual presence" of the members of the community one to the

other, a presence that should not be taken by any means to
be a state of permanent tranquility. The locutor of the ostensive, in evoking this presence from the asymmetrical position
of the original victim, judges that the information conveyed
by his act will *guarantee* his usurpation of this position. The
virtual presence of human communication is not—today nor
in the beginning—simply an "open channel," but an essentially *suspicious* one. It is this suspicious nature of linguistic
communication, its requirement of guarantees, that is at the
basis of the severity of the norms which pervade language at
all levels, from the phonetic to the logical and esthetic. Each
speaker in proposing his linguistic model to one or more of
his fellows in effect recreates a crisis in which the significance
of the information conveyed provides the power of reconciliation.

It is the need to guarantee the asymmetric situation of the
speaker that is the motivation for communicative efficiency
and, in particular, for lexical diversity. The internal time of
linguistic presence is not taken into account by the communicative intention, but for that very reason it affects this
intention from without, as an acultural psychological reality.
To take too much time in communicating a piece of information is to commit an error not linguistic but practical, the
hearer's potential for anger tending to increase with the duration of his subjection to the speaker's linguistic model. Thus
this time will tend to approximate the minimum required for
the hearer to absorb the information conveyed. Now if we
begin with a simple designative sign, the sign conveys only
the information that its object is significant, in addition to
(perhaps) giving a directional indication of its location. Such
a unique sign could only be justified by a referent endowed
with the same "power" as the sacred object, because any
object of lesser interest would not be able to forestall the
mimetic conflict aroused by the mobilization of a communal
presence identical to that of the original event. Thus a single
sign could not take on the task of designating a plurality of
referents without differentiating itself into a plurality of
signs, each one of which would convey information about its
referent proportionally to the member of such signs available,
that is, to the size of the lexicon.[4]

This differentiation would begin as soon as the original sign was applied to a referent other than the original one; for the intention to designate the object to the community as other than the preexistent sacred object could only express itself through some modification of the original sign, for example, a diminution of its intensity. This first differentiation would create a two-place hierarchy of signs constitutive of the opposition between sacred and profane representations. The virtual presence of the community incarnated in the sacred object would at this point become the ground of the communication of a significance that could not in itself justify this presence. This development is dependent on the power of the sacred object to maintain peace in the community; but fear of this power is precisely what motivated the modification of the original sign in the first place. Now within the domain of profane representation the same dynamic of differentiation would continue to operate. For if we assume that the "profane" sign attracts from its addressee an interest of a certain intensity, then this interest too can be deceived by a relatively insignificant referent, which will therefore tend to acquire for its designation a newly differentiated sign. But this differentiation must not be merely quantitative, but qualitative as well; two objects that are perceived differently by the group will tend to acquire two different names. This process of lexical differentiation must remain, in its beginnings at least, purely hypothetical, although it can still be observed in the evolution of modern language.

The need for guarantees of significance against what we might call the suspicion of nonsignificance thus determines two distinct elements of linguistic development. The potential danger aroused by the actualization of communal presence requires an originally high threshold of significance; the gradual lowering of this threshold leads in turn to the distinction of categories of reaction to signs themselves increasingly diversified. No doubt the differentiation process has already begun with signals, and in several highly publicized instances, such as the directional signals of bees or the less clearly understood calls of dolphins, has produced within a limited domain of signification a kind of signaletic substitute for language. But those who would make use of such phenomena to cast doubt upon the distinctiveness of human language and to reject the "subjective" concept of intentionality are guilty of a grave misinterpretation.[5] Evolution offers many cases of functional parallelism. And rather than vainly dispute about the relative "value" of human and animal communication, we would do better to begin by recognizing that they are in any case of very different natures. The evolution of highly specific signals is merely a striking example—but no more so than many others—of the Darwinian process. By no stretch of the imagination can it be said to be the result of a need to guarantee the "speaker" against the potential suspicions of his audience. If the human lexicon is vastly more varied than that of bees or dolphins, this is not a mere difference of degree but the result of the general impetus to differentiation given by human suspicion, whereas evolutionary pressure must confine itself to maximally essential areas. Human presence, unlike that of a swarm of bees, is fragile and apt to be transformed into unanimous aggression against the speaker. As the threshold of danger is lowered in conjunction with ritual reinforcement of the communal solidarity produced by the sacred, the reaction of the community of hearers acquires more degrees of freedom and thereby provides the impulse for a vocabulary richer in information. Such a development is foreign to animal ·"languages," the evolution of which is limited by the requirements of instinctual drives which are not themselves subject to the retroactive influence of language.

This differentiation of reaction to the sign can only be understood in the context of the *deferral* of action which was already the effect of the sign in the original situation. The presence in which communication takes place can be thought of as a time of deferral separating an original virtual presence from a final action. In the original event designation of the victim-object led, as we have seen, to its sacralization and, presumably, to reverential acts taken by the community to preserve it not only from the danger of possible appropriation by individual members of the community but from reintegration in the processes of nature. The remains of the victim, we have assumed, are preserved by their deposition in a tomb or "monument" of some sort which serves as a quasi-permanent referent for future uses of the designative sign.[6] But we should not forget that the original event, which results in the nonviolent resolution of a general crisis, is not the inevitable outcome of such a crisis but a memorable success preceded, and in its early instances presumably followed, by numerous failures. The virtual presence of the community brought about by the attraction to the victim as an object of aggressive appropriation is converted by the original *successful* sign into the object of communal reference and the guarantor of peaceful cooperation.

But in the event that instead of the abortive gesture we have hypothesized one or more "natural" gestures—that is, signals—of appropriation continue to occur, these would lead not to nonviolence but to a renewal of collective violence, now directed at the individual or individuals who are perceived as threatening to appropriate for themselves what is already considered, if not a sacred object, then a particularly "attractive" one. The evolution of the crisis situation as a whole according to the hypothesis has been in the direction of increasing concentration on a victim singled out to take the blame for whatever unpleasantness set off the crisis in the first place. And in each case the collective choice must have been dictated by the victim's possession of some unusual trait that served the others as a "sign," perceived if not as "intentional"— for the conditions for intentionality had not yet been brought into existence— at any rate as punishable. The cessation of hostilities around the cadaver of some specific victim, designated finally not merely by his own acts and qualities but by a collective gesture independent of him, and standing in relation to him, so to speak, as the first "linguistic model," qualifies this latter sign as a uniquely successful communication which, instead of merely rendering its referent a more attractive object of aggression, leads to its sacralization and collective preservation.[7]

In this perspective, unavailable, of course, to the participants in the original act of signification but accessible to the community at the "second moment" in which the category of signification-in-general already exists, the consequence of the success or failure of acts of signification as such can be seen to reproduce in structure, if not in intensity, the violence/nonviolence polarity characteristic of the original event. The successful act of signification leads to cooperation between speaker and hearer(s), and the unsuccessful act, to the mobilization of the latter against the former. Hence we have on the one hand the threshold of significance, which separates successful from unsuccessful acts, and on the other the tendency toward lexical differentiation, which corresponds to the differentiation among potential acts of cooperation. In the original event the single sign could only distinguish success from failure, violence from nonviolence; but as the virtual presence assured by the sacred object is reinforced, and the threshold of significance is lowered, or, in other words, as nonviolent cooperation is brought about by reference to objects that inspire increasingly less terror of mimetic violence, the multiplication of potential responses will lead to a corresponding multiplication of the number of signs. The constitution of a lexicon of signs thus goes hand in hand with that of a set of social forms, that is, forms of secular, "functional" interaction. The codification of these forms in the lexicon preserves them in the significant memory of the members of the group and permits their further elaboration by future generations. It is only because human communication, unlike that of animals, must pass through the "infinite" risk of violence that characterizes the actualization of communal presence that human language has accrued the "infinite" gain of intentional deferral of action and the concomitant lexical differentiation. But the evolution of language is not confined to the mere differentiation of signs. These signs, as we have seen, give rise to desire, to paradox, and thence to new linguistic forms in which the paradox is resolved. The next stage in this formal evolution will be described in the following section.

Linguistics of the Ostensive

Thus far we have been concerned with the hypothetical preconditions for the existence of the linguistic form of the ostensive and for the differentiation of the signs or "words" available to this form. Under the assumption that these preconditions have been met, we shall now attempt to elabo-

rate a "linguistics" of the ostensive language thereby constituted. This construction, unlike those of the hypothesis, can
be controlled by direct observation of ostensives in our
own language.[8]

Because the ostensive construction lacks any internal
structure its vocabulary is not divided into parts of speech. In
particular there can be no distinction between nominals and
verbals. More fundamental still is the nature of the relationship between the word and its referent. We have described
the first ostensive as a designating gesture referring to the
"sacred" object. At the same time, as we have already pointed
out, the object is in itself not detachable from the communal
presence in which it appears. In the "profane" world, however, such presence is realized in the communication situation, but no longer appears as the principal attribute of the
object. This is not to say that the ostensive simply signifies its
object in the same way as, in developed languages, a proper
noun signifies its bearer. The ostensive offers, within the presence of communication, an intentional model of the universe
limited to a single present reality. The internal differentiation
of the ostensive lexicon can increase the precision of the
model, but without modifying what we are calling its *intentional structure*, the relation of the model to the world. The
ostensive designates as significant an element of present
reality observed by the speaker but not (yet) by the hearer,
who is in any case assumed to be able to verify this presence
for himself. "Significant" here means worthy of eliciting
cooperative action on the part of the hearer; the intentional
nature of such action, as opposed to examples of instinctive
cooperation, is dependent on that of the linguistic communication that brought it about in the context of communal
presence. Thus a visible element of reality is singled out from
a neutral ground as requiring action, or minimally, attention
of some kind. In the model created by the ostensive, the
recognition of the designated object is assumed to be sufficient to incite such action. But the question as to whether
the designated object is effectively *named* by the ostensive
has not really been answered.

Let us consider the expression "Fire!" This utterance is
immediately recognizable as an ostensive. The speaker com-

municates to his audience the presence of a fire, to which they are expected to react by taking appropriate measures. These measures are not spelled out, and could not be within the ostensive construction regardless of the refinements in its vocabulary, although a possible differentiation between, say, "Oil fire!" and "Forest fire!" might lead to a difference in response. We may indeed go further and claim that an ostensive language would only possess such a distinction were a difference in response anticipated, that is, implicit in the intention of the speaker. But in no case does this intention *specify* the response; the existence of lexical differentiation simply implies that the hearer would expect to be given the information it contains before preparing his course of action. The time of linguistic presence being of necessity short, the deferral of action is itself brief, and thus we can assume that lexical differentiation would remain limited to a small number of basic situation types, such as that signified by "Fire!"

Two further features of this last ostensive should be noted: First, its object is not an individual thing but a state, not necessarily limited in extent to a small area such as would be consonant with a gesture of pointing; and second, the significance of this state, its requirement of an urgent response, is precisely a result of its unlocalizable nature, its tendency to spread beyond its current spatial limits to engulf the entire community. This last characteristic is shared by many objects of ostensives, such as dangerous animals ("Wolf!" etc.), which are, to be sure, individual beings, but whose danger lies in their unrestricted mobility. From this example the ostensive is seen to be something other than the mere designation of an object. This latter is indeed "named," but implicit in the naming is the sense that if urgent action is not taken, the referent of the name will no longer be confinable within a linguistic model, because its continued existence will destroy the physical conditions of virtual presence in which the model can be communicated. In contrast, the action anticipated by the ostensive is such that the referent, if not simply annihilated as a fire is extinguished, will not in any event remain an object of significance after its execution. In these characteristics the "secular" ostensive differs markedly from the original sign, which by its very existence put an end to the threat of further violence. Now the threat of violence is still the motivation for the sign, but it is that of an agency (which could of course be an alien human) external to the presence of the speaker and his hearers. It is the externality of the threat—the significant object—that permits it to be isolated within the linguistic model, whereas the precarity of this isolation is in effect the motivation for the linguistic act.

As a control of the last example, which we might call a "denunciatory" ostensive, we may consider an example of the "annunciatory" ostensive, such as Xenophon's θάλαττα! θάλαττα! or the exclamation "water!" on the lips of a thirsty traveler sighting a stream. Here the significance of the referent is not a threat posed to the survival of the group but its contribution to this survival, which was at least implicitly threatened by its absence. The urgency here is, however, not an attribute of the threat but of the newly discovered resource, which might be fast disappearing, like a beast of prey, but in any case is to be profited from immediately. In this type of ostensive, as in our previous example, the anticipated cooperative action may involve genuine working together—as in a hunt—or, minimally, "communion" in a life-giving activity (like drinking from a stream); the group's solidarity is affirmed, and the designated object rendered, for the time being at least, "insignificant." Whereas in our first example the referent was isolated as an external threat to the collectivity, here the linguistic model serves to isolate an externally given benefit—threat and benefit being both present as constitutive moments of the original act of signification, which consists of nothing but an oscillation between the responses—approach and flight—appropriate to each.

Although ambivalent cases, as we should expect, can exist (the dangerous animal which is also edible), our two examples illustrate the two polar tendencies of significance. Objects neither dangerous nor beneficial will remain insignificant, although the lowering of the threshold of significance will tend to enlarge its domain. We may assume that the ostensive, which lacks a nominal/verbal distinction, can designate "actions" as well as objects, an expression like "Fire!" although unambiguously a noun, referring indiffer-

ently to the fire and to its burning. Taking advantage of the
English language's diminished morphology, we may conceive
of ostensives like "Run!" which would refer to the action of
running without identifying the runner, and which would
occupy a linguistic category more general than either nominals (*a* run or running) or verbals ([something] runs). Such
constructions must indeed have existed in ostensive language
if we are to assume that it provided the basis for the lexicon
of higher stages. But epistemologically speaking it would
seem more reasonable to classify all ostensives functionally as
nominals. If we consider a highly specified action, the ostensive "Stampede!" is a verb as well as a noun, but until such
time as the verbal form becomes a true *predicate*, and thereby takes on a tense relating a linguistic temporality to that of
the real world, the stampede or stampeding is simply, like a
fire or a wolf, a thing to be reacted to.

Our examples up to this point have illustrated the salient
features of the ostensive by reference to real and imaginary
"scenarios" of appropriate usage. In the remainder of our
discussion we shall attempt to create a more formal model
of ostensive language in order to make explicit what we have
called the *intentional structure* of this construction. Traditional linguistics has concerned itself exclusively with the
internal structures of language. The recent and indeed welcome trend toward "speech-act" linguistics has emphasized
the pragmatic functioning of language, but in doing so has
altogether neglected the genesis of the linguistic forms this
functioning depends on. Thus some linguists now study
function, others form. But the proper task of linguistics as
a branch of a general theory of representation is to study
how form structures function. It is this interaction between
the linguistic model and the real world as a potential object
for action which we have referred to as the domain of intentionality; the intentional structure of linguistic forms, of
which the ostensive is the most primitive, can be defined as
the set of intersubjective relations produced by these forms
within the presence of the communication situation. These
structures, as is evident from our genetic perspective, do not
possess the absolute stability of "pure forms" but are only
metastable; their full explicitation leads, through the dialectic

of desire and paradox, to the emergence of higher structures. The simple structures remain, however, because this explicitation is unnecessary and indeed impossible in the vast majority of practical cases. But their apparent stability is no excuse for an empiricism that takes its forms where it finds them without ever seeking to understand their genesis or to discover their potential for evolving into higher forms. The study of language is in dire need of the Socrates who would confound its learned practitioners by simply asking "What is a sentence?"

The Intentional Structure of the Ostensive

The speaker of the ostensive creates by his utterance, which we should not hesitate to call a sentence, a linguistic model of reality. The simplicity of this model may make the very notion of a "model" appear inadequate, but its extreme impoverishment should rather serve to indicate the complexity of the cultural experience that has been necessary to permit the evolution of the vastly more adequate models provided by scientific discourse. The distance traveled by human representation—a "distance" that, in spite of the image, is anything but linear—separates us from nature and the nonrepresentative, nonintentional forms of animal communication. The ease with which we construct complex declarative sentences inspires in us the illusion that such sentences simply reflect, "transparently" as it were, the order of things, so that a primitive structure like the ostensive strikes us not as an "objective" model but as an expedient inspired by practical necessity. Thus we think of declarative sentences as true or false, whereas ostensives, if we think of them at all—and linguistics has done nothing to make us aware of their existence—stand outside the pale of "objective" truth. Surely it will take more than the "deconstruction" of the discourse of "Western metaphysics" to make even a dent in the stubborn "logocentricity" of this perspective. The "truth" of the ostensive is by no means that of the declarative, of the complexity of which we have not yet given the slightest notion. But to describe the ostensive as itself a model of reality, subject to verification within the limits of its information-bearing power, will only make us more deeply appreciate the immense superiority of the declarative, whereas those whose notion of "objective reflection" or the like is limited to the declarative consider that they are not thus electing a "higher" form, but merely a "natural" one.

Considered from the standpoint of mature language, the ostensive .sentence lacks the two "shifters" of *person* and *tense* which explicitly relate the present of linguistic communication to the real-time present to which the communication refers (and which is suspended or *deferred* in the *presence* within which the communication takes place). From this standpoint the ostensive model is incomplete, and the ostensive can only appear as a "defective." sentence, if indeed it be considered a sentence at all. But from a genetic perspective the ostensive is simply the first and most primitive linguistic form. It needs no tense because its referent is present to the speaker and verifiably present to the hearer. Similarly it lacks person because the hearer is intended to stand in the same relation to the referent as the speaker. Thus after hearing the ostensive and observing its referent for himself, the hearer may repeat it for the benefit of others; the first person to cry "Fire!" has no monopoly on his utterance. Even in the case of "Ouch!" as we have seen, what is referred to is not the internal sense of pain so much as the verifiable violation of a social norm. The ostensive sentence presents its model and does nothing more, it being assumed that its referent is of sufficient significance to the hearer for him to wish to learn of its presence as soon as possible. The hierarchical relation between speaker and hearer during the (brief) duration of linguistic presence thus gives way to a symmetrical sharing of the information, and presumably, to cooperative action. But we should note that, unlike the imperative, the ostensive does not itself refer to such action. Its only reference is to the present, which its does not yet distinguish linguistically from the presence that is the ground of linguistic communication in general.

Within the intentional structure thus outlined the ostensive can already, in theory at least, make use of a lexicon including the totality of perceptibles—things and actions. Thus the semantics of an ostensive language may be indefinitely rich. But we must be careful to avoid attributing to ostensive language the signifier/signified realtionship that is dependent on the existence of the fully developed declarative model. Because ostensives are only employed in the presence of their referent, they express an ontology of events rather than of beings. Because they designate their object as significant in a given situation, and their enunciation necessarily implies this significance (danger or benefit), they cannot be reduced to the pure models of conceptual thought, which simply signify without themselves participating in the significance of their object. The ostensive "name," itself a complete utterance, has no means of acquiring the subsentential, conceptual status of our own vocabulary. The ostensive lexicon is a list of "expressions," as we might call them, for which no acontextual definition is conceivable, because their context is not a merely linguistic one. Such a lexicon must nevertheless be conceived to have constituted itself in the significant memories of speakers of ostensive language, associating its words with mental images of appropriate use. With the constitution of this lexicon and its criteria of appropriate and inappropriate use the ostensive is established as a genuine linguistic form, but at the same time the contradictions latent in its model of reality can begin to reveal themselves.

Dialectic of the Ostensive

The lexicalization of ostensives is one and the same with the explicitation of their appropriateness criteria. The original sign had no place in a lexicon, not simply because it was unique, but because in its evocation of the sacred object as bearer of the communal presence in which alone the sign could function it was always appropriate. This ever-appropriateness of the sign makes it inadequate to reinforce the presence it merely designates, and it therefore evolves into ritual, the action contained within the representation as participation in this presence becoming increasingly elaborate, until it englobes the totality of the original crisis situation. Thus the crisis is reduced to a mere preparatory stage in the birth of presence through the intermediary of the sacred object. The formal, as opposed to the institutional, evolution of the sign takes place, as we have seen, through functional differentiation. But this is synonymous with saying that it takes place through the establishment of appropriateness criteria because it is the criteria that determine the functionality of the sign. As a result, the ostensive, which is the immediate product of this differentiation, is no longer merely a self-guaranteeing reference to communal presence but must find the guarantee of its appropriateness in the specific situation in which it is employed.

Now this guarantee is required on two levels, of which the first is prerequisite to the second. In the first place the very act of speech must be justified, as opposed to saying nothing at all. In the second, the specific utterance used must be shown to be appropriate to the situation. We may call these criteria the significance-criterion and the signification-criterion, the first requiring the utterance to be significant, that is, worthy of actualizing the presence of communication, the second requiring it to signify what is actually the case. We might indeed call it the truth-criterion, although the notion of truth in a strict sense is narrower than that of appropriateness, being confined to declarative sentences that alone possess a "truth-value." We should note that the hierarchy of these two conditions is historical, not logical, because it is perfectly possible for a sentence, ostensive or otherwise, to be true and yet insignificant. But such an observation is only possible a posteriori; where a high threshold of significance exists, the danger of falling below it makes the criterion it imposes considerably more important than that of appropriate signification, with the result that the lexicon at this state will remain relatively undifferentiated. Lexical differentiation and the consequent refinement of the signification-criterion depend, as we have seen, on the lowering of this threshold. Thus the significance-criterion is seen to exercise a restraining force on the progress of the linguistic dialectic, although it is not an element of this dialectic.

The history of representation may indeed be understood uniquely in terms of these two criteria. The intersubjective basis of the significance-criterion is simply that of communal presence; hence this criterion is applied to ritual as well as language, and indeed to all forms of representation. In contrast, the signification-criterion, because it measures the correspondence between the linguistic model and its referent, is nothing other than a measure of the fulfillment of its intention; for this criterion is not applied from without as a measure of the precision of the lexicon or of the quantity of information it carries, but from within the language as it is constituted at the time of usage. Thus in a 100-word language the signification-criterion would be satisfied more easily than in a 400-word language where the domain of each original word is divided among four new ones.

Significance and signification are nothing but justified presence and fulfilled intention. But whereas presence has no structure, and its justification simply depends on the threshold of the audience (with which the speaker can be expected to be familiar), intentional structures increase in complexity at each stage of linguistic evolution. The speaker's intention and the implicit intention of the utterance as it appears to the hearer in context are never simply identical. And, contrary to what one might think, the divergence is greater at the early than at the later stages, the dialectic of desire and representation being motivated by the need to reduce the contradiction within the individual lexicon—what we have called "significant memory"—between these two intentions. The use of the term "signification" has generally avoided the complexities of intentional structure and been limited to individual words, which correspond if not to a specific referent then to an idea or "signified." But our examination of ostensives, in which the basic form of the utterance consists of a single "word," demonstrates the necessity for a broader notion of signification. As we will use the term, signification will refer to the "objective" or hearer's understanding of a linguistic form in general, whether it be a complete utterance or an element separable from it.

Let us now consider more precisely the implications of the constitution of an ostensive "lexicon" in the significant memory of an individual speaker. Each ostensive utterance, or word, will here be associated with its appropriateness conditions of signification. (We may disregard significance-criteria because the very existence of the word implies that they must at some point have been met, and because we are not concerned at this point with the pragmatics of the speech situation.) These words are conventional and must therefore be passed on from speaker to speaker. Their usage further implies a certain period of apprenticeship, during which they may conceivably be employed inappropriately; and in any case, the very constitution of appropriateness conditions of any kind carries with it the possibility of intentional or unintentional inappropriateness. Now in the lexicon of a developed language—one possessing declarative sentences—a word is not an utterance, and its "meaning" can be considered conceptually, apart from any given sentence in which the word might be included. But in the case of the ostensive, the "word" can only be associated with its appropriateness condition, which is the presence of the object that it can be said to designate. We may say that "fire" means a certain state of matter, of which we can assume that the significant memory preserves a certain number of images; but "Fire!" means the presence of a fire. Here the lexicon may contain similar images of reference, but the relationship of the word to them is very different, because in one case the image is a pictorial synonym of the word, whereas in the other it is the motivation of the utterance. Or in other terms, to think "fire" is to imagine a fire, but to think "Fire!" is to think of a situation where the cry would be appropriate. This imaginary cry would, at least implicitly, be accompanied by its imaginary results: panic, flight, organization of a bucket brigade, and the like. The ostensive possesses the power to realize a linguistic presence that exists only as an instantaneous deferral of action, and this power, which accrues to its speaker, is itself an element of the "definition" because the appropriateness condition for a specific ostensive like "Fire!" is the existence of a situation where the exercise of this power would be appropriate: the speaker observing the presence of the fire before his hearers.

Now the power of the ostensive, like that of the sign of the sacred object, is not only an attribute of the word, but of the community whose presence, in whole or in part, is required for it to be operative. And the thought of the ostensive, like the thought of this sign, is not a "reduced" conceptual thought but an imagined exercise of power. Thus the thought does not merely give rise to desire but is in itself an expression of desire. The possession of the representation, now as before, is the imaginarily represented possession of the power of the object represented to compel the presence of the community. But now this representation is possessed in the absence of its object, as an element in a lexicon. Thus whereas the designation of the sacred object in the original event led to the collective attribution to the object of the power of nonviolent presence exercised in reality by the community, in the case of the ostensive the power of its real object is attributed to its representation. Using the name of the sacred object meant evoking a power that remained in any case its own, although one could imagine possessing it. But using an ostensive even in the absence of its appropriate object—as in the familiar case of the boy who cried "Wolf!"—is usurping the power of the object for the duration of the linguistic act and for the brief period that follows until the inappropriateness is discovered.

Thus the very existence of an ostensive lexicon contains a contradiction, and the thought of any of its constituent elements presents the thinker with a pragmatic paradox. It is no doubt true to say that "Fire!" *means* that there is a fire, but the word "Fire!" possesses its effect at least momentarily independently of the presence of its referent. (This is only residually true of the truly lexical word "fire," the "effect" of which is entirely subordinate to the constitution of a linguistic model of fire that makes no postulation of the real-world existence of its referent.) This contrast can be stated in terms of the double intentionality discussed above, the necessarily self-contradictory structure of which is the source of the pragmatic paradoxes that motivate the dialectic of representational form: From the hearer's point of view, "Fire!" means the presence of a fire, whereas from that of the speaker, "Fire!" means the hearer's anticipated reaction. In the case of the sacred object the paradox implicit in its imaginary possession, which in the original situation would in fact have nullified its "powers," led to the quasi-permanent attribution of these powers to the object independently of the communal presence in which they were originally exer-

cised. In the same way the solution of the paradox posed by
the ostensive is simply to consider the utterance of the word
as guaranteeing not the actual presence of its object but the
desire of the speaker for (the power conferred by) its presence. An ostensive pronounced in the absence of its object is
prima facie inappropriate, and as in the case of the boy who
cried "Wolf!" is eventually treated as such. The actual
outcome of the story, in which even the appropriate use of
the ostensive is treated as inappropriate, with unfortunate
consequences to the speaker, illustrates a "conservative,"
nondialectical solution to the paradox of the ostensive:
Inappropriate usage leads to expulsion of the speaker from
the linguistic community, or in other words, to the rejection
of his utterances as a priori lacking in significance.

Here as ever conservatism consists in the application of the
significance-criterion, whereas formal evolution would have
resulted from the lowering of the threshold of this criterion,
in which case the utterance would have to be "understood"
on its own terms, and the structures of signification modified
accordingly. But in this latter case, where the inappropriate
ostensive is understood as having a meaning for the speaker
despite the absence of its object in practice, the conduct of
the hearer will itself be modified. To react to this ostensive as
though it were simply appropriate, which is to say, on
hearing the word "Fire!" to pretend one is in the presence of
a fire although one knows that one is not, is no doubt a
conceivable solution to the paradox. But although it might
remain useful for dealing with paranoids, particularly those in
authority, it could never become formalized in the language.
For if inappropriate ostensives are to be treated identically
with appropriate ones, then the ostensive as a whole ceases to
have any significance.

We have already observed in general terms that the revelation of the latent contradictions of an intentional structure,
although leading to the creation of new structures that
abolish the contradiction and thus avoid the pragmatic
paradox it arouses, does not for all that lead to the abandonment of the old construction. For because the situation for
which the original construction was evolved is not itself a
linguistic but a real event, it is not affected by the internal

evolution of language and therefore continues to require the same form of communication. In the case at hand fires will continue to break out as before, and their significance being no less than before, they will continue to call forth ostensives as the most immediate and consequently most efficient means of mobilizing the presence of the community. This of course in no way excludes the supplementing of the simple cry of "Fire!" by more highly evolved forms conveying further information; but it is inherent in the formal dialectic that an evolution motivated by resolving contradictions in intentional structures will produce models of greater objectivity at the necessary cost of immediacy. The most primitive forms remain the most efficient within their original domain because they are not only historically but ontologically closer to original presence, which they consequently evoke with greater urgency. But if "Fire!" continues to be used in the case of real fires, its accepted use in the absence of such fires would destroy the significance of the former use.

Yet although the distinction between appropriate and inappropriate use of the ostensive must continue to be drawn, it does not follow that the inappropriate use cannot itself evolve into a new form, one which, if successful, will presumably inspire the differentiation of the utterances, so that all possibility of ambiguity is avoided. The possibility of this evolution depends on not only the lowering of the threshold of significance from that of communal danger to that of individual desire but on the possibility of successfully distinguishing between the two levels as implicit, respectively, in the "appropriate" and "inappropriate" constructions. The latter can indeed only acquire an independent status in situations the relative insignificance of which would make the true ostensive inappropriate.

Thus we have made reference to the situation of linguistic apprenticeship which plays a major and in fact essential role in linguistic evolution. The language learner generally speaking must learn the words of the language before grasping the totality of their appropriateness conditions.[9] In the case of the ostensive, where the very constitution of a personal lexicon involves the speaker in a contradiction, *no* appropri-

ate practice use of language is possible because the ostensive
cannot be used in "true" statements outside its normal
sphere. Thus to learn the ostensive at all is to disassociate it,
albeit temporarily, from its normal usage. Even if we assume
that the child will learn the ostensive through experience of
its appropriate use rather than through any deliberately conducted apprenticeship, he cannot be expected to learn to use
a word appropriately without a few trials. This point need
not be belabored as it is not essential to our argument, the
contradiction being in the lexical sense of the ostensive
irrespective of the circumstances of its acquisition.

The ostensive, like any representation, arouses in the
individual contemplating it in his imagination the desire to
possess the power exercised by the representation over its
potential audience. To think of the ostensive is in effect
to imagine its usage and the exercise of power that it implies.
But this power can in the communication situation be
effectively exercised only in the presence of the object. Thus
the inappropriate ostensive, if it is to be interpreted at all as
possessing significance, can only be understood by its hearer
as an expression of the speaker's desire for the object in
question, the presentation of which would convert the
originally "false" ostensive into a "true" or appropriate one.
The "false" ostensive would then be interpreted as requiring,
in order to become appropriate, the presence of its originally
absent object; it would become, in a word, an *imperative*.

The apprenticeship situation lends itself to many plausible
scenarios of this development, of which the most familiar
from our own experience is doubtless that of a child, having
learned the word for "mother" as an ostensive, calling this
word in her absence to bring about, magically as it were, her
presence. We should note the simplicity of this example, in
which the object of the "imperative" is identical with the
addressee, and where the presence of communication is
simply converted into visual presence. Such a usage is indeed
not "inappropriate" at all, rather it illustrates the standard
vocative use of personal names. But this illustration of the
ostensive-imperative dialectic is thereby all the more pertinent, because in learning to use the name the child in effect
relives in his own linguistic universe the evolution we are now

describing. Surely he does not learn the imperative use of the name by example; nor does he know, upon being taught the name ostensively, that this imperative use is indeed acceptable. Thus, motivated by the desire for his mother's physical presence, he recreates the imperative for himself in the same way that its creation must have occurred in the course of the formal evolution of language. From the near-instantaneity of this evolution in the child—this assumption can no doubt be confirmed by experiment—it does not follow, however, that the historical evolution was equally instantaneous. For the identification of the name with the person by its very nature avoids the problem implicit in the "lexical" identification of the ostensive with its object, which came about, as we may recall, as a result of the contradiction inherent in the transfer to the ostensive word of the presence-creating power of the object in situation. The only presence established by calling the name is that of its bearer; knowing the name gives power over the person, but in general this power is freely given by the bearer of the name. To return to a familiar example, the boy who cried "Wolf!" did not desire the presence of wolves but of his fellow humans. His difficulties stemmed from the fact that, limited as he was to the ostensive construction, he could not appropriately obtain the one without the other. The word "Mommy" would no doubt have served his needs far better.

We may sum up our discussion of the dialectic of the ostensive by remarking that, despite its secular character, the ostensive "word" is incapable of attaining the stable lexical status of a concept-sign or "signifier" because, although it has acquired a practical, secular function, its ontology remains that of the sacred, and as such shares the paradoxical status of more explicitly theological concepts. In the absence of the participatory solution furnished by ritual, which avoids contradiction by reproducing the temporal constitution of the divinity in the original event, the community provides in the imperative a secular resolution of the paradox.

In St. Anselm's famous "ontological proof" of the existence of God, our possession of the concept of the "most perfect being" (*ens perfectissimum*) itself implies that being's existence. Kant's refutation of this proof attempts to invalidate it by claiming that existence is not a predicate. But precisely on the level of language at which the concept of the sacred was generated, the predicative function of the declarative sentence had not yet been conceived. The ostensive word may *name* its object, but its use *means* its object-as-present. Thus to conceive of using the word is to conceive its object as present, and to pronounce the word is to provoke this conception in its hearer. The ontology of the ostensive is thus identical with that of the sacred as expressed by St. Anselm, and whatever punishments may have been meted out to its first "believers," with the emergence of the imperative, their obstinate faith in the ontological proof at last obtained its reward. The desire of the individual soul, to which the ostensive gave a means of expression without, however, providing a guarantee of communication, had attained significance in the eyes of the community of his fellows.

Part 2

The Imperative

Traditional grammar, and the linguistics that is derived from it—and which despite its methodological innovations remains far more dependent on its analytic perspective than most linguists would care to admit—does not recognize the existence of the ostensive. It is willing, at least, to grant syntactic status to the imperative, which it considers as a poor, or as the grammarians would say, "defective," relation of the declarative sentence. The imperative, in this perspective, never quite succeeds in being a declarative, but is at least commended for trying. Thus although it has no true tense, it does have a verb that one may if one likes consider a sort of immediate future. Similarly, although its nearly universal zero-morphology attests to an apparent ignorance of the category of person, it can generally be classified functionally with the second person, a decision all the easier to justify because it does, in some languages, possess contrasting third-person forms.

Yet from the standpoint of the genesis or linguistic forms, which linguistics is, if not functionally unable, theoretically unprepared to consider, the imperative is not a "defective" form of the declarative but its ancestor. The word "defective" is merely a symptom of the metaphysical reliance on the declarative sentence as the fundamental linguistic model, so that a manifestly more primitive construction like the imperative is described, in the Chomskian terminology that formalizes without genuinely revising the discursive analyses of earlier grammarians, as a *transformation* of the declarative. Nor is it sufficient to explain that genetically speaking the imperative may well be more primitive, but that the linguist's analytic model, because it is synchronic, need not take this genetic priority into account. "Synchronic" or not, the analysis constructs its object, and it must pay the price if the real object is in fact constructed differently. We shall have more to say on this subject when we come to speak of the declarative, to which linguistics has done a grave disservice by postulating it as the fundamental form of the sentence. In passing, however, we may remark on the peculiar prestige that was at least until quite recently attached among social scientists to the word "synchronic," as though the heuristic elimination of temporality were the high road out of the cave into the Platonic sunlight. The act of ontological faith implicit in the construction of synchronic models is that of Ockham's razor. Unfortunately this credo, admirable in its intentions, places far too great a burden on the analyst's intuition of simplicity. For the most difficult problem in the study of human representations is not to find the simplest formulation, but to decide what to formulate. The quantitative objectivity of the natural sciences keeps their practitioners honest by forever obliging them to "save" new and unanticipated phenomena; in the human sciences, our intuition of the "simple" can eliminate the crucial problems by considering them, not merely as already solved, but as "simply" nonexistent. Thus nothing is simpler in appearance than the Chomskian model of the declarative sentence, which is "simply" NP plus VP. Anything less, according to the lights of structural analysis, would be no structure at all, or, like the imperative, at best a "defective" structure. But once we even begin to attempt to formulate a hypothesis concerning the genesis of this structure, to explain how indeed, *à partir de rien*, NP became associated with VP, we discover that the synchronic model not only does not provide us with an answer, but does not even permit us to ask the question. Thus we find in the most "advanced" of the human sciences the most fundamental matters surrounded by taboos more constraining even than those of primitive religion, which at least attempts through etiological myths to explain the origins of cultural forms.

From our perspective, then, the imperative is characterized not by "defective" but by nascent grammaticality. But the category of grammaticality, which reaches its full development in the declarative, must itself be explained in genetic terms. We shall define the grammaticality of a linguistic form as its degree of self-containment or "context-free-ness," considered as an intentional model of reality. From this definition the situation of the imperative between the ostensive and the declarative on the grammatical scale follows immediately. The ostensive is meaningless in the absence of its object; the declarative can do without a real-world object. The imperative operates in the absence of its object-nominal or -verbal, but can only be satisfied upon the object's being made present. The declarative stands at the end of the scale of grammaticality; the higher forms of language, that is, the various forms of *discourse*, which we shall touch on in a later chapter, are not properly speaking linguistic forms at all but forms of cultural expression not capable of being formalized, as are linguistic forms, independently of their content. Thus the declarative can be considered as the telos of linguistic evolution, after which no substantial progress is possible. This explains, if it does not excuse, the temptation of the grammarians to treat all other forms as imperfect declaratives, irrespective of their evolutionary status; one might just as well consider both snakes and worms as imperfect quadrupeds, although the first have lost their legs whereas the second never had any. The analogy is imperfect, of course, because whereas both worms and quadrupeds engage in locomotion, imperatives and declaratives can only be considered in the most general terms as offering competing models of the universe. It is not indeed the forms but their intentional structures that evolve, and this evolution is not a linear but a branching one that, although reaching new points of equilibrium, leaves the old ones virtually intact. It is to this evolution that we must return in order to pursue our analysis of the imperative.

The imperative, as we have seen, is in its origins an ostensive uttered in the absence of its object and interpreted by its hearer as an expression of desire for the presence of the object. This would imply that the primitive form of the imperative is a nominal, although, as we have had occasion to note, the ostensive makes no formal distinction between verbals and nominals; because verbality proper is a quality of *predicates*, the very term "verbal" is at this stage an anachronism. The imperative, in its origins at least, does nothing to modify this situation. Thus if, for example, the imperative "Stone!" means to bring a stone whereas the ostensive "Stone!" means the presence of a stone, in the same way, whereas the ostensive "Run!" designates the presence of running, the imperative "Run!" which we interpret today as a verb form, would request the presence (or more precisely, the *presentification*) of running from the interlocutor, a request which would be a nominalized manner of asking him to run or to "do a run." In either case the provision of the object of the inappropriate ostensive makes it appropriate. The "nominality," or we should rather say the *substantivity* of this object, is important because only as a substance capable of being an independent object of the imagination can it become an object of desire. But the fact that in mature languages the imperative is considered to be a form of the verb, whereas nominal imperatives like "Scalpel!" are categorized, if at all, as defective forms of the verbal imperative, cannot simply be attributed to the perversity of grammarians. What it demonstrates is that by subordinating the appearance of the desired object to the action of the interlocutor the imperative has already taken a major step in the direction of predication. We shall return to this point later.

Let us now consider more precisely the intentional structure of the imperative. The ostensive is an expression not of individual but of social concern, the significance of its object being measured by its capacity to arouse the community to action. The individual speaker of the ostensive thus expresses an interest in the object no greater than, and possibly even less than that of his addressee, because the speaker, being already aware of the significant object, may be assumed to have already at least begun whatever action its presence might require. (The ostensive may thus be wholly altruistic, for example, warning the hearer of a danger to which the speaker is immune.) As we have noted the ostensive creates a symmetrical situation with regard to its object which it constitutes within linguistic presence as equally present to all interlocutors. Thus the ostensive retains the nonviolent symmetry of the original gesture designating the "sacred" object.

Now it is not a priori apparent from the consideration of the two forms simply as grammatical structures that the imperative should be a less "social" form than the ostensive. If the ostensive points out significant present objects, the imperative might equally well refer to significant absent ones. The ostensive reference to a present object creates a model of reality—the simplest possible—in which this object becomes the unique and therefore unifying object of attention. The imperative could use essentially the same model, although now its referent would become the object of a communal effort at "presentification," that is, procurement. Examples of a collective imperative are indeed abundant; the sanguinary shouts of crowds, like "Kill the umpire!" or "Down with X!" especially come to mind, although less violent examples like "Three cheers for Y!" also exist. In these cases the imperative functions to "spread the word" within a group and to reinforce a particular decision concerning what is to be done, the content of which may be nominal as well as verbal.

A closer examination of these "collective imperatives" reveals their apparent symmetry to consist rather of a reciprocity that is necessarily unstable, hovering between the asymmetry of the true imperative and the group identification of the first-person ("Let's . . .") construction. The collective functioning of the imperative is worthy, however, of consideration in itself, precisely because it does not share the strictly hierarchical, asymmetric structure of the basic construction. The origin of this basic construction has been traced to the inappropriate use of the ostensive; yet inappropriateness implies lack of integration into the linguistic community, something that can hardly be the case for a group composed of an appreciable portion of this community. But to assume that the collective imperative preceded the individual, which would then become but a special case of it, would be to suppose that a judgment concerning appropriateness conditions could be made spontaneously by the group as a whole, acting under its own internal dynamism. Thus in the midst of crying "Fire!" some members of the group would suddenly take to shouting "Water!"; or to take another example, the ostensive "the enemy!" would lead to "Weapons!" or "Kill!" or something of the sort. Or in the fire situation one might imagine that the first discoverer of a supply of water would announce this to his fellows by an ostensive that would be taken up by the others as an "imperative." This scenario is, however, as the slightest reflection reveals, totally implausible. In order for "Water!" to have an imperative meaning in the fire situation, this meaning must be established beforehand, because otherwise the utterance would simply be interpreted as indicating not the absence but the presence of water. But if we suppose that in his panic someone having heard the (ostensive) call of water, but lacking his own supply, begins to call out "Water!" in the "Anselmian" belief that his use of the word will make the water appear, then we are simply reproducing our earlier analysis of the dialectic of the ostensive, the panic of a fire being substituted for the inexperience of the language learner as a possible source of "inappropriate" linguistic behavior. This is not to deny categorically the possibility of such a collective origin of the imperative, although one may wonder why in such a situation anyone would take the trouble to supply the speaker with the needed substance rather than, understanding his cry as a true ostensive, simply seek to obtain some for himself.

This appeal to relative plausibility can serve to underscore a methodological problem of scenarios in general. The

depiction or "scenario" of the original event is a necessary
link between the theory of representation and the original
representations about which it theorizes, the contents of
which, if it take these representations as its own true ancestors, it must extrapolate into a hypothetical approximation
of the truth. This hypothetical extrapolation does not,
however, apply directly to the form of representations but
only to *presence* as the precondition of representational form
in general—or, in other words, as the real-world situation that
permits the separation of content and form. Hence, once a
hypothetical genesis of presence has been constructed, the
theory of representation, insofar as it is indeed a formal
theory, has rigorously speaking no further need of scenarios
and can content itself with elaborating the dialectic implicit
in the forms, or rather in their use by "presentifying" beings
such as we. The only concrete or "scenic" element required
by this dialectic is the expansion of the original presence to
permit the intersubjective communication of contents
originally spawned by individual desire—the process that we
have earlier referred to as the lowering of the threshold of
significance. This process, although itself affected by the
progress of the formal dialectic, and increasingly so as this
progress continues, with the result that in the modern era the
whole system of socioeconomic relations is drawn into its
sphere, is always essentially external to the dialectic because
it is dependent on the resistance of the social order to internal violence. Thus our dialectic of forms is not, like that of
Hegel, totally self-contained, and it is precisely this factor
that permits it to subsist in historical time, where the threshold of significance acts as a check on a formal evolution that,
as our contemporary experience has only begun to show, is
intrinsically no more bounded than desire.

The origin of the imperative is consequently sufficiently
explained from our standpoint by a lowering of this threshold, and, whatever may have been its specific context, we
should assume the process to have been a gradual one. From
an idiosyncratic action taken in response to an inappropriate
ostensive, the supplying of the desired object became a
regular practice and was thereby formalized in the intention
of the nascent imperative. Even were such actions to arise in

a collective context, the birth of this form would still be explicable as the lowering of the threshold of significance to include, beyond the present factors affecting the presence of communication, those absent ones imagined by one or more desiring subjects. It is indeed noteworthy that the typical example of the "collective imperative" is the expression neither of the need of a community genuinely threatened by some outside agency nor of its pleasure on the discovery of an object of collective satisfaction, but rather the cry of the mob intent on discharging its violence on a designated victim. The reader needs no reminder of the parallel that can be drawn here with the original event, where the aggressive gestures of the assailants toward the victim served as prelinguistic, instinctual "ostensives." But in the historical moment at which we now find ourselves, the chaotic violence of the original mimetic conflict has been replaced by the ordered forms of ritual in which the foreordained acts of aggression, as well as those that only mimic real conflict, are carried out under the aegis of the sacred being. In contrast acts of mobs in which violence is neither feigned nor controlled no longer create a new communal presence nor, although they may contribute episodically to the solidarity of the existing community, do they provide it with a sacred guarantee of future nonviolence. For the threat of death cannot spread, as in the original crisis, from the victim to his persecutors who act within the protection, as they see it, of a preexisting sacrality. And because they lack the original risk, they fail to produce the original reward, which is that of a sacred guarantee against further violence.

Thus we may categorize the actions of the mob as motivated not by instinct but by desire—a desire founded on representations. The collective imperative, in this case, is not an expression of a true but of a spurious community created to satisfy the desires of its members which, in the perspective of the real community, are lacking in significance. Mob violence, no doubt, did not require for its existence the linguistic form of the imperative—the ostensive designation of the victim being sufficient—but, once available, the imperative cries that accompany it are overt expressions of its origin in desire. An additional feature of the collective

imperative confirms these observations: It is very often
addressed not to the group formed by the speakers but to a
real or undefined figure of authority who is called upon to
carry out the desires of the mob. Thus when the spectators at
a baseball game shout "Kill the umpire!" they have no intention of performing the murder themselves, or even of inciting
the other spectators (or the players) to perform it; rather the
murderer is someone totally undefined who is to satisfy the
collective desire while the collectivity incurs neither danger
nor guilt. A closely related if more sinister phenomenon is
that of the cries that formerly accompanied the execution of
"enemies of the people"; here they are indeed genuine
imperatives addressed to the executioner, but the mechanism
of desire remains the same.

The imperative is not the first creation of the dialectic of
desire: The secular ostensive and, before it, the sacralization
of the sacred object were products of the tendency of desire,
which attaches to the designated objects of preexisting
representational forms, to find expression, on the one hand in
the sacralization (and later through the "esthetization") of
the objects, and on the other, of particular concern to us
here, in the creation of new forms in which the subject's
relation to the desire-object can be translated from the
individual imagination into a communication to others within
the de-temporalized sphere of communal presence. But in the
ostensive what was at first an individual desire or apprehen-
sion of the object is converted directly into a collective
concern in which the speaker's asymmetric role is annulled.
In contrast the imperative overtly expresses the desire qua
desire, which is to say, claims for it communal significance.
But this is not to say that the imperative, or even the ostensive, should be conceived as necessarily pronounced before
the community as a whole. Linguistic presence, once established in a communal context, can be recreated between any
two members of the community, because once the protection
of nonviolent presence vested in the sacred object was
deemed to extend over nonritual communication situations
the size of the group involved would be unimportant. Yet the
imperative, as an expression of individual desire, is certainly a
more "private," more "secular" mode than the ostensive. Its

existence along with the ostensive allows for continued dialogue—for example, the operating surgeon's "conversation" with the assistant who presents him the requested instruments: "Forceps!"-"Forceps," and so on. This was not possible with the ostensive, which is rather a means for revealing an unusual presence than for facilitating continued action. It is indeed difficult to imagine a cooperative work situation without the imperative, the use of which would tend to contribute to the linguistic categorizing of necessary implements and therefore to their distinctly cultural quality as tools.

The Intentional Structure of the Imperative

1. Constitution

The intentional structure of the ostensive can be summed up in a few words: The speaker transmits to the hearer an immediately verifiable model of the universe as containing one significant present object. That of the imperative is more complex, and this complexity is expressed as well in the existence of variant forms, such as the "collective imperative," already briefly discussed, and the third-person and first-person forms. In accordance with its foregoing derivation from the ostensive, we will consider the primitive form of the imperative to be substantival, the imperative sentence consisting of a word designating the object to be supplied. Although the most natural examples will be true nominals, we should recall that at this stage the nominal/verbal distinction has no formal basis, so that an imperative requesting an action ("Run!") is structurally identical to one requesting a physical object.

The imperative is, with respect to what we might call its "linguistic substance" (the linguistic elements it employs without regard to the specificity of their use), identical to the ostensive. In its primitive stage the imperative, once it is no longer considered simply inappropriate, would necessarily be experienced as a variant of the ostensive, distinguished from it only by secondary (intonational) elements. Whether language at this point consists of sounds or gestures, this identity of linguistic substance is only conceivable if the words of the ostensive are fully lexicalized and unambiguously differentiated.[10] The utterance of a word designating a potentially desirable object would then create a model in which the object would appear as significant irrespective of its presence or absence. The appropriate reaction would depend on the interpretation of the situation with regard to the model: Either the object is present, and is being designated, or it is absent, and being requested. There exists a third possibility that combines both alternatives: The object is present to the hearer but not to the speaker, who can then be thought to be either simply designating the object or, in addition, demanding to be presented with it. In cases like the last when an ambiguity arises the dynamic of the situation will tend to lead to the dominance of the imperative, because once there is no clear social or "symmetric" reason for the designation of an object, the speaker's desire for it will be presupposed. Or in other terms, because the speaker's designation of the object indicates that he, at least, is interested in it, whereas the ostensive presupposes the interest of the other interlocutors as well, the imperative will be preferred as the form of lesser a priori significance and, by the same token, of greater informational value because it communicates not merely the verifiable presence of the object but the desire of the speaker. It is precisely by means of this information concerning the speaker's desire, which thereby defines the speaker's relation to the object, that the imperative, despite its lack of any morphology or of any specifically verbal element, is a protogrammatical form, possessing in its intentional structure if not its morphology the fundamental grammatical relations of person and time.

We may suppose that the more grammatical form consolidated itself through being preferred in ambiguous cases as defining more precisely the desire of the speaker and as making fewer presuppositions concerning that of the hearer. But this is only another way of saying that the model intended by the more grammatical form contains more information about not the "world" so much as the communication situation. In the present case the identity of "substance" between ostensive and imperative corresponds to an identity of information about the world. The result of the fuller grammaticalization of the imperative is that it destroys the symmetry of the ostensive communication of significance. The ostensive communicated nothing about the desire of the speaker that it did not at the same time presuppose in the hearer; the imperative accentuates the asymmetry of the speaker's role as conveyor of information by making his desire serve as a mediator of the desire of the other. In certain social contexts this mediation can be taken to imply the existence of an asymmetric authority relation that transcends the immediate speech situation.

But it is important to explain why this need not be the case, and is indeed from a formal standpoint a quite unnecessary presupposition. It is *the situation of linguistic presence* that is the original source of the "authority" of the imperative. To be a participant in this situation the hearer must, as we have already seen, defer his attention to worldly tasks in order to attend to the intentional model constructed by the speaker. In the imperative the speaker takes the greatest possible advantage of this attention in order to extrapolate his linguistic intention into a worldly one aimed at the appropriation of its object. The ambiguity of the word "intention" here is not coincidental, nor is the instrumental nature of the imperative that exploits it. (It is thus understandable that for a pragmatic explorer of the "language-game" like the later Wittgenstein the imperative is always made the prime example of the practical use of language. One might indeed describe this author's intellectual career as a regression toward the source of language from the declarative of the *Tractatus* to the imperative/ostensive of his later work, although he never attempted to develop a *genetic* language theory that alone could have brought unity to his researches). This identity of linguistic and practical intention resolves the paradox arrived at in the dialectic of the ostensive and thus produces a stable linguistic form, although, as we shall shortly see, the use of this form will produce a paradoxical situation of a different sort.

The extrapolation of linguistic into practical intentionality in the imperative leads to a characteristic modification of the presence situation and of the accompanying deferral of appropriative activity by which the hearer permits it to prolong itself until the end of the communication, undisturbed by the claims of worldly time. The end of the ostensive utterance was the end of linguistic presence, albeit the successful ostensive may normally have been followed by a collective action directed toward its object. In contrast the imperative prolongs this presence to include the performance of the requested act. Where the ostensive merely supplied the information on which action might be taken, the imperative includes the hearer in its intention as the performer of the action. Thus the imperative, although its duration as a speech act may be as brief as that of the ostensive, does not terminate as an act of communication until this action is performed. The deferral constitutive of the presence situation now becomes an *awaiting* of the anticipated action that is not merely a subjective attitude on the part of the speaker but an element of the intentional model.

2. *Grammatical Form*

Our discussion up to this point, concerned exclusively with intentional structure, has maintained the assumption that the primitive form of the imperative was substantially identical to that of the ostensive. As we know, however, the imperative in developed languages is normally considered a verbal form, although the nominative imperative, ignored as such by grammarians, continues to exist. In the present inchoate state of the study of language universals, undertaken generally speaking in a cyclic rather than truly genetic perspective, it would almost certainly be impossible to give a satisfactory explanation of the genesis of the specific forms of even so simple a construction as the imperative, and in any case we shall not attempt this here. Our discussion of grammatical form will therefore be limited, here as in our discussion of the declarative below, to the categories of tense (linguistic time) and person, both of which, irrespective of their morphological expression in specific languages, are fundamental categories of the intentional situation, and to the relations of dependency ("governance") between elements of a given form.[11]

Any future discussion of linguistic universals within the context of a theory of representation will have to construct its models not by working backward from empirical data, but, as we have done here, from the ground up. And without prejudging the case for a complete theory of universals, such as this present work does not intend to be, we can at least claim with some assurance that it would be obliged to construct its fundamental grammatical categories before and not after its constitution of the declarative sentence (in which alone, however, as we shall see, they can truly be said to function "grammatically"). By presenting a hypothesis for the evolution of linguistic form in general up to its culmination in the declarative, we are in effect elaborating a speculative theory of language universals, but one that from the standpoint of a linguistics founded on a genuine theory of representation—a linguistics that has in fact never existed— would require extensive ramification to be brought into contact with the vast quantities of empirical data that have been made available from the analysis of past and existing languages.[12]

The preceding analysis has already pointed out the source of the tense of the imperative in the prolongation of linguistic presence in "awaiting." It must be emphasized, however, that at this point the notion of tense has not yet been constituted within linguistic form. In particular the imperative offers no choice of tenses and thus creates no need to distinguish among them. At the same time the association of tense with the imperative is not the result of an arbitrary decision by grammarians. The time of awaiting, prolonged beyond the time of the utterance, is both real, lived time standing outside linguistic presence *stricto sensu* and a prolongation of the presence intended by the utterance. Thus the imperative includes in itself a model of a time other than that of its presence. We should contrast this with the simple identity of linguistic and real time in the ostensive, where the time of linguistic presence remains, as in the original event, merely the time of deferral of action in attention to the speaker. The ostensive model has no temporal dimension, the word and its referent coexisting in the same present. The imperative presents the word without the referent, or in any case without the referent's being in conformity with the model. The temporality of the imperative is not a true tense like that of the declarative, linguistic time as represented in the model being not independent of the presence of communication but merely a prolongation of it. At the same time this prolongation, if not yet a temporal mapping of reality on the model, is already a mapping of the model on reality. The hearer of the ostensive can immediately verify its informational content for himself, and so to speak discard the linguistic model that conveyed it; the hearer of the imperative must retain the model as a guide for his conduct in the immediate future, "verifying" it only upon the conclusion of his performance.

None of the features referred to in this analysis requires that the imperative be in fact a verb. But because whether a nominal or a verbal form is used the anticipated result of the imperative is an action by the hearer, the verbal form is a more explicit model of the action. This is not true merely in the trivial sense that "bring the hammer!" or "Give me the hammer!" is more explicit than "Hammer!" If we compare "Hammer!" (conceived as a nominal) with "Run!" (at this stage of our analysis more a verbal substantive than a verb), the former requires the performance by the hearer of actions not explicitly stated, whereas the latter is a fully explicit instruction. And this is because the hammer is a concrete object whereas the run or running is merely an "accidental" attribute of the hearer. This difference between nominals and verbals was not visible in the ostensive, where in either case the significant phenomenon was merely a "thing" present both to the speaker and (at least potentially) to the hearer. In the imperative the hearer can perform the action but can only supply the object. This divergent relationship to nominals and verbals in effect implies the possibility, which we may assume to begin to be realized at this stage, of the governance of the former by the latter, although, as is the case with tense, this "governance" is not yet the fully realized model of the declarative which presents the relationship of agent, verb, and object independently of any action of the hearer.

It is nevertheless this action that permits us to explain governance from a genetic perspective. It is perfectly conceivable that "double" or even "triple" ostensives may have existed, consisting of a verbal and one or more nominals; for example, on observing a flight of crows, "Fly! Crows!" or even something like "Burn! Fire! House!"[13] But it would be a grave mistake to consider such utterances as true linguistic forms and thereby as the direct ancestors of the declarative. The elements of such compound utterances remain independent and therefore separable as complete utterances in themselves, whereas the declarative sentence is not complete until all its positions have been filled. And if it be claimed that the habit of such compound utterances may have led to their expectation on the part of the hearer, and thereby to the loss of independence of their separate parts, we would answer that such an explanation simply begs the question by referring to a "habit" that could have in fact no possible motivation. For not only do present-day ostensives dispense unconcernedly with such scruples—and this in languages where the declarative is not merely available but where speakers are taught from their childhood that it is the only legitimate constative form—but it is inconceivable that such a "habit" could take root in the presence of all the elements of the model. The sort of analysis of the situation prerequisite to the formation of this "habit" could not evolve unless the originally independent elements were somehow felt to lack sufficient significance in themselves, and in the ostensive situation this significance is guaranteed not by these elements but by the presence of their referents. Within this presence the elements of compound utterances remain separately observable phenomena; to claim that these phenomena provide in themselves, by their interrelationship, sufficient motivation for the institution of a normative model of the declarative is to return to the logic of Port-Royal and to suppose that the declarative sentence is simply inscribed in nature.

The fact is, however, that no governance relation, even the inchoate one of the imperative, is conceivable in an ostensive language. "Fly! Crows!" is no more a "sentence" than "Fly! Sky!" or "Sky! Crows!" or indeed any other combination of ostensives. Governance, which is a generic term for the relations between linguistic elements of an utterance as opposed to the intentional relationship (expressed in tense and person as well as in the reference of substantive words) of the utterance to reality, cannot be derived from the mere observation of relationships in nature but only from the significant functioning of these relationships within the situation of linguistic presence, that is, as human interaction. In the ostensive model this interaction is reduced to the mere existence of linguistic presence, within which the utterance points out a significant phenomenon present in the real world to which the mobilized attention of its audience should turn. The imperative model, however, includes not the mere presence of its object but the relationship to be assumed toward it by the hearer. If a compound ostensive like "Fly! Crows!" merely presents two independent significant observations related at most as two different models of the same reality, a compound imperative like "Bring [the, a] hammer!" or, if the notion of "bringing" be thought to beg the question, "Come! [with] hammer!" requires of its hearer not a contemplative analysis of the relation of its elements but a performance in which the referents of the elements are combined.

We need not suppose the analytic counterpart of this practical operation to somehow be present in the mind of the hearer. It suffices that this performance be more explicitly determined in its verbal than its nominal aspect so that, in the example at hand, the hammer cannot be provided without the hearer's coming to the speaker, although the action of coming can be performed without the hammer. And in general the verbal element will be performed by the hearer as agent accompanied in some way by the nominal element as object or instrument. Thus although a bystander could describe the performance in our example by means of an ostensive identical in substance to the original imperative, the meaning of which would be something like "there is coming, and there is a hammer" (just as the meaning of the preceding example would be "There is flying, and there are crows"), the performer of the act could not be unaware that his coming was "governing" the appearance of the hammer. The speaker of the imperative, like the bystander, might be considered indifferent to this subordination because the need for performance analysis is in the first place that of the performer. If, however, we consider the practical function of the imperative as well as the absence of any need to assume that its asymmetry be founded on a permanent social hierarchy, we may assume that the speaker would be aware of the relations implicit in the requested action. The essential point is, of course, not the state of awareness that we wish to attribute to speaker or hearer at a given moment but the availability of this awareness within the communication situation. The phenomena described by the ostensive, whether or not they involve human agents, are independent of the linguistic model that refers to them, whereas the imperative specifically requests a human performance.

A similar analysis makes clear why the notion of *tense* or linguistic time, which we have observed to arise in the imperative from the prolongation of the time of linguistic presence per se in the awaiting of the requested performance, is specifically attached to the verbal element of the imperative, with the result that this verbal element may acquire in its most primitive form the character of what in developed languages we call a *verb*. In the nominal imperative the requested object is simply made present, but its existence as such is generally speaking independent of the action in which it is thus involved. In contrast the performance requested by the verbal imperative is a *creation* of its object. "Run!" requests not merely the presentation but the creation of a "run." Thus it is the existence of its object that puts an end to the awaiting, and this "object" is defined within the temporality of the waiting and its resolution. Or in other terms, the same hammer may be requested today as yesterday, but not the same run. What is requested now is a run-present, a run to which the imperative model attaches a specific linguistic time. Here again the contrast with the ostensive brings out the increased grammaticality of the imperative model: The ostensive, concerned only with the presence of its object, is indifferent to its temporal specificity. The "run" observed today is no more different from that observed yesterday than today's hammer differs from yesterday's hammer. In fact, given that the function of the ostensive is to designate potentially problematic phenomena, if for some reason the hammer was yesterday the object of an ostensive, perceiving it as *the same* hammer today would make its further designation unnecessary. Conversely, objects problematic in themselves are always "the same" object because their appearance leads to functionally identical situations. Thus we say that "Fire breaks/broke out," as though today's and yesterday's fire were merely two appearances of the same object. The ostensive is unconcerned with the distinction between the identity of phenomena and their repetition. The imperative is not, because it requests its hearer to present the identical and reproduce the repeatable—and it specifically designates the latter to occur within linguistic time.

The greater specificity of the verbal as against the nominal imperative is thus seen to generate a primitive notion of verbal tense. It is important to note that this notion does not contain a distinction among verbs of different tenses, but only the more fundamental distinction of the verbal, which possesses a tense, from the nominal, which does not. The genesis of the notion of person follows similar lines, although in contrast to that of tense it can undergo internal differentiation within the context of the imperative model. But the verbal imperative can be said to be personalized even in its basic "second-person" form because, again in contrast to the nominal, it requests an action to be performed, and thus made to exist, by the hearer. Just as we have seen that the "run" requested is a "run now," so we may say that it is also a run-by-X, which is by no means identical to a run-by-Y. And, as in our preceding discussion of governance, the specificity of action on the part of the hearer of the imperative can be supposed to become included in the intention of the speaker as well. Thus if several hearers are present and the speaker requests a hammer ("Hammer!"), the intentional model includes only the hammer. And even if one person is specifically addressed, this model is not violated if someone else brings the hammer, although of course the speaker's expectations may be. But if he says "Come!" to one of the group, then the "come" he is requesting could not normally be performed by any other member. The object is presented, but the person *presents himself*, and it can be assumed that the request for the presence of one person cannot be filled by another. Thus the verbal imperative may be said to have from the beginning a "second-person" form.

Now at this point "person" simply means second person, the contrast with the first person not having any basis in the intentional model. The speaker is of course normally at least the "dative" object of the imperative, and he may on occasion be the "accusative" object, as in a request to help him up or to perform other personal services. But although the presence of the gestural element in language makes it obvious that personal "shifter" pronouns must have been among the first "words," each individual being obliged to refer to himself or to the other by means of symmetrically "shifting" gestures, the speaker even as the accusative object of an imperative verb is never in a symmetrical position to the hearer. The intention of the simple imperative is to request a performance of the hearer in which no contrast with a possible performance by the speaker is implied. If we assume that the verbal imperative was originally conceived analogously with the nominal as a personless form, the accretion to it of the category of person would at first include only the person of the addressee.

Here we are not concerned with demonstrating the formal existence of this intentional category, which would require the presentation of evidence in the form of a minimal paradigm or "significant pair," because we are merely describing the process by which verbals acquired the intentional features that distinguish them from nominals. This is a process which we need not assume to have led to morphological differentiation within imperative langauge, but without which the future emergence of the declarative sentence would be inconceivable. The "tense" of the verbal imperative may be said to remain at this stage a *latent* element of intentional structure, visible only to the extent that we may be permitted to assume that the verbal form, being perceived as a more explicit linguistic expression of this structure, eventually displaced the nominal as the dominant or "unmarked" form. (This displacement would presage the grammarians' classification of the nominal imperative as a mere "contraction" of the verbal form, in which the verb is "understood.")

In the case of person the specification of the verbal imperative as a "second-person" form can at least in developed languages be confirmed by paradigmatic evidence from within the imperative.

If we now consider a group of hearers to whom a unique speaker is assigning respective tasks—a scene that evidently connotes a certain level of social organization—the series of imperatives, each preceded by the gestural and/or verbal identification of the individual addressee, will be in effect addressed in a more general sense to the group as a whole; the intention of the speaker will be not only to request a specific task of each individual but to make the tasks of each known to all. From such an intention to that expressed by the third-person imperative the only extension required is the absence of the performer of the action. Thus the true third-person imperative establishes a linguistic chain of command, the functionality of which would no doubt be tenuous—as distinct from that of the simple imperative that functions within a single linguistic presence—without the existence of a social hierarchy (at least a work hierarchy) of some kind. Within this chain of command the second and third persons form a paradigmatic opposition (which cannot be extended to the first person, however). This opposition remains, as we have defined it, merely intentional, not formal, because the chain of command is independent of the use of the verbal rather than the nominal imperative. But the verbal imperative, being already personalized as the nominal is not, will thereby tend to reflect morphologically the change in person. As we might say, a "you-hammer" and a "he-hammer" are still the same hammer, but a "you-come" and a "he-come" are two different actions. Regardless of morphological differences, the intentional distinction will here again contribute to the dominance of the verbal form, because in the context of a possible choice between two persons, the "personlessness" of the nominal imperative will be perceived as an ambiguity, or more precisely as a zero-degree of personalization.

The "first-person" (plural) imperative is not a simple parallel to the second- and third-person forms. The speaker merely includes himself in the proposed action rather than opposing his performance to that of the hearer. A similar situation can be found in the "collective imperative" discussed above, the only difference being the specific use of the first-person plural form in developed languages. If we seek the origin of this form in the intentional structure of the imperative itself, however, we can at best have recourse to analogy with the second/third-person distinction: The tendency of the imperative verbal toward personalization will tend to distinguish this general collective form from the more specific personal forms. Morphology aside, the difference between the collective and first-person forms of the imperative would appear one of degree of significance, the collective form implying a communal indifference to individual persons, whereas the first-person form specifically defines the collectivity to which the action is proposed as the group of persons being addressed. But the most important point to be made concerning the first-person imperative is rather a negative one. It is not a true first-person at all, and cannot by any stretch of the imagination be reckoned as the origin of the first person that we find parallel to the other two in the declarative. The "objective" reflection on one's action necessary to motivate this parallel is not yet available in the imperative.

Elementary Forms and Grammatical Structures

The preceding discussion has shown that the requirement of human performance in the imperative is the source of the categories of tense, person, and governance which will become the touchstones of the grammaticality of the declarative sentence, by which we mean its capacity to present a model of reality no longer dependent on the conditions obtaining during the communication situation, having corrected by means of "shifting" elements chosen from these categories for the specificity of time and speaker. But we cannot discuss these categories purely in terms of our hypothetical imperative language, and our presentation has unavoidably been oriented teleologically toward the declarative. Tense and person have been associated with the verbal imperative as a first-order justification of its morphology in developed languages, but this association has not been demonstrated to be the necessary resolution of a paradox inherent in the primitive conception of the imperative as an "inappropriate" ostensive. It has rather been considered as a development internal to the imperative, operating as a "tendency" rather than as constituting the dialectical emergence of a new form. We should not take these assertions to contradict the formal dialectic to which we shall return in the following chapter, or to imply that a fuller analysis, for example, one making greater use of empirical data, would conceivably have produced results of a different kind. The formal dialectic as here conceived does not generate paradigms but the intentional forms within which paradigms can come into existence in answer to the needs of the general speech-situation. Thus to take the simplest example, the ostensive permits of indefinite lexical differentiation, but that this differentiation actually occurs is not a formal but a practical truth. But the same can be said for the distinctions we have drawn between the verbal and the nominal imperative. Once it has been shown that the intentional structure of the imperative, which is at the minimum a model of the addressee's performance, direct or indirect, admits of the additional specificity of formally distinguishing between "tenseless" nominal and "tensed" verbal, or between the addressee and the performer of the action by means of person-markers, the question of whether languages in general have taken up these options must be left to empirical research.

Because all known languages make use of the categories of tense and person, the preceding considerations may appear unfounded; these are certainly language universals as much as any that can be said to exist. But here we must make an important distinction between the elementary linguistic forms that we are still discussing and the "developed" form of the declarative. The paradigms of the declarative and of the forms derived from it (subjunctive, interrogative, etc.) are in many languages of considerable complexity, and our general discussion of the intentional structure of the declarative will be obliged to ignore them, the divergence among the formal options taken by known languages being such that, at the present time at least, no theory could hope to derive these options in detail; this is still a domain for empirical, classificatory research. The primary task of a theory of representation with regard to the declarative is to explain not the specific categories of its paradigms but the quality of its intentional structure which permits such a variety of categories to exist.

The categories of person, tense and governance (case) are precisely those that give rise to the most familiar paradigms of the declarative and its related modes, as a glance at a Latin or Greek grammar will show. Even in languages with few or no paradigms these categories must be marked in other ways. For these categories are constitutive of the notion of grammaticality itself, and the declarative sentence is inconceivable in their absence. Thus the intentional structure of the declarative not only admits of the possibility that oppositions between persons, tenses, and so on will generate paradigmatic combinations in a given language, but, regardless of the morphological means employed, the declarative sentence presents a model that is situated with regard to the time of utterance and to the speaker and his audience, and where the relations among nominals and verbals are, within certain limits, specified. The constitution of this intentional structure, which we shall take up in the following chapter, is indeed the result of a dialectical process generated by the internal contradictions of the imperative.

The intentional structure of the imperative does not require the specification of these categories, although if we would explain the genesis of the declarative from the imperative, it is reasonable to assume their inchoate existence in imperative language. The imperative model minimally requires only the definition of the phenomenon the presence of which is requested. The time of the action is not a true tense, but an extension of linguistic presence, and whatever analysis of the situation we may wish to suppose on the part of the speaker, "governance" of the passive object by the active performer is a matter of practicality and not truly of grammaticality. Or in other terms it is senseless at this stage to speak of "correct" and "incorrect" utterances because the only relevant criterion, assuming that the addressee accepts his role in the intentional structure, is whether or not the task itself is well-defined in context. The verbal form of the imperative is, as we have said, more explicit, and we may wish to assume that, given its dominance in developed language, this same dominance was a "tendency" of imperative language. But the superior explicitness of the verbal form does not make it any more correct—or even necessarily any more practical, as is evident from the survival even today of the nominal imperative in contexts where it can be unambiguously understood. For the notion of correctness presupposes the possibility of metalinguistic dialogue to "correct" the faulty construction, and this is not yet possible in imperative language.

The category of person appears at first to constitute an exception because in contrast with that of tense it can be said to possess a true paradigm in the opposition between the second- and third-person imperatives. But for proof that this paradigm is not essential to the imperative we need look no further than our own language, where the third- (and first-) person imperatives employ a periphrastic construction whereas the basic second-person form simply uses the root form of the verb. (Even in Greek, where the third-person imperative is classified as part of a paradigm, it contains a true ending $[-(\epsilon)\tau\omega]$ in contrast with the "zero" -ending $[-\epsilon]$ of the second-person form.) But morphological evidence aside, the question to be asked is whether the basic form of the imperative is truly a "second-person" form involving an implicit opposition to third- and/or first-person forms. And the answer to this question is undeniably negative. The nominal imperative has not even the possibility of personalization, and whether or not the verbal form actually becomes personalized, in imperative language the action to be performed remains the only essential component of the imperative intention. If we again imagine a collectivity of hearers awaiting their orders from a single speaker, the imperatives addressed to the others are not understood by each hearer as "third-person" but simply as not addressed to them. If in this context a "third-person" form should be developed to designate the task of absent parties, the hearer who transmits the message is simply relaying the original speaker's request, thereby maintaining the symmetry of the collective situation in which each individual has his own task to perform. Even in a situation in which a well-defined chain of command exists, and where, let us say, the chief says to his aide "let the prisoners be executed," the aide will simply understand that he has been requested not to execute the prisoners but to give orders to others who will perform the task: The effect is the same as if the chief had said "tell [the guards] : 'Execute the prisoners!' " The contrast is never a symmetrical opposition, as in the declarative, between, "You do X" and "He does X," but rather an asymmetrical contrast between the awaiting of a performance by the addressee and an awaiting that includes the latter's own awaiting of a performance by a third party. Thus either, as in the first instance, the "third person" imperative is simply an imperative addressed to someone else, or, as in the second, it specifically requests a second-level imperative on the part of the addressee, so that his relation to the third party is either not defined at all, or it is defined not paradigmatically but hierarchically as that of speaker to hearer. This is not at all to say that the speaker of an imperative language would be in some sense unable to distinguish between his actions and those of others, but that the intentional structure of the imperative, even in the most favorable case, would not make it possible for this distinction to appear in itself abstracted from the particular action in question, because the awaiting of this or that action, which may on occasion be specified as to its performer, cannot distinguish between the hearer and a third party as potential performers of the *same* action. If I say "John runs, and you run" the hearer will understand the model as placing the two runners in a parallel situation and will imagine them as such. But if I say "Run! and let John run!" either my hearer will consider the second part of the sentence as inapplicable to him, as merely on overheard order to John, or he will take it as a second order of a different kind from the direct command of the first part. It can never appear as equally significant that the verb "run" have a second- or a third-person subject because ultimately the imperative has only second-person subjects, even if on occasion a second speech situation must be created to realize them.

We may sum up the foregoing discussion of the grammaticality of the imperative by saying that, in a word, the elementary linguistic forms lack true grammatical structures because they are not independent of the linguistic presence in which they are uttered. This is really only to say that they are not declaratives. This equivalence is, however, a fact of major importance not immediately apparent from the structure of the declarative. It can be made more explicit if we remark in addition what precisely is lacking in the paradigms of the imperative, for this lack is not simply the absence of one member among several: It effectively destroys the symmetry of the paradigm in question, or rather makes it impossible for a true paradigm to exist. The imperative verb is seen to lack, on the one hand, a true first-person (singular) form, and on the other, a linguistic subject. The latter absence is only perceptible from the standpoint of the declarative, but its association with the first absence is anything but coincidental. The speaker has no "person" in the imperative because he cannot as speaker create a model of his own action. But this lack of symmetry with regard to the performance requested in the imperative, and thereby with the "verbal" form that it may take, makes it clear that the "subject" of the imperative verb, even when expressed, is not an element of a linguistic model but a person in the real world. The difference between "You do this" and "You, do this!" independent of the morphological specificity of English, is that the first "you" is a linguistic subject, parallel to the other persons: he, I, we, and so on, whereas the second is really a vocative or "phatic" employed to establish linguistic presence with the hearer, and thus to assure him that it is really he who is being asked to perform the task. Thus it is the real-world person, not the linguistic "person," who is the true subject of the sentence, and this being the case, no true grammar is possible because these sentences are not opposable to unsaid sentences, but being themselves events in the real world, to other events.

The imperative and ostensive are pragmatic, not theoretical, which is to say that the linguistic *present* internal to the utterances is not fully separated from the linguistic *presence* in which they are uttered. The elementary forms have not yet fully emancipated themselves from their origin in the original crisis: Presence is still a deferral to permit cooperation, not contemplation. Thus even if the imperative takes different forms, these can never be grasped as paradigms of possibilities inherent in the imperative intention; their use merely corresponds to different real-world situations.

Language even at this stage is anything but instinctual, but there is still a sense in which behavioral models apply: Each word is still "associated" directly with the real or desired appearance of its object. Thus not only an ape but even a rat could be trained to "speak" by pressing one lever when a cat appears and another when it is hungry, the two levers being connected to a mechanical voice which would produce, respectively, the ostensive "Cat!" and the imperative "Food!"[4] Such models of human language, because they neglect the crucial element of presence, are both etiologically inadequate to explain elementary forms and incapable of even conceiving an explanation for the higher forms; conditioned reflexes produce only insoluble paradoxes and are thus incapable of formal evolution. The fact remains, however, that so long as we confine our analysis, as we have done thus far, to the practical functioning of the imperative, we will not touch on its contradictions and the forms generated in response to them and thus will remain on a level of explanation consonant with the conditioned reflex. Our assertion that the proto-grammatical developments to which we have referred do not make use of true grammatical categories is in effect equivalent to saying that they could be described as hypothetical accretions to the original model arrived at under the pressure of "conditioned reflexes," that is, by mere trial and error. Here again we should note the significance of the absence of a first-person form at this stage. If utterances are to be explained as resulting from "association" with the presence of their objects, then the self, because it is by definition always present, must either be spoken of constantly or not at all. This observation alone should suffice to demonstrate the inapplicability of behaviorist theory to mature languages.

4 The Origin of the Higher Linguistic Forms

Dialectic of the Imperative (I)

The intentional structure of the imperative has up to this point been discussed as a structure in equilibrium: A verbal request establishes an awaiting of performance by its hearer, compliance with which abolishes the awaiting and terminates the prolonged presence that it maintained. Indeed, this is how imperatives are supposed to function; to borrow a term from Austin, we might say that this process constitutes the "felicitous" performance of the imperative. Because, however, felicity requires in this case the action of someone other than the speaker, it cannot be predicated of the utterance alone, the expectations of which, whether or not reasonable in their context, may or may not be fulfilled by the addressee. The ostensive can only be verified; the imperative must be fulfilled, and thus as an utterance is not complete in itself. Thus the asymmetrical positions of speaker and hearer are not simply those of the speech situation; the hearer must, within the linguistic presence created by the speaker, not only hear but act. It is the contradictions implicit in this asymmetry that will lead to the creation of the "objective," information-bearing declarative form.

The dialectic of the ostensive, as we may recall, was motivated by the power implicit in the (ostensive) word in its capacity to generate linguistic presence. Once this presence has been actualized by an inappropriate ostensive utterance, the hearer may fulfill the expressed desire of the speaker for the object designated by supplying it, whether to avoid conflict with the speaker or simply in order to render his utterance appropriate. Thus the contradiction between the speaker's power in the linguistic situation and his symmetry with the hearer in the real-world situation of the ostensive (where the referent is at least potentially present to both) is resolved in favor of the former, as alone it could be, because outside the nonsignifying framework of ritual a purely symmetrical speech act is inconceivable, and the only possible "resolution" available in this direction would result in the symmetry of silence. In the imperative the implicit asymmetry of the ostensive speech-act becomes explicit so that the speaker commands not only linguistic presence but extra-linguistic actions of the hearer within the extendable limits of this presence. But by the same token, from the standpoint of its own autonomy, the speech act overextends itself, leaving itself open to disconfirmation or "infelicity," not on its own merits but at the hand of another.

The ostensive can be "inappropriate" if it refers to an absent object, but this is a feature of the real-world situation. The imperative eliminates this possibility by ordering the hearer to himself modify the situation. But at the same time it creates a new possibility of "infelicity" that has no analog in the ostensive and which points up a latent contradiction in the intentional structure of the imperative between the status its model of reality holds for the speaker and that which it holds for the hearer. This contradiction is not the effect of a "misunderstanding" but of the limitations placed by the imperative intention on the hearer. For the speaker the imperative is in effect nothing more than an extended ostensive, as it was in its origin. The presence of the referent gave him power over the other; now he employs this power to demand the presence of the object, and the hearer's performance justifies this employment, because, the act once accomplished, the original "ostensive" has indeed been made correct. The speaker's awaiting, as this analysis shows, is not merely in origin but in function a prolongation of the deferral of action characteristic of linguistic presence from the beginning. In the true ostensive this deferral lasts only the instant of the utterance, followed immediately by its confirmation by the hearer; in the imperative the same deferral of the hearer's own activity, "instinctual" or simply self-motivated, is prolonged until such a time as the utterance, like the ostensive, can be "verified."

It must again be stressed that this prolongation, although it of course lends itself to exploitation by those who possess authority over others, is a formal possibility of linguistic presence itself and thus perhaps as much a source as a product of social authority. But although the imperative obtains its original force from the sanctity, so to speak, of linguistic presence, from the hearer's standpoint the awaiting of his presentation of the object is not a simple equivalent of the deferral required in order that he may understand the speaker's message. Here we need not even speak of an unwillingness to perform the requested action, although the very possibility of this unwillingness is already a distinguishing feature of the situation. Linguistic deferral, although not "instinctive," is very nearly automatic, and in any case the act of will it might require is different in kind from that necessary to the performance of a worldly action. The first deferral is merely that of linguistic presence as such; the second, although it be in the case at hand derived from the first, must be maintained throughout the duration in real time of the requested performance. And in general the necessity of this performance, however brief, makes the imperative dependent on extra-linguistic real time in a way the ostensive is not. This the hearer, however great his good will, cannot help but experience, whereas the speaker, however well he may understand this truth, cannot put his understanding "into words," that is, into the intentional structure of the imperative.

To say that from the speaker's standpoint the imperative is no more than an extended ostensive is, in more rigorous terms, to say that for the speaker the hearer's performance is not a voluntary act, not a worldly act at all, but merely an element of a linguistic construction. The supplying of the object that will convert the imperative as "inappropriate" ostensive into an appropriate one is thus awaited in linguistic time, although it must take place in real time. The hearer, insofar as he performs this act, is not truly the addressee of the imperative but only its *agent*. The asymmetry of the construction is such that if the symmetrical communication situation of the ostensive be taken as the criterion of linguistic presence, the imperative can be said to have no addressee at all, its "apparent" hearer annulling his hearer's role on completion of his performance. This implicit denial of the role of interlocutor to the hearer can be realized explicitly in a situation where a third party is present; thus if a fashion designer showing his dresses to a prospective buyer says "summer dress" and a model wearing the appropriate clothing appears, his speech act is an ostensive addressed to the buyer and only secondarily an imperative because the presentation of the dress is simply assumed to take place upon the utterance of the ostensive.[1] Or one might think of a mother presenting her children to a guest, each one standing when his name is called, etc. In these examples the action of the "addressee" of the imperative merely takes the place of or supplements a deictic gesture by the speaker of the ostensive, and could be replaced by the operation of a mechanical device controlled by the latter.

This analysis is, however, made from the speaker's point of view. The hearer of the imperative, however "mechanically" he obeys it, is never reacting instinctively but through the mediation of linguistic presence, so that his act of obedience is not merely "voluntary" but *intelligent*, in the sense that it is mediated by a prior representation. And thus not only nonperformance but deliberate disobedience is possible. Here again we must stress that there is no reason to assume the speaker to be ignorant of these facts; but the intentional structure of the imperative has no place for them. The performance is implicit in the structure, which would otherwise be simply "infelicitous," a noncommunication. Conversely, the hearer can well understand the absolute nature of the imperative; but its intentional structure from his own viewpoint, by the very fact he has a "viewpoint" and is not simply an element of a linguistic construction, cannot be the same as that of the speaker. The hearer can only interpret the imperative as expressing the desire of the speaker, as indeed was the case of the original "inappropriate ostensive." His performance is thus for him a worldly fulfillment of the speaker's desire, whereas for the speaker this desire is fulfilled

in linguistic presence, the performance being merely a prolongation of this presence.

The inherent contradiction of these two versions of the
intentional structure of the imperative remains latent in the
case of satisfactory performance. In the event that the task is
not performed, however, it manifests itself openly. In effect,
whatever his intentions the hearer who does not satisfy the
imperative request restores the imperative to its original
status as an inappropriate ostensive. Now if this is indeed the
hearer's intention, that is, if he simply ignores the imperative
and considers the absence of its referent not as an indication
of an act to be performed, but as an impropriety on the part
of the speaker, then he will react as a speaker of ostensive,
not imperative language. In imperative language, however,
this reaction can only be understood as a refusal of linguistic
presence, for within this presence only performance is a
satisfactory response to the imperative. The hearer who is
unwilling or unable to accede to the request is thus faced
with the latent contradiction of the imperative situation: The
response demanded by the imperative is representational for
the speaker, but real for the hearer, and if this real response
cannot be made, then the latter has no representational
response available. The hearer thus can be said to feel the
need to maintain linguistic presence, as the speaker wished,
even if he cannot provide real-world satisfaction for the
latter's desire. It is this need that will give rise to the creation
of the declarative form.

The Fundamental Asymmetry of the Speech Situation

The contradiction in the intentional structure of the
imperative between what we may call speaker's intention and
hearer's intention is dependent on the fundamental asymmetry of the speech situation, which emerges at this stage and
which is not so much resolved in the higher forms as made
explicit and thereby discounted. This asymmetry was of
course present from the beginning. In the original event each
individual's participation in the designating of the sacred
object, although productive of the same representational
model as that of the others, was, as we have observed, at the

same time an imaginary possession of the object at the other's expense; and in the absence of a "subjective" linguistic model in which representation is productive of desire, the very sacralization of the object by means of which it came to retain its "powers" outside the original context would have been inconceivable. From the vantage point of the imperative, however, and a fortiori from that of higher forms, we may now express this asymmetry in more formal terms because the significance expressed by these forms is no longer simply an attribute of communal presence but is itself mediated by the desire of the speaker. This mediation occurs in its most overt form in the imperative, but it is discounted rather than simply eliminated in the declarative. The earlier forms do not contain it explicitly, and the locus of desire in their intentional structures is therefore still hypothetical; but we may apply our formalization to them retroactively.

The "objective" formulation of the distinction between speaker's and hearer's intention requires that we consider linguistic presence as a virtual relation actualized voluntarily by the speaker but entered into by the hearer without question as a duty incumbent on him qua member of the community. The enforcer of this duty in the original event was the community, and its enforcement became by our hypothesis incarnate in the sacred object. But even the de-ritualization of the modern world has not lessened this dissymmetry. On the contrary, the rise of the "media" tends only to accentuate it—and this is no technological accident but of the very essence of modernity. Thus the speaker chooses to speak, but the listener cannot help but listen, although means are of course available to avoid or terminate the speech situation. It is not that the preexistence of virtual linguistic presence confers on the speaker a permanent advantage; the community imposes certain appropriateness-conditions or guarantees of signification which if violated will be punished a posteriori. His only "advantage" is one that compensates him in advance for the presumed significance of his communication—the possibility of such communication being the original and fundamental raison d'être of the very existence of linguistic (or more generally, representational) presence. It consists in an *economy of intention*. Viewed from without,

speaker and hearer in the speech situation are equally present
to one another, yet from the virtuality of linguistic presence
before the speech act it follows that the speaker need not
"present himself" to the hearer otherwise than through the
linguistic model expressed in his utterance.[2] The speaker's
intention then is simply the correspondence between this
model and reality.

For the hearer, however, the model does not appear alone,
but spoken by the speaker-speaking-the-utterance, and thus
the hearer's own intentional model of reality in the speech-
situation is complicated by the addition of a supplementary
factor. The speaker intends the linguistic model alone, but
the hearer intends the speaker's intention. If this were not
so the communication situation would not be "intentional,"
that is, interpersonal at all. To understand the speech act as
something other than a signal or other instinctual or involuntary form of communication (and in this context any distinctions we might wish to make between the instinctual and the
involuntary are unimportant), it must be seen as an *intentional* actualization of linguistic presence. On this point it
might be said that hearer and speaker are in accord because
the latter is certainly aware of his own intentionality. But the
speaker does not intend this intentionality; it is not an element of his model. Were this not so his speech act would be
logically impossible because it would suffer from infinite
regression, as do in fact all theories that attempt to propose
a completely symmetrical (or we might say "metaphysical")
model of the communication situation. Linguistic presence is
not a "channel" of communication, even if the higher linguistic forms make the channel analogy a reasonably accurate
approximation—one that cannot contribute, however, to the
understanding of the origin of these forms, which are thereby
made to appear "natural." *The speaker's model of the communication situation must be incomplete if it is to exist at all.*
Thus he acts as though indeed such a "channel" existed into
which he may pour the information he desires to communicate, whereas for the hearer the actualization of this "channel"
is not the result of the words and of the information they
convey, but of the intentional act of the speaker. Linguistic
presence, it must be remembered, is a form of communal

coexistence, and only abstraction can eliminate its intersubjective nature.

Before pursuing our formalization of the speaker-hearer asymmetry and the analysis of the dialectic of linguistic forms on which it directly bears, we should dispose of an epistemological objection that our exposition of this asymmetry would otherwise not fail to provoke. Is not the logical impossibility of complete representation of the communication situation independent of the anthropological hypothesis we have taken such pains to present? And if this is the case, then are not the forms of representation in general, specifically including the declarative, all equally "natural," and their contradictions and resulting dialectic merely gratuitous assumptions because, as the channel analogy implies, the form and content of the communication situation (the channel and the current, as it were) are simply of two different natures, incapable of any dialectical opposition? Ultimately the point of this objection is this: We communicate through language and can only conceive of this communication as "transparent," that is, as permitting us to say what we think, the proof of this being that we can express any qualifications we may feel pertinent to add to our previous statements; in Peirce's terms, to every sign there corresponds an "interpretant" that may be made as explicit as possible. But even if in some undefined sense this is not true and language is indeed "opaque," then there is no vantage point from which we may speak of the inherent contradictions of linguistic communication because our own discourse must remain subject to the limitation we purport to denounce. This objection, then, has a double expression, "optimistic" and "pessimistic," the one "metaphysical" and traditional, the other, post-Nietzschean and nihilistic, using language only to "de-construct" its earlier pretensions.

Our response to this double objection is at the same time a justification of the need for and of the possibility of a scientific theory of representation—the first, in answer to the "optimists" who find it unnecessary, the second, to the "pessimists" who think it inconceivable. It is nevertheless very simple. The transparency of communication does not consist in the presence of a "pure intuition" but simply in the capacity of language to include indefinitely many levels of metalanguage. This capacity is virtual and by definition cannot be exhausted; thus what we say on any subject can never be a definitive "last word". And precisely because this virtuality is an element of the intentional structure of discourse, our communication remains "transparent," that is, open to explanation and eventual refutation. But this condition of language is not inherent in the extant forms of language; it consists rather in a capacity for further construction on them. Here we use the word "form" to refer not to linguistic forms like the imperative or even the declarative sentence but to the forms of discourse. In particular, we claim that this present analysis represents a new, "hypothetical" form of discourse in human science, the realization of a possibility latent, but certainly not preexisting, in its earlier and, from this writer's point of view at least, less satisfactory forms. But in this perspective all these forms, including the linguistic forms, did not "preexist" in a metaphysical concept called "language," but were at one time or another constructed on the basis of earlier forms, to account for the earliest of which we have proposed the hypothetical origin described herein. The dialogic "transparency" of discourse itself was not available a priori, but only became even a virtual reality through the construction of the general form or "type" of dialogue which is itself based, as we will attempt to show, on the preexisting form of the declarative sentence. This "transparency" being merely a potential openness to further discourse, it does not abolish the original asymmetry of the communication situation, but merely permits its effects to be indefinitely reduced. And once the founding hypotheses have been made explicit—which in the domain of human science means providing an epistemological link between the subject matter and the theory that purports to explain it, as we believe we have accomplished here—the discourse that performs this task can properly claim for itself the name of science. The "logical impossibility" of complete self-inclusion by the linguistic model does not prevent, from this perspective, the construction of forms to resolve whatever contradictions thus arise, beginning with the most intolerable, and it is to our analysis of this process of construction that we now return.

The speaker intends his words as a model of reality; the hearer intends them as intended by the speaker. This opposition can be expressed schematically in very simple terms: if S says "X," then

Speaker's model: X
Hearer's model: S (X)

The simplicity of this schema, although mnemonically convenient, masks the fact that as a "mapping" of the linguistic situation it only really applies to developed language, because only by means of the declarative sentence can the "hearer's model" actually be formulated. At the more elementary levels this model cannot be expressed linguistically and so cannot be said to exist even implicitly within linguistic presence. Although the hearer, of course, "realizes" that the words are being pronounced intentionally by the speaker, he cannot say this himself—for example in repeating the speaker's words to others—and therefore cannot conceive that his model of the situation might possess the same objective status as that presented by the speaker. In the words of the preceding discussion, therefore, language at this level is not "transparent" but opaque. No metalinguistic levels are available for discussion of another's words, and thus no interpretation of their "subjective" meaning, and conversely, no judgment of their truth, is possible. Even these statements, unobjectionable as they may appear, are unavoidably anachronistic because they judge the deficiencies of elementary language from the standpoint of later developments. Their relevancy begins, as we shall see very shortly, with the problems occasioned by the hearer's model of the imperative. It will be useful, however, to briefly recapitulate the preceding stages of linguistic evolution in terms of the schema just proposed, precisely in order to demonstrate its less than total applicability to the forms of "elementary language."

In the original event the individual "speakers," as we have already noted, can be supposed to have experienced, through their construction of linguistic models of the sacred object, an imaginary participation in the mediating or presence-compelling power of this object. To describe the "hearer's" point of view in this situation it would certainly be inaccurate to make use of our schematic S (X). Although the designation of the object by the others is indeed perceived as intentional, this intention appears as something essentially negative, a withdrawal from the appropriation of the object in the presence of the community, this presence being itself seen to be mediated by the object as focus of "noninstinctual attention." The individual-as-hearer's appetite for the object is contravened by the presence of the others, which forces him to participate in the general symmetry of this presence. His own designative gesture is, more than a sign of the object, a sign of his participation in the communal attention to it. This sign is adequate to its referent; the model of the central sacred object is justified by the communal presence around it, and the signification of this model is indeed this presence. Thus the "speaker" in this instance evidently needs no further introduction to the group; the significance of his act is fully guaranteed. And conversely, from the "hearer's" standpoint, there is no element of subjectivity to be accounted for in the intentionality of the "speaker" because the latter coincides with the community as a whole, and the intention manifested is none other than the formation of the community, that is, of nonviolent presence mediated by the sacred object.

It is therefore evident why our schema is inapplicable; yet we also know that the perfect symmetry of the communal intention is disrupted, privately as it were, by desire. In the schema, the means for understanding and discounting the element of desire in linguistic intention are given, but the participants in the original event do not possess these means. But at the same time the "means" are unnecessary because the linguistic expression requires no explanation, being wholly significant. Insofar as this expression is for the individual speaker an expression of desire, it is "private," outside of linguistic presence. Now if we examine precisely how desire nevertheless exerts a dialectical pressure on representation, we see that is through the isolation of the formal power of presence in the object and the concomitant liberation of its field of attention to include other, profane objects, while the sacred guarantee of this presence is reenacted and reinforced through ritual. It is only at this point, then, that representation truly becomes a *form*, and within this form, the sacred object can be represented as possessing the *power* to compel and guarantee presence, without its representation being the simple equivalent of presence.

From the standpoint of our schema this evolution has taken place *as if* the individual-as-hearer were interpreting the others-as-speakers' designation of the sacred object as the expression not of a collective but of an *individual* choice of referent, so that the sacred object becomes a referent as "arbitrary" as any other, and the form of the ostensive-in-general can come into existence. Now evidently there is no question of such an interpretation having actually taken place: The sacred powers of the object were the effect of its desirability. But what else is the "desirability" of the object than the fact of its designation *by others*? The dialectical functioning of desire thus appears here in its purest form, fully mystified, as it were, because language at this elementary level offers no possibility to represent its working even in others. The individual here not only cannot see the beam in his own eye but he is blind to the one in the eye of his neighbor. The spectacle of this blindness illuminates for us the entire dialectic of representational forms, which can now be seen as the progression of the understanding of desire. Yet at the same time it permits us to grasp the partial truth of the enduring notion of the lost paradise of the original presence, the falling away from which is described by Heidegger as a "forgetting of being" coeval with the institution of "metaphysics," that world view that considers representational form as at the same time independent of and transparent to its content. For stripped of its theoretical reinforcement in philosophical doctrine—as though the problem were caused by the doctrine rather than the other way around— "metaphysics" is merely a nonrecursive understanding of representational form expressed in our schema; that is, capable of seeing desire in the representations of others, but not in our own and therefore not in the form itself.[3] The original innocence of desire was not, certainly, absence of desire, but its blindness at least remained symmetrical, whereas the establishment of the higher forms of language coincides with a fall from grace in which each speaker begins to denounce the "subjectivity" of his fellows. This denunciation is of course the road to the objectivity of scientific discourse, and ultimately—one hopes—to "objective" nonviolence as well. Yet from the vantage point of our postpositivist epoch it is easy to denounce the arrogance of the metaphysical notion of objectivity, more difficult to understand it as a step toward the understanding of desire.

The second stage in our dialectic, the passage from the ostensive to the imperative, requires less comment. Here we are much closer to the opposition represented in our schema, because the hearer of the inappropriate ostensive can only treat it as an imperative if he understands it as the expression of a subjective intention of the speaker, that is, of his desire. The imperative sign, which denotes an absent referent significant, in the first place at least, only to the speaker, is thus antipodal to the ostensive that designates a present phenomenon of general communal significance. But if in the ostensive the role of individual desire was neglected, in the imperative it is exaggerated. The ostensive purported merely to represent objects of communal significance, so that the speaker's own intention was absorbed immediately into that of the community, and his original initiative perhaps forgotten altogether in the general repetition of his words. In the imperative quite the opposite is the case: Whether or not the referent is of communal significance, this significance can only appear through the mediation of the desire of the individual subject.[4] The origin of this polar opposition is of course the polarity between the presence/absence of the referent, and when this absence is only relative to the speaker, as in the case where he requests that a nearby but "distal" object be placed in his immediate possession, this polarity is not mitigated but is rather all the more striking because it is unambiguously clear that what is desired is not the mere presence of the object but its appropriation by the speaker. In the imperative model the linguistic presence of the referent reflects its real absence, and by responding to the "inappropriate ostensive" the hearer demonstrates that he understands that such possession in language is a sign of desire for real possession, or we may say with more precision, of a desire model of possession.

But although his furnishing of the desired object will normally satisfy the speaker, and thus produce a return to equilibrium, it does not correspond to a genuine understanding in terms of our schema of the asymmetry of the speech situation; the literality of its interpretation of the desire of the speaker fails to do justice to the essentially paradoxical, or more accurately, paradox-producing nature of desire. To the extent that the speaker of the imperative does not simply need but desires the referent, his desire will not be satisfied but merely "deferred" by its possession. And thus in a case where the hearer is for whatever reason—socially grounded authority, or his own desire, as in a "fatal" love relationship—committed to supplying at all costs the referents of the imperative, these referents will simply prove more and more difficult and eventually impossible to obtain. (This progression to a "bad infinity" is of great interest to historians of social relations. It represents a "resolution" of the paradox of desire which pushes the asymmetry of the imperative to its extreme, and for that very reason is not dialectically productive of higher forms of representation.)

If we now examine the ostensive-imperative progression in terms of our schema, we observe that if the ostensive utterance is interpreted not as $S(X)$ but simply as X, the imperative interpretation must be expressed as something like $S \rightarrow X$. The absence of parenthesis represents the lack of a formal barrier between the speaker and the referent, so that his utterance is interpreted not as his significant model of reality, but as the significant model of *his* reality. That the speaker comes to accept this interpretation, which realizes in the world the merely formal asymmetry of the speech situation, is not of course unimportant. Indeed, this acceptance, except in the extreme case where the speaker's authority over the real (and not merely linguistic) time of the hearer is understood by both parties to be limitless, permits the imperative to establish itself as a linguistic form and to acquire a practical function. This functionalization of the imperative in turn tends to limit its referents to objects the appropriation of which by the speaker can somehow be considered "socially useful," or at least socially appropriate, and thus serves to "educate" desire, no longer merely a subjective phenomenon but one capable of being communicated in linguistic presence and in consequence obliged, in its expression at least, to take the criteria of communal significance into account. Thus a point of equilibrium is established at which the speaker of the imperative can continue to profit from his command of linguistic presence to realize his desire, but where his desires are functionalized in the service of the community, in which service they are, indeed, more likely to be adhered to. From the standpoint of intentional structure, however, the functionality of the imperative request is irrelevant because the speaker's desire must by definition be taken as significant.

Imperative Dialogue

The addressee of the imperative, by his acceptance of the speaker's desire, becomes not merely his hearer but his interlocutor. Thus he hears not only the utterance but the person, and by hearing the speaker's utterance as a personal one, he is able to assume in linguistic presence the "nonpersonal" role of member of the community and respecter of its norms of significance. In this fashion the addressee of the imperative creates the possibility of *dialogue* with the speaker, the most primitive form of dialectic *proprement dit*, and the distant ancestor of our own. But a glance at the sort of dialogue imperative language makes possible only confirms our observations concerning the inadequacy of the imperative model to the fundamental asymmetry of the speech situation as expressed in our schema, an inadequacy that nevertheless contrasts with the total blindness of the ostensive. The ostensive is totally unproductive of dialogue: A hearer of the ostensive who then repeats it to others is not responding to the first at all, but on the contrary is demonstrating the impersonal symmetry of his position toward the designated object. The imperative at least permits of an elementary form of dialogue, an example of which has already been given: at the operating table—"Scalpel!"-"Scalpel"; "Forceps!"-"Forceps," etc. Here the ostensive serves as a reply to the imperative. The addressee interprets the desire of the speaker as significant, or in other terms accepts it as an appropriate utterance in linguistic presence. His ostensive reply in a sense "corrects" the first speaker by designating the presence of the object, but more importantly "corrects" his *personal* expression of desire by designating its object in this impersonal, communal mode. Of course this reply implies no disagreement with the imperative, to which it is a sign of obedience both in the linguistic model and in reality, the "communal" significance of the ostensive being in effect guaranteed only by the first speaker's desire as expressed in the imperative. Instead of "correct" we may equally well write "perfect" because the passage from imperative to ostensive is also that from absence to presence, or simply from the "inappropriate" ostensive to the "appropriate." Whichever word we use, however, we cannot fail to note that this dialogue in no way transcends the asymmetry of the imperative intention. The second speaker responds in a form different from the first, and which permits of no further dialogue; the content of his utterance is entirely determined by that of the first speaker, which he simply mimics. The identity in linguistic substance of the two utterances is indeed anything but accidental: It reflects the totally dependent, parasitic character of the second speaker's role. But in this role the utterance of an ostensive reply is not indeed the essential feature, for this utterance is only possible upon prior completion of the performance requested by the interlocutor. The ostensive can mimic the words of the imperative only once the deed required for its realization has been performed. Thus the imperative-ostensive dialogue represents the expression and annulment of desire, the successive pairs of utterances marking the beginning and end of successive periods of awaiting. But the fundamental asymmetry of the two speakers with respect to this desire and this awaiting is never called into question.

The addressee of the imperative, the second speaker in this "dialogue," demonstrates in his reply that he has understood the imperative on its own terms. His utterance, although peripheral to the imperative situation, is a valuable indication of the precise degree of this understanding, which is, as we have noted, only partial. For a full understanding, in terms of our schema, would grasp the onesidedness of the imperative model and permit a "dialogic" reply to correct this partiality, whereas the ostensive reply can only be given, as we have seen, when performance of the speaker's request is not only possible but already carried out. The awaiting fundamental to the imperative model is an awaiting of performance which blocks any purely linguistic response.[5] The addressee is in effect included as agent in the intentional structure of the imperative; his performance, or at any rate its result, is a part of the linguistic model, and until it be completed the speaker still "has the floor."

But even if the addressee fully understands the imperative and accepts the role it designates for him, he may not be able to carry out the required performance—a case more significant, from our point of view, than that of a simple refusal, which is in effect a prima facie refusal of linguistic presence. Here, lacking performance, no linguistic response is possible; yet by hypothesis the addressee has no desire to violate the linguistic presence in which he stands with the speaker—a violation that might indeed be productive of unfortunate consequences. In this situation the contradiction inherent in the imperative model becomes explicit. It is to be noted that this "contradiction" is not a purely private one, as was the case in the sacralization of the original object, or one standing in an ambivalent position between the "private" and "public" spheres, as we found in the second stage of our dialectic, where the "inappropriate" ostensive, expression of an individual desire, came to be interpreted as an imperative, that is, a legitimate speech act of genuine, although mediate, communal significance. Here the contradiction overtly involves the distinction between the speaker's and hearer's model of the imperative. This is not yet a fully dialogic conflict because it cannot be assimilated into a disagreement in which one speaker contests the other's objectivity; the fact is merely that the hearer's model permits him to understand the situation in a way that is closed to the speaker, for whom the possibility of nonperformance cannot arise because performance is already included in his intention. It would therefore be a mistake to view this situation as one merely of the contradiction between the imperative model on the one hand and "reality" on the other. This contradiction of course exists, but from a representational standpoint it is mediated by the speaker's relationship to the hearer. For the referent of the imperative model is not merely an object of desire but the object of a desire expressed in linguistic presence, and its impossibility of fulfillment, before leading to a contradiction in the sphere of reality, provokes a contradiction within the limits of this presence. This fact is certainly obvious enough to the addressee, to whom "reality" is apt to afford little protection from the wrath of the speaker.

Now the hearer's model of the imperative is not indeed blind to the possibility of nonfulfillment, because the speaker's request appeared in it from the very beginning, not as an objective model of reality but as the expression of a desire. But the nonidentity of the hearer's intention with the speaker's remained only latent so long as the former was able to bring the two into coincidence by fulfilling the expressed desire of the latter—a coincidence expressible, as we have seen, in his ostensive "reply." In the present case the non-coincidence becomes a contradiction, although this contradiction is, as befits the asymmetrical structure of the imperative, visible only to the hearer. It is "reality" that is the ultimate source of this contradiction, but the situation would in fact be little different if this source were the recalcitrance of the hearer. For in any case the problem at hand for the latter is to retain, despite the contradiction, his relation of linguistic presence with the speaker. But this implies that instead of using an ostensive to express the presence of the object, he must find a way to communicate its absence. It is this need that leads to the creation of the declarative.

The speaker of the imperative awaits an object, or more generally, a performance through which his utterance will be realized as an ostensive (whether or not this latter is actually spoken by either party). The addressee, lacking the possibility of producing the object, must produce an utterance that will have to be accepted in lieu of the object. What is required is, so to speak, a negative ostensive—the *contradictio in adjecto* being merely a reduced form of the contradiction between the hearer's and the speaker's intention. Once the reduction is accomplished, however—that is, once the necessity of expressing the contradiction by an utterance is recognized by the addressee of the imperative—the negative-ostensive resolution of his paradoxical situation will be able to be found. It suffices that the materials of which this solution is constructed be available: the ostensive, and the concept, or more precisely the *operator* of negation.

Negation and the Imperative

The ostensive admits of no negation because its referent is required to be present, and this is true even if the referent is itself "negative" in character. Thus, for example, we may consider the familiar utterance "Help!" despite its imperative appearance as in reality a form of the ostensive. Although from a semantical standpoint help is obviously what is lacking to the speaker, and what is being requested, we cannot presuppose in the cry any sort of imaginary preconception of the aid that will be furnished, and thus any element of desire. What is being expressed is rather the presence of a help-requiring situation. This analysis may well appear to the reader as overly subtle,[6] but its point is to state the most favorable possible case for a "negative ostensive." And if this analysis be accepted, what is revealed is that the cry for help once taken as an ostensive, the hearer's response can no longer be considered as "supplying" help but simply as "coming to the rescue." That is, to the extent that no imagined help precedes the cry, no imagined help exists in the mind of the rescuer. What is in his mind is rather the peril being undergone by the speaker. This peril may require the former to seek what is needed to extract the latter from it (such as a life preserver for someone in danger of drowning); but this analysis is extra-linguistic, its materials not being supplied by the imperative. A true imperative like "Water!" involves a very different intentional structure.

In the imperative, in contrast to the ostensive, negation is common, and there is no reason to exclude it from imperative language. In its simplest form it might originate in the refusal of a proffered object. Such a refusal is not in itself a negative imperative; it is not in fact a negation at all because mere refusal is not a representational act. But gestures of refusal not only supply a plausible source of negative lexemes but are fully compatible with the intentional structure of the imperative. Just as the positive imperative expresses a desire to appropriate an object, the negative form refuses such appropriation to the hearer—what is awaited is not the appearance of the object, but a gesture óf renouncement. From this perspective, indeed, the original sign designating the sacred object can be looked on as a negative imperative *avant la lettre*, indicating through its mere existence, and through the nonviolent representational presence that it creates, that its referent is not to be appropriated by the other members of the group. Interdiction is indeed an original element of the ostensive, and in the passage from ostensive to imperative a communal interdiction is transformed into one imposed by individual desire: Just as the object of the ostensive is in general not to be appropriated (at least not individually), the object of the imperative is designated for appropriation by the speaker, and by the same token refused to the hearer.

We have already referred to the desire aroused by the ostensive as the motive force for its inappropriate use and thereby for the emergence of the imperative form. The expression of desire by one speaker should not be taken as a sign of its extinction in others, however, but rather of the contrary. The power of linguistic presence gives a supplementary force to expressed as opposed to unexpressed desire and thus permits the constitution of the imperative; but the imperative, as an expression of individual desire, can only strengthen mimetically the nonspeaker's desire for the object. This desire does not contribute as such to the dialectic of linguistic forms, which as we have seen no longer takes place in the domain of "private" desire but in the "public" or "dialogic" arena constituted by linguistic presence at this stage. Or rather its contribution has already been made, that contribution being the explicitation of the interdictive element of the ostensive in the negative imperative. The positive imperative expresses the desire of the speaker; the negative imperative presumes the existence of similar desires in the hearer. In reference to a particular object the negative complements the positive because once the object has been demanded by the speaker it is likely to have to be refused to the hearer. But we need not be content with such episodic explanations. The very existence of the imperative makes explicit not merely the existence but the significance of individual desire, which has now received its right of entry into linguistic presence. In this situation the interdictive element of the ostensive is no longer sufficient, or more precisely, it is ambiguous as it stands because designation of an object can now simply signify desire for that object. Hence the imperative must come into existence in both positive and negative forms—or more precisely, prescriptive and interdictive, for no formal notion of negation is yet present. Thus, although their social functions are undoubtedly different, the prescriptive imperative being more closely associated with practical (profane) activities and the interdictive with ritual, their intentional structures are not antithetical, but identical. Interdiction, as we have just observed, implies an understanding of the desire of the other, and might therefore appear to transcend the limitations we have attributed to the speaker in the general imperative model. But we must be careful to distinguish this sense of understanding from that represented in our schema. The speaker of an interdiction recognizes in the other desires as similar to his own, and which may not yet even have led to actual behavior. But within the intentional structure of the interdiction, no symmetry is established between these desires and that of the speaker which contravenes them. On the contrary, the interdiction does not address itself to the desires of its hearer at all but to his actions. And if anything the asymmetry between speaker and hearer is even greater here than in the prescriptive (positive) imperative because the desire of the former is now realized explicitly in the negation of the activity of the latter.

The interdictive imperative thus tends to imply more readily than the prescriptive the preexistence of a well-defined authority relation between the interlocutors. The strength of this relation is most evident in a phenomenon we may call "normative awaiting." which is particularly although not exclusively characteristic of interdiction. In such cases the linguistic presence of the imperative is not terminated by any specific performance, but prolongs itself indefinitely into the future. Thus a father who tells his son "Don't take candy from strangers!" does not await any specific act, even an act of renouncement, although a sign of such renouncement will normally be expected to terminate linguistic presence *stricto sensu*. He simply states a general rule of conduct, and will consider the interdiction to be violated if candy is accepted at any future time. The same situation can result from a positive imperative like "Eat an apple every day!" or "Keep your hands clean!" In normative awaiting the linguistic presence of the speaker is in effect indefinitely prolonged, so that any offending conduct becomes a violation of this presence, which is to say, not merely of the desires of the speaker but of presence-in-general, guaranteed by the community as a whole through the mediation of the sacred. This form of the imperative thus plays a major role in the maintenance of the social order. The normative propensity of the interdictive form is worthy of our notice because it serves to emphasize the opposition between the two "understandings" of desire implicit in the imperative model. The speaker's desire, here as always, is identified with the maintenance of communal presence, whereas that of the hearer, insofar as it may be a source of potential action, is opposed to the former as incompatible with this presence. In the normative imperative (prescriptive or interdictive) the mediation of communal significance by the individual desire of the speaker may well be purely derivative, the spoken rule being merely the repetition of one that has already received general acceptance, the original pronouncement of which may even be attributed to a sacred being. But even in this case the mediation is real, and the ritual or collectively based authority of the rule is only realized in the speech situation through the intermediary of the speaker's own, even if this latter merely serves to reinforce a normative awaiting already established in another ritual or profane context.

The negative imperative, as it appears from this discussion, is not an independent linguistic form. It differs from the prescriptive variety only in content. It would even be a mistake to classify the positive/negative dichotomy as a grammatical paradigm like that of person. For, as we have defined

the grammatical, it functions to objectify linguistic intentionality by discounting the particular temporal or spatial conditions of the speech acts. The declarative is more grammatical
than the imperative because, for example, it contains a paradigm of tenses (however they may be morphologically
expressed) which permit the time designated in the utterance—linguistic time—to be situated with relation to the time
of the utterance. In this sense the persons of the imperative
form a partially complete paradigm. The positive-negative
dichotomy is not paradigmatic at all, however, because the
relation between speaker and hearer remains fundamentally
the same, affirmation and negation not being in any sense a
pair of "shifters." The role of negation in imperative language
is rather better described as that of an *operator* that affects
"adverbially" the whole content of the performance requested by the speaker.

The notion of an operator must be distinguished from that
of a simple *modifier*, which in imperative language can only
express a modality of the object requested and not the
performance. The available etymological evidence supports
the view that the modifiers of developed languages (adverbs
and adjectives) were originally derived from substantial words
(nouns and verbs). This view is fully compatible with the
dialectial process of formal evolution outlined here in which
the first proto-linguistic sign was of substantial nature, as
were the communally significant objects through which, in
the ostensive form, the power of compelling linguistic presence was extended to worldly phenomena. In ostensive language, although the combination of various substantive
elements in a "double" or "triple" ostensive is easily imaginable, just as it is impossible to conceive of the existence of
true governance-relationships between distinct categories of
"nouns" and "verbs," it is equally impossible to conceive of
the existence of true modifiers, that is, of degenerate substantive words no longer utterable in themselves but dependent
on nondegenerate substantives. Even in developed languages
the use, for example, of adjectives as nouns, is possible in
many contexts, and the distinction between the two categories is often something of a fine point of grammar. But our
argument on this point can be given a firmer epistemological

basis. A "double ostensive" like "Forest fire!" or even "Big fire!" involves, in comparison to the simple "Fire!" which functions as little more than a signal, a minimum of analysis on the speaker's side and construction on the hearer's. But just as in the case of the flying crows of the preceding chapter, the intentional structure of the ostensive precludes the formation of any genuine notion of subordination. There is a fire that is big; but there is just as much something big that is a fire. To the extent that the image of a fire is more explicit than that of bigness, we may speak of a psychological tendency toward subordination. But in order for this tendency to be realized in a grammatical category it is necessary that the relationship between the two elements be defined, or more precisely, be obliged to be defined, within the linguistic model. In the case at hand we may well admit that "big" is less significant in the communication situation than "fire," less specific in its mobilizing action on the community. In the context of the ostensive, however, this difference is merely relative, not, as in the case of true modification, absolute, because either word is sufficient by itself to turn the attention of the community toward its object. Modification, like governance, must await the inclusion of its constitutive hierarchical relation in the intentional structure of linguistic form.

In the imperative modification, again like governance, receives a primitive form of grammaticalization. Requests for physical objects, for example, must in practical contexts make a distinction between the category of things and that of qualities; here again the performative nature of the imperative model provides the impetus for grammaticalization. This development can be stated more schematically: it is the asymmetry of the imperative that permits the "informal" grammaticalization of asymmetrical relations between the elements of its intentional model. Thus the subordination of adjective to noun in the nominal imperative is dependent on the subordination of the addressee to the speaker's desire. Here we mean not that the speaker can be presumed to be "more interested" in the nominal than the proto-adjectival component, for such relative differences could be traced to the ostensive, but rather that the relative difference in significance from the standpoint of the original model is translated into an absolute difference in the performance of the addressee, precisely because in fulfilling the model maximally he must convert an "analog" to a "digital," a relative to an absolute relation. Thus if a big hammer is requested, a small hammer will be generally more acceptable than a big basket. The same analysis evidently applies to constructions like "Come quickly!" where a verbal rather than a nominal request is qualified, verbals being at this stage, as we have seen, not yet formally distinguished from nominals.

To sum up our analysis of imperative modification up to this point, we can consider it to be, like governance, in a state of incipient grammaticalization. Whether or not specialized lexical terms existed, the intentional structure of the imperative provided in its asymmetry a model for asymmetrical relations of both kinds. It would not be accurate, however, to speak of grammaticalization in the sense in which it occurs in the declarative form because the asymmetry is not fully realized in the linguistic model. Thus as in the case of governance, analysis into, for example, "noun" and "adjective," although it may in fact be carried out by the speaker, is structurally speaking a problem only for the hearer because it develops from the analysis of his performance. But in more formal terms this is only to say that the asymmetry that provides the foundation for this analysis is at the same time an obstacle to its formalization in the linguistic model because the speaker's words, unlike the hearer's actions, are intended to produce fulfillment through purely linguistic means—the imperative remaining always, in essence, an "inappropriate ostensive."

The use of operators that modify the imperative performance model as a whole constitutes the limit of grammatical polarization possible within imperative language. In "Big hammer!" or even in "Run fast!" the requested performance is merely more specific than in "Hammer!" or "Run!". In a case like "Run again!" or "Two hammers!" however, what is added by the modifier is not a specification of the object/action requested, but of the performance in which this object/action is included. The difference between operators and ordinary modifiers may appear to be one of degree, particularly in those cases where action and performance coincide (so that if "run fast!" merely specifies, "run faster!" implies a comparison with a previous performance taken as a whole). In contrast in a command like "Hammer (n.) fast!" "fast" clearly operates on the requested act of presentification rather than modifying the hammer. But the point of the distinction is clear: Operators take the substantial part of the linguistic model not merely as designating an object or action, but as in themselves complete performances. And in negation, the operator most clearly distinguished from a simple modifier, it is all but impossible to suppose that a quasi-grammatical analysis has not been carried out, not only by the hearer, but by the speaker. On hearing "Don't walk!" not only the hearer but the speaker as well must consider that the command cannot be separated into the substantive action of walking and a secondary but never totally dependent quality that attaches to it. In "Run fast!" "fast" may be an afterthought, a quasi-independent request to be combined with "Run!" and thus perhaps expressed in imperative language in something lexically similar to "Run! hurry!". Whatever its lexical form, however, "Don't run!" can scarcely be analyzed in this manner. Even if we consider the primitive form of interdiction to be something like "Run! No!" with the imagined referent or "image" of running as occurring first independently and then "operated on" by the negative, the reinterpretation accomplished by the latter is such as to transform it from a model of requested behavior into precisely the opposite. The unambiguous example of negation may be presumed to lend strength to a similar operator/substantive distinction in other cases, although only negation will concern us here.

Interdiction, as we have just observed, operates not on the substantive content of the imperative model but on the model as a whole conceived in a positive sense. Schematically we may represent this situation by the equation: Perf $(\sim X) = \sim[\text{Perf}(X)]$, where "Perf" refers to the performance requested by the speaker. Now we must be careful to distinguish this equation from the apparently similar but incorrect: Imp $(\sim X) = \sim\text{Imp } X$, where "Imp" stands for the entire intentional structure of the imperative, the sense of which would be that to forbid something is simply not to order it. This distinction may appear merely logical, unconnected with any particular theory of the evolution of linguistic structures. But this objection misses the point that the negative operator has been specifically defined in imperative language, and that the "logical" limitations on its function are entirely dependent on the anthropological premise that such a language existed. For the only thing wrong with the second equation is that it contradicts the normal functioning (and, we might add, the linguistic structure) of imperatives as we know them. Declaratives do not function in this manner (thus There is ~ man = ~ [There is (a) man]), and the "illogicality" of such constructions as "must not," which ≠ "~ must," is indeed traceable to their connection with the imperative. The fact is, then, that in the imperative the operation of the negative is fixed at the level of performance. Within the linguistic model the performance of the addressee is described as the negation of a possible ("positive") performance, but the fundamental elements of the intentional structure remain the same—the nature of the awaiting merely being altered to fit the nonperformative (indeed antiperformative) nature of the request. This situation merits particular consideration because it represents the extreme point of grammaticality within imperative language and thus its highest level of what we may call "thought" or "reasoning"—manipulation of linguistic models as context-free substitutes for reality.[7]

So long as we remain close to the origin of the imperative in the "inappropriate ostensive," its specifically linguistic character, like that of the ostensive, remains limited to the more or less explicit communication, in linguistic presence, of a significant phenomenon that the addressee is now called upon to presentify. In this function the formal or "arbitrary" nature of linguistic signs is essential only in one respect, which is the capacity of such signs to actualize representational presence in other members of the community, a function that is directly dependent on their noninstinctual (and therefore nonsignaletic) nature. But this relationship between a formal noninstinctual sign system and linguistic presence, although evidently the key to our whole hypothesis concerning the evolution of linguistic form, has not yet been demonstrated to result in any significant functional superiority of formal over instinctual signs as models of reality. (This is, indeed, the crucial point of distinction between our "formal" theory of representation and the "institutional" theory that gives primacy to the analogical type of representation embodied in ritual.) Because the use of such signs constitutes the specific difference of human language from the signals of animals, or, more crucially, from imaginable iconic forms (such as pictures), it can be said that until such time as the forms generated by our dialectic provide evidence of a functional capacity for "thought" greater than what can be obtained by such other forms, our hypothesis remains simply gratuitous. And it will not do to merely allege the undeniable existence of the "higher forms" of human thought inconceivable without language, for these forms can only enter our purview once they have been constructed within our dialectic.

Now the "primitive" function of the imperative, to which we have just alluded, could be accomplished as well by analogical as by formal means: A picture of the desired object or activity would serve as well as a linguistic utterance, and can still do so when linguistic communication is impossible. This assertion, however, becomes problematic once we include within the possibilities of the intentional structure of the imperative those relations that we have categorized as proto-grammatical, and it appears *all but* incompatible with the existence of the operation of negation. The qualification of the last statement is essential to our argument, which makes the declarative form the watershed of formal thought per se, and must therefore be fully justified. This justification may be seen as an outgrowth of our discussion of the limits of the grammatical categories of governance and modification in the imperative.

From a grammatical standpoint operators are different from, but similar to, modifiers, traditional grammarians emphasizing the similarities, modern linguists, the differences. Negation is, in imperative as in developed language, the most extreme case because it is the most unambiguously transformational in character, requiring for its application an already-existing linguistic expression. In the imperative, as we have seen, negation (or more properly interdiction) requires for its formulation the designation of a substantial performance that could always, at least in principle, be equally the object of a prescriptive imperative. As we shall attempt to demonstrate in the next section, it is the lexical expression of interdiction which supplies the first declarative predicate. At the present stage, however, negation can exist only as interdictory, and we must be careful not to read into it the characteristics that it will only acquire in the declarative form. Now interdiction, as previously discussed, shares the asymmetrical structure of the imperative in general. It does not negate the subordination of the addressee to the desire of the speaker, but only the performance that, formulated in the same words, the latter might in another context have requested. In the sense, then, that these words might be replaced by the imaginary representation of this performance to which they correspond in the significant memories of both speaker and hearer, interdiction is truly meta-representational, involving as it does an inversion of the positive relationship between image and performance which obtains in the prescriptive form. But the factor that stops interdiction short of the truly context-free—or in our terms, truly grammatical—functioning of negation in the declarative is its continued dependence on imperative awaiting, which limits its field of operation to the linguistic presence between speaker and hearer.

Thus nonperformance remains always, even when it consists in nonaction, a performance in real time which fulfills this awaiting, just as, conversely, the performance of the forbidden action constitutes a violation of it. And this means that imperative "negation," although independent of the imagery of its substantial content, retains a common ground with this content in the lived time of the imperative performance. This performance, as we know, occupies an ambivalent role in the intentional structure of the imperative, being for the speaker simply a prolongation of the deferral intrinsic to linguistic presence in general, whereas for the addressee it is real time subordinated to the "mobilization" made possible by this presence. "Negation" in the imperative is not, so to speak, an act of the intellect, but an act of the will. And as such it remains bound by its temporal limitations. Thus the substantial performance is refused, but its shadow haunts the nonperformance and by doing so deprives it of the freedom of a purely formal operation. In the last analysis, then, the interdicted nonperformance is still a variety of performance: Not-running in an imperative context remains a kind of running because its satisfaction of the interdiction will be measured by both parties by the degree of its correspondence to the criteria that constitute running.

The situation in the declarative is quite different. If I say to someone "John is not running," my statement will be judged true or false by those criteria. John's activity, however, is not itself governed by them: He may in fact be making an effort not to run, but the model established by my statement is free of this presupposition. Negation here is pure formal, or more rigorously, metalinguistic manipulation: Whatever else John may be doing, I may if I like interpret his activity as not being running, thereby totally cutting off my linguistic representation of it from analogical images of any kind, but at the same time liberating my imagination to grasp analogies with areas of experience not intended by John in his action. Such liberation, which is the formal basis for metaphor and for intellectual creativity in general, is not attained by "negation" in imperative language, which offers at best a real-time approximation of it. Thus if I say to John "Don't run!" I may then observe what he will actually do instead; but whatever else he may be doing, he will also be "not-running"—that is, fulfilling the awaiting instituted by the imperative. Or indeed he may decide to run in spite of my command, or even in deliberate defiance of it, thereby obliging me to consider his running not as a phenomenon in itself but as a defective form of not-running—in fact, as not-not-running. Because by my interdiction I have not negated the imperative but only the performance its prescriptive version would have requested, I have not liberated my interlocutor from a requested performance, nor myself from the criteria it imposes on my judgment of the situation. Such considerations, of course, exceed the scope of imperative language as such, in which it is difficult to conceive of experimental activity. Their function here is solely to exemplify the limitations of "negation" in imperative language as opposed to the fully conceptualized negation of developed language.

We may thus sum up our discussion of the negative imperative by the statement that, like governance and modification, the operation of negation (and a fortiori the use of other operators such as "again," "twice," etc.) is not fully grammaticalized in imperative language. But a distinction still must be made between the nature of this incompleteness here and in the previously discussed constructions, because interdiction, unlike these, involves the use—and hence the lexicalization—of an operator not independently realizable as a performance, and therefore would appear to create a first generic distinction between "parts of speech" linked in a formal hierarchy. Here again the point under discussion is a crucial one because the lexicalization of the negative is necessary to our hypothesis concerning the origin of the declarative. Now if we can say that interdiction is still a request for performance, and thus that not-running is still a kind of running—a zero-degree, so to speak—it is more difficult to consider the "not" a separable element, capable, like "fast" or "big" (if we consider not English usage but the semantic content of the words), of being used as an imperative in its own right. Yet that this is indeed the case is suggested by our own usage of the expression "Don't!" which is evidently parallel to the basic interdictive construction "Don't talk!" rather than to "Talk not!" "Do" here is not a general verb of action but a purely functional auxiliary. (That this is so is demonstrated by the existence of the more or less synonymous expression "Don't do that!" which, unlike "Don't!" is clearly not elliptic.) The obvious objection to the allegation of "Don't!" as an independent use of an interdictive lexeme is that, like the declarative "No" in answer to questions, it is merely an ellipsis for "Don't do X!" But although this may often be the case, for example, when it occurs as the answer to "Should I close the door?" it need not be so: the woman who exclaims "Don't!" to a lover's tentative caresses is a familiar, and quite revealing example.

In claiming that such examples are not cases of ellipsis we are not merely playing with words. It is useful to be certain of what "ellipsis" really means because this concept (often under different names) plays a crucial role in the linguistic reduction of elementary linguistic structures to the status of "defective" forms of the declarative, as well as providing in Chomskian linguistics a blank check for the inclusion of any convenient unexpressed elements in the "deep structure" of a sentence.[8] The notion of ellipsis is, in our view, only justified if it is defined as the omission of an already-present linguistic element. By "present" here we mean actual in linguistic presence, not merely presumed to be present in the mind of the speaker. Thus the answer "No" (or "Yes") to a typical interrogative may be called an ellipsis because the replying speaker is stating his disagreement (or agreement) with the words of his interlocutor. The reply accepts or rejects a linguistic model and can be said to refer to reality only through this mode. It thus involves no decision concerning the representation of specified elements of reality within the model. "(Please) don't" in reply to "Should I shut the door?" is by this criterion a true ellipsis, in fact a quasi-synonym of "No" which would be the more normal reply.[9]

The woman's "Don't!" to her would-be lover is another case entirely. One might imagine various verbs to fill out the meaning of this expression ("Don't touch me!", "Don't try to seduce me!" etc.) but the very lack of a verb that can truly specify the interdicted performance is most significant. By thus failing to present a linguistic model of her partner's behavior, the speaker perhaps purposely avoids any character-ization of its intentionality and thereby disallows any attempts by the former to reinterpret his actions to her satisfaction. The relevance of this strategy to the specific situation is dependent on the preexistence in the minds of both of what we might call a behavioral complex of seduc-tion in which the previous sexual experiences of the couple and their general expectations concerning the patterns of such experiences all participate. "Don't!" thus interdicts by association the totality of this complex, far more effectively than "Don't do that!" which focuses on the specific act performed. To characterize "Don't" as an ellipsis here would imply at the very least the existence of some specific verb in the mind of the speaker (and, presumably, of the hearer), whereas, as we have just seen, the specification of the exact meaning, even assuming there to be no distinction between meaning and language (as is supposed to occur in "deep structure"), is effectively impossible. The negative imperative is used here to request nonperformance, not merely of a specific act but of an entire behavioral complex, and this is only possible because in the imperative, negation refers not strictly to linguistic models, as in the declarative, but to performances that, although they are indeed normally specified by such models, may simply be exemplified in reality.

Thus we see that the operator of interdiction, although specifiable lexically, retains sufficient substantiality to stand alone when its real-world referent is sufficiently evident. And this is not an accident of modern usage, but a necessary consequence of the intentional structure of the imperative in which the linguistic presence of the interlocutors is not fully divorced from their real temporal presence. Interdiction is not true negation, as we have argued above, because it directs itself to the "will," not to the "intellect," to performance and not to a context-free model of performance. And by the same token, it is not wholly devoid of substantiality because it can assume as its content that of the present moment. Taken out of its temporal context, it is no doubt true that the lexeme of interdiction appears as a pure operator lacking in substantiality, but in imperative language this purely lexical abstraction is impossible. There is no pure linguistic space available in which to ask the metalinguistic question of what "Don't!" *means* because its utterance intends unavoidably its real temporal context. Its evolution into a true negative, which is at the same time the genesis of the declarative form, must therefore depend on its *inappropriate* use.[10]

Dialectic of the Imperative (II)

In our previous discussion we have assumed that the hearer of the imperative, knowing the requested object to be unavailable, requires a means of expressing this fact to the speaker. But we cannot consider that on the one hand he possesses the "thought" of the absence of the object, but on the other, he is unable to "express" it and must therefore invent a new form for this purpose. Rather, the "thought" itself is the invention, and if we can specify precisely what the thought should be, we will find it already expressed. For whether or not thought be deemed possible without language the desire to express a thought to another, as is the case here, can only be formulated in the terms of whatever system of representation is available. Thus the imperative did not arise when, desiring to command the presence of an object or action, someone decided to use the ostensive for this purpose in the absence of its referent. Rather, the "thought" of the desire for the object was simply expressed by the means at hand, without deliberation on the change in linguistic convention that it would entail. And the response of the second party, by correcting this "inappropriate" usage and at the same time satisfying the speaker's desire, led to its reinforcement and to its eventual acceptance as an appropriate linguistic act. Similarly, in the present case the second speaker does not seek the means to express the absence of the object—for if he sought them, he would find them wanting—but expresses it simply as he has formulated it to himself. The model he creates may not be immediately comprehensible to the first speaker. But because all members of the community have been on occasion in the same situation as this interlocutor, and have thus expressed, to themselves if not openly, the same thought, he, or another, will eventually grasp its meaning.

The creation of new linguistic forms thus passes through a moment of subjectivity in which desire is expressed as faith. In the case of the nascent imperative, the object of this faith was the "ontological" power of the ostensive to compel the presence of its object. In the case now at hand the desire of the second speaker is no longer purely private, but specifically takes as its object communication with his interlocutor. The absence of the object is not desired, but known; what is desired is to communicate this knowledge. Now for the two interlocutors it is the absent object that is the focus of their attention: the first speaker desires its presence, the second knows that this presence cannot be obtained. This object is designated by a linguistic expression, a word or combination of words, which has already been employed by the first speaker as an imperative, and which, if the object were indeed presentifiable, could be employed anew by the second speaker as an ostensive, as in the "Scalpel!"-"Scalpel" dialogue earlier discussed.

But it is we who have classified these two usages as belonging to two linguistic forms, linked by a historical dialectic. For the speakers who make use of ostensive and imperative utterances in the process of communication, they do not possess, as they do for us, the discrete existence of elements in a paradigm. The forms represent for us two different intentional structures, but these structures cannot themselves be "known" to the speakers, and are not perceived as such even by a speaker of a developed language in the course of his own speech. They are conventions of communication the choice among which is never overtly made because this "choice" is predetermined by the needs of the situation in which the speaker finds himself. Now if, in ostensive language, the word designating the object could be said to "mean" or intend its presence, this was because the usage of the word in linguistic presence always accompanied, and specifically designated, the object-as-present. In the significant memory of the members of the community, even at this stage, the word could be said to possess the same lexical *signification* that its counterparts possess today, that is, it is simply the *name* of the object. The "ontological faith" that we have attributed to the user of the ostensive is not the product of the signification of the lexeme, but of its *meaning*, which is nothing but the memory of its *usage* in linguistic presence. Were the word, even at the most primitive level of language, endowed with the same intention as its usage, there would indeed be no need to use it.

The speaker of imperative language possesses two linguistic forms that are in effect conventional uses or *meanings* for the word, not significations of it. "Hammer" simply signifies "hammer"; it is the *usage* of the word that is limited, and this not because the word could not be pronounced independently of either the imperative or the ostensive form, but because this pronunciation could be given no other meaning. One cannot simply "talk about" a hammer, because there is as yet nothing to say about it, save that it is present or that one wishes it present. This is not to say that the words need be lacking to describe the hammer's size and shape, or even its location, but simply that a sentence *merely* describing its size or location is not yet conceivable. To combine the words "big" and "hammer" in a sentence tells us, of course, that the hammer is big, but the meaning of the sentence is either that the big hammer is here, or that the speaker wishes it delivered. That it is big is not information conveyed by the sentence, because it is presumed to be known already (assuming its referent to be definite); the use of sentences is not in fact to convey information at all, but to designate significant phenomena. In the "Scalpel!-Scalpel" conversation the word designates a specific object of interest to the speakers (but to the second only through the mediation of the first). Both surgeon and assistant are no doubt capable of formulating sentences of indefinitely great complexity concerning the scalpel, of describing its real qualities and of attributing to it imaginary or hypothetical ones, but in urgency of the operation at hand, such sentences, even though they be in the linguistic competence of the speakers, would be inappropriate. Nor is it at all likely that the speakers would be aware that their dialogue consists of an imperative followed by an ostensive, even assuming that such terminology were available to them. Their conversation uses the word simply as a means of communication, the intentional structure created in each utterance being an appropriate model of reality: The surgeon says "Scalpel!" because he wants the scalpel, and his assistant repeats the word to show that it is now available for the surgeon's use. In both cases the word simply signifies the object; its place in the intentional structure is in each case determined by the context. We should suppose this to be the case as well for the speakers of imperative language. Thus for the second speaker in an "infelicitous" imperative dialogue, the word used by the first to demand the object is simply its name and not itself either an imperative or an ostensive. And by the same token his own (ostensive) reply, were the object in fact available, would repeat this name. We can thus assume that, whatever else he may be "thinking," the requested object is imagined, but the image once evoked is understood to be, at the present moment at least, inactualizable.

This situation bears a certain similarity to that of the original speaker of the imperative, who, imagining an object in its absence, called its name to make it appear. But this role has already been preempted by the first speaker whose ontological faith the second knows is in the present case not justified. It is in fact this nonjustification that constitutes the object of his desired communication. Calling the name of the object will not in fact make it appear, whatever the sanctity of linguistic presence. The knowledge of the second speaker demystifies the faith of the first. The name of the object, in other words, can be presented in linguistic presence without the object appearing. This knowledge is the negative moment of the declarative, or of higher linguistic form in general: The use of the word is now divorced from the presence of the object. But from the standpoint of the first speaker, one still implies the other; it is not *his* usage that is meant to exemplify this knowledge. The first speaker uses the word as an imperative; the second, knowing the fallibility of the imperative, has not used it at all. Yet he is aware that his interlocutor awaits the desired object. To fulfill this awaiting with the object is impossible, yet all he can produce is its name. But at the same time there is an awaiting that would indeed be fulfilled by the absence of the object: the negative imperative consisting of the name of the object and the operator of interdiction. Now uttered in linguistic presence the name-plus-operator would indeed be an interdiction. In thought, however, it evokes simply the image of the object as absent, or in other words, it is the *name* of the object-as-absent. The second speaker is aware that to say the name of what is not will not necessarily make it appear. But to say the name of what is, even if all there is is the absence of an object, is to use the name not as an imperative but as an *ostensive*. The negative-ostensive is at the same time a correction of the first speaker's utterance, which, insofar as it is an imperative, is itself a transformed ostensive no longer "inappropriate," no doubt, but deferred. The second speaker's ostensive, then, in its negativity, is already fulfilled, but at the same time, by presenting in ostensive form the object requested by the first speaker, even if it is presented-as-not-present, his utterance has at least the potentiality of putting an end to the awaiting created by the original imperative. There is no guarantee, of course, that this communication will be successful, because the ostensive offered in the dialogue is not what was originally expected. But in the genesis of the imperative there was no reason either to assume that the inappropriate use of the ostensive would be automatically rewarded. What is essential is that the new form exist as an intentional structure for the speaker, so that the hearer, who at first finds it inappropriate, will come to use it when he finds himself in similar circumstances, that is, with a similar desire to express.

The negative ostensive can thus arise as a possible negative "reply" to the imperative. Its acceptance by the first speaker in lieu of the requested object, as opposed to the more violent response that might be expected in a case of inappropriate fulfillment of his request, constitutes a further lowering of the threshold of significance from that which gave rise to the imperative. At that moment it was individual desire that was accepted as a possible source of significance; now it is the unfulfillability of this desire. But this is too negative a formulation: What the negative ostensive presents is simply the state of affairs, not as a matter of interest in itself but insofar as it withstands a desire to modify it. This purely negative trimuph of reality over desire is, in the sphere of representation, an immensely significant triumph of objectivity. The inappropriate (positive) ostensive opened the domain of linguistic representation to the infinity of desire; the inappropriate negative ostensive, in representing the limitations of desire, permits the dialectic of desire and reality to be comprehended entirely by language so that linguistic models can henceforth mirror and anticipate the results of our attempts to realize our representations. But this development is predicated on the prior acceptance of the significance of those facts of reality which oppose desire. In urgent situations these facts in themselves are without value and must be overcome through action. In those less urgent the facts, although negative, may acquire communal significance in themselves. Thus if our "Scalpel" dialogue occurs during an operation, the answer "Scalpel-no!" to the doctor's question is not likely to be of help. If no scalpel is present then a substitute must be found immediately, and the assistant would do better to rush off to seek one than to attempt to "correct" the doctor's imperative. But were the request made in more leisurely circumstances, say in the course of taking inventory, the negative reply will permit the functional act of ordering the missing item. The key criterion here is the immediacy of the universe of discourse in crucial situations. When the horizon of the interlocutors is limited to the present moment—to the moment of presence—the negative ostensive is functionless. Conversely, its functioning makes the universe beyond this presence and its extension through awaiting for the first time a possible source of the significant.

Negation as Predication: The Origin of the Declarative

The negative ostensive is a new linguistic form certainly not assimilable to the ostensive; we are not yet ready, however, to call it a declarative. Before we can consider its generalization outside the specific situation of the imperative dialogue, we must first examine its functioning in this dialogue more closely.

The original imperative-ostensive dialogue took place around the successful presentation of the object. The two utterances of its name mark the beginning and the end of the first speaker's awaiting, which is also, from the standpoint of the dialogue, the period of focusing on the particular object or class of objects. If we imagine a "conversation" consisting of a series of such exchanges, the objects requested and furnished will constitute the *topics* of conversation. All that can be said "about" them is their name, that is, just enough to identify them, but each object is at a given moment a topic, a focus of both linguistic and real interest. Now if we consider the negative ostensive as acceptable to the first speaker, that is, as terminating for the present moment the awaiting created by his request, then the role of the object as topic would remain limited by the imperative and ostensive just as before. But now the object would never have been made present: It would have been spoken of entirely in its

absence. The imperative of course intends the presentification of its object; the negative ostensive, on the contrary,
merely expresses its nonpresence. Thus it is the first linguistic
form we have met with that *says something about* its object.
As a "name" for its absence it is not unlike other names, but
precisely, it is not the absence that is the topic of interest but
the object. Absence is not an essential quality of the object in
general but merely pertains to the situation at hand. Whereas
in the negative imperative the operator of negation was never
totally separable from its object, both elements—negation/
interdiction and substantial content—being ultimately, as we
have seen, conjoined in the model as two names for the same
reality, the "not-hammer" being both a kind of hammer and
even a kind of "not-," here the preexistence of the hammer
as topic makes its absence not a subcategorical modifier but a
true *predicate*. The negative ostensive thus offers the most
primitive example of predication.

In the negative imperative, to be sure, the object (or
action) is the primary focus of attention. In forbidding the
bringing (or taking) of the hammer, the speaker, whether or
not he reacts to a specific appropriative gesture by his interlocutor, presupposes on his part at least a possibility of desire
for it. It is even conceivable that the hammer has already
been mentioned in speech, either as an ostensive or indeed as
an imperative: One party requests the hammer, the second
forbids it. But this "dialogue" would not involve predication.
The negative imperative creates a model of reality in which
the absence of the object, either from the field of perception
as a whole, or from the immediate possession of one or both
of the parties, is significant not as a fact but as an object of
desire. Thus although it evokes the image of a hammer, it is
not "about" the hammer at all but "about" the speaker's
desire. As opposed to the prescriptive imperative, where the
mental image aroused in the speaker provides a model to be
realized in practice, here the same model is evoked as precisely what is to be avoided. But in the negative ostensive this
model is made to include the absence of the object as a state
independent (and implicitly beyond the reach) of any present
performance. Whereas the negative and positive imperatives
still had in common, beyond their substantive content, the

necessity of a performance focused on this content, the negative and positive ostensives have nothing in common but their content, posited as present in one case, absent in the other. But the (positive) ostensive does not predicate presence. It merely names the object and in so doing presents it. In the negative ostensive, however, nonpresence is a true predicate, the subject of which is an already-established topic of "conversation," of interest in itself whether present or not.

The negative ostensive is the germ of the declarative sentence. The widespread existence, along with the familiar subject-predicate form, of the so-called "topic-comment" sentence, dominant notably in Chinese and several other Oriental languages, lends support to the view that in the declarative form a topic is first established then commented on. We shall deal more fully with this typological question in the following chapter. In the case at hand there is no need to distinguish between the two types. The topic exists à priori as supplied by the desire of the first speaker, and the "comment" is at the same time a predicate. The negative ostensive falls short of the declarative model only in the limitations it imposes on predication, which is still dependent, albeit negatively, on the presence of the object. But once this purely verbal reply to the imperative is no longer considered as "inappropriate" and is accepted as adequate in certain situations, the admission of other predicates will follow from the necessary modification of the conditions of dialogue. For an "imperative" to which a predication is an adequate response is no longer truly an imperative. The acceptation of such a response is, of course, never a foregone conclusion: Like the ostensive, the imperative leads to the generation of a higher form without itself becoming obsolete. The criterion, here as before, is the level of significance of the imperative situation. If this level remains high the imperative retains its exigency. But if a verbal reply comes to be expected the imperative is transformed into an *interrogative* and presumably pronounced in the hesitant tone, raised at the end as a rifle barrel is raised to demonstrate the absence of violent intention that remains in most languages its distinguishing characteristic. "Scalpel?" is thus only a softened form of

"Scalpel!": The request for information is a direct descendant of the request for the object. But once information concerning an object is requested the possibility of new predications other than mere nonpresence follows in short order. It suffices that the category of predication exist as an intentional structure. And this development is a direct consequence of the modified imperative-ostensive dialogue.

There is already in imperative language no shortage of potential predicates, neither predicate nominatives/adjectives nor verbals. The imperative speaker could no doubt request a big hammer or a small one, a green branch or a yellow one. The passage from the imperative to the declarative is thus not, in the beginning at least, from sentences poor in informational content to richer, but in fact the opposite. The lowering of the threshold of significance implied by this passage means that what was formerly only the object of an imperative request ("Big hammer!") can now become an information-presenting utterance in itself ("[The] hammer [is] big"). This is not to deny all validity to the transformational analysis of adjective-noun constructions like the first, which considers them to be derived by reduction from sentences like the second. But this analysis applies only to declarative, that is, mature language, within which all the proto-grammatical relationships of ostensive and imperative language are fully formalized in rigorous hierarchies of dependent and independent terms. Within imperative language "Big hammer!" was not quite a true grammatical construction because no one could simply say that the hammer was big, and therefore there was no way of discriminating between the hammer being big and the big (thing) being a hammer. It is only in the declarative that, the sentence topic having an a priori existence, its qualities can be predicated of it as accidents of a substance—the substance/accident dichotomy being of course a product of the existence of the declarative rather than the reverse. But the lack of fully grammatical constructions should not lead us to assume that imperative or even ostensive language need be lacking in the lexical "raw material" of predication.

As an example of the evolution that led to the multiplication of predicative terms, we may take the case of locatives.

Clearly locative expressions, which can be formulated gesturally by pointing, were among the earliest linguistic terms. Thus a speaker of ostensive language, seeing or hearing the arrival of, say, a herd of buffalo, would not only pronounce the word "Buffalo!" but indicate gesturally and, eventually, verbally as well (by an expression such as "Over there"), the location of the herd. It should not be necessary to repeat our previous discussion to demonstrate that this usage in ostensive language is not predicative; it merely expresses a "modification" of the presence within which the utterance is made. Now let us suppose that, in answer to an imperative request for a hammer, the addressee, rather than producing the object himself, simply replies that it is "over there." Whereas, in ostensive language, "over there" was included within the domain of presence with which the speaker and his audience could consider themselves vitally concerned, in this reply it is located *outside* the immediate presence defined by the speaker's request. It thus becomes a modification not of presence but of absence. In this light the reply is simply an elaboration of the negative ostensive; the hammer is not-present, and furthermore it is over there. Given an appropriately non-crucial situation, this reply will be not only understood by the first speaker but accepted as supplying information adequate to his request; he wants the hammer, and he learns where to find it. Such an "imperative" is thus already little more than an interrogative. We would tend to express it not by "Give me a hammer!" but by "Do you have a hammer?" or "Is there a hammer around here?"

This example can serve to indicate the indefinite variety of nuances theoretically available between the simple imperative on the one hand and the simple interrogative on the other. The possible degrees of urgency of the situation and the spatial extent of "presence" for the speaker define a continuum between the surgeon's request for a scalpel and a casual request made to an indifferent stranger. Those "speech-act" theorists who tirelessly compile lists of quasi-synonyms in order to demonstrate the absence of one-to-one correspondance between the form and function of sentences should realize that from a genetic perspective their conclusions are at best a point of departure.

5 The Declarative

With the derivation of the declarative sentence we have reached the final moment of the dialectic of linguistic form per se. The further evolution of linguistic representation will take place on a higher level, that of discourse, within which the declarative sentence is predominant. This closure must be demonstrated from the standpoint of our theory, and the major implications of the intentional structure of the declarative drawn. But the grammatical infrastructures of the declarative, to the analysis of which modern linguistics, particularly since the rise of transformational grammar some twenty years ago, has devoted so much of its energies, will not be discussed here in detail. This is not either to accept or to condemn this collective effort in toto, although we cannot avoid taking a stand on the general theoretical questions it raises. Our purpose here is not to offer an alternative to modern—that is, in the broadest sense, Saussurian—linguistics in its own domain, as the significance of that domain is defined by linguistics in its own terms, but rather to formulate what we conceive to be the principal elements of a theory of representation. Whether this theory will prove in the long run incompatible with modern linguistics not merely in its main thrust, as is already apparent, but in its concrete analyses, and consequently be both compelled to formulate, and capable of formulating an alternate analytic methodology, in the domain of syntax at least, and possibly in semantics or even phonology (assuming that these categories themselves must be retained), remains always an open possiblility. Our unavoidably limited and schematic discussion of the declarative

169

form may suggest to the reader evidence either for or against such a possibility, but, for the present at least, no conclusions will be drawn.

The Declarative Model

The chief obstacle to the comprehension of the intentional structure of the declarative is its familiarity to us, not only as users of language in general, but more pertinently, as theoreticians. We write of the lower forms from the telic perspective of the higher. But having attained the final stage of linguistic evolution, we find ourselves writing about the structures of the declarative sentence in declarative sentences. That this situation does not present more of a problem than it does is already a significant phenomenon. The metalinguistic capacity of the declarative is unlimited, although it is only in discourse that it can be systematically exercised. Thus the declarative, unlike the lower forms, offers its user the possibility of reflection on its own form. The paradoxes generated by desire can, in the declarative sentence, be converted into "logical" paradoxes. Before we can examine the significance of this and similar developments, however, we require a more rigorous understanding of the form of the declarative in general.

In its most general terms the declarative sentence is a predication about a topic. In its origin, as described in the preceding chapter, this topic was preestablished by the objective desire of an interlocutor as expressed in an imperative. One may say that in any declarative sentence some a priori interest by the locutee in the topic is still implicit, and that the topic-comment form makes the objectal focus of this interest clearer. It is, however, obvious from our own usage that this interest need not be previously expressed, and certainly not in imperative form. The threshold of significance in mature language has been sufficiently lowered in many situations so that the speaker may introduce the topic if he has reason to believe that it might prove a posteriori interesting to his audience. This phenomenon cannot, however, be satisfactorily explained in one-dimensional terms. It is influenced by the existence of discourse, and more specifi-

cally by the desire-generating character of the declarative.
For the moment the assumption of a priori interest, even in
the absence of overt supporting evidence, will suffice for the
definition of topicality. The topic is always a substantive,
even if it refers to an activity, in which case we may think of
it as a verbal noun (like the present participle in English).
This restriction can only appear arbitrary in the perspective
of an insufficient grammar, which makes verbs "coequal"
with nouns; but as we shall attempt to show, inflected
verb-forms are in fact de-substantivized verbals.[1] Thus verbals
are not a nominalized variant of verbs, as the grammar books
teach us. It is rather the latter that have lost, for reasons we
shall touch on below, their substantive character in becoming
predicates.

"Predication" is a term that, unlike "topic," is rich in
philosophical implications. Certainly our use of it here should
not be understood to imply that the evolution of language is
somehow telically subordinated to logic. The topic-predicate
relation can only be defined more rigorously than the linguistic form of the declarative if it is constructed not, as here,
out of a historical dialectic, but on the basis of formal ad hoc
definitions—the possibility of such constructions being, of
course, one of the benefits accruing from the existence of the
declarative form. To attempt to define predication as anything more than saying something about a topic would at this
stage be self-defeating because the formal dichotomies like
substance/accident, being/modification, or subject/predicate
in any one of its logical formulations are simply ex post facto
formalizations of the topic-predicate relation found in the
declarative. To attempt to specify this relation on the basis of
the forms it takes in various languages would be an even less
rewarding task. Our choice of "topic" rather than "subject"
to designate the chief nominal has been made specifically to
avoid giving currency to the view, expressed in the *Grammaire de Port-Royal* and elsewhere, that the grammatical
agreement between subject and predicate in Western languages possesses a peculiar ontological significance. It would
appear rather that the topic-comment declarative form
(which appears historically the more primitive), once established, can evolve into the subject-predicate form by a tight-

ening through habitual usage of the morphological links between topic and verb.[2] This evolution is not, however, irreversible, for the concomitant reduction of the topic to a merely coordinate rather than superordinate position in the sentence will tend to generate a new emphatic topic not bound by rules of agreement. Such emphatic constructions (e.g., compare "My sister, she likes spinach" with "My sister, her teeth are crooked" or "My sister, I don't like her") are available in English, and, we may assume, in all subject-predicate languages. The significance of this hypothetical but highly plausible cyclical alternation between topic and subject is that it demonstrates the resistance of "natural" language to grammatical formalization, which is also a fortiori a resistance to the rigor of logical formalization. The logical proposition is no doubt a sentence, but the assimilation of sentences to logical propositions, however justified by the inherent potential of the declarative for the formulation of "context-free," de-temporalized models, eliminates from consideration precisely that small but not insignificant element of temporal urgency, or in other terms, of *significance*, without which the existence of no linguistic form can be understood. If the grammarians and linguists fail to comprehend the elementary linguistic forms because they see them as degenerate declaratives, the logicians and language-philosophers misunderstand the higher linguistic forms by viewing them *avant la lettre* as elements of discourse, and logical discourse at that.[3]

In languages that possess the topic-comment sentence form, the topic is not always identical with the grammatical subject of the verb. But we may consider this distinction a secondary product of linguistic evolution, the grammatical subject in our hypothesis having formerly been itself a regularized topic. In the primitive form of the declarative we must suppose topic and subject to be identical, the very existence of inflected verb forms (and hence of "grammatical" subjects) being inconceivable unless they were originally attached to the chief nominal of the sentence. Thus we may without loss of generality consider the subject-verb sentence form as simply included in our basic "topic-predicate" model.

The original "negative-ostensive" form of the declarative does not possess a verb; the subject and negative operator are simply "coupled," as in the typical Russian copulative, without a verb "to be." In this latter example, however, a verb has been omitted which is supplied in other tenses than the present; in the primitive case there is no verb to omit. The specific question of the origin of the copula is not of interest to us here. But we cannot avoid the more general one of the origin of the verb because the latter is ubiquitous, and the markers of tense and person which we have cited as the most fundamental grammatical categories are in all languages attracted to it, if not actually contained within it as inflections. Indeed, the ubiquity of the verb as bearer of these markers has led grammarians to consider it a more fundamental constituent of the sentence than the subject; a verb alone (as in the imperative) may constitute a sentence, a noun, never (except of course in "elliptical" constructions). This grammatical prestige of the verb appears paradoxical in the light of the unquestionably more fundamental character of nouns as the names for persons and palpable objects. But the paradox remains only so long as we consider the declarative as the "natural" sentence form, in which case the very existence of syntactical relations requires the simultaneous genesis of both nouns and verbs. It vanishes in our hypothesis, where nominal forms (whether semantically nominal or "verbal") are seen to be more primitive, and where the first sentence-forms are precisely lacking in verbs. The verb is the sign of the declarative only because it is the more evolved of the two substantial forms, through an evolution that is at the same time a degeneration because the original verbals were, like nominals, capable of serving as topics in themselves. But whether the topic be nominal or verbal in nature, it is not a verb; if a verb be present, it can only serve as a predicate. The verb may in fact be defined simply as a predicate verbal. There are two observations to be made concerning this definition. In the first place, whether nominals or verbals constitute the most fundamental lexical elements, words denoting objects are particularly likely to be found as topics, and words denoting actions as predicates. But in the second the universal existence of the noun-verb dichotomy transcends this merely relative distinction and must therefore have an additional cause, not to say a different one entirely.

If we return to our derivation of the negative-ostensive, we note that the negative operator, which we consider to be the first predicate, can apply equally well, if not better, to verbal as to nominal imperatives, but that *as a predicate* it is more readily associated with nominals. This is in both cases because of the performative nature of the imperative verbal as opposed to the objectal nature of the nominal. Thus if one is equally likely to request an object or an action, the action, being available to the imperative addressee independently of any requested object, is more likely to require interdiction. Conversely, this same performability of the action by the addressee makes it a far less likely candidate for unavailability than the object. Thus if indeed an action cannot be performed, merely presenting it as unavailable conveys no information beyond a simple refusal, whereas the absence of an object is prima facie a verifiable fact. This original superiority of nominals as topics is only relative. But if we suppose the differentiation of predicates along the lines that we have suggested in our locative example, the new predicates, which carry supplementary information beyond that of mere unavailability, will apply even more exclusively to nominals because an absent object exists and can thus be otherwise qualified, whereas an absent performance exists only in its absence. In particular the absent object may be participating in some other action, but an absent action cannot involve some other object. Thus if we assume that the original function of the declarative is to express unavailability for presentification, nominals will tend to appear more frequently as topics and verbals as predicates.

In the case of predicate adjectives and nominals ("the scalpel is broken." "That tree is an X" [and therefore not good for tool-making] , etc.) it is difficult to suppose that the "verb" provided by the copula is anything more than the result of assimilation of this sentence form to the true verbal form, presumably in order to bear the grammatical burden of person and tense already attached to the verb. Which is to say that the existence of the verb as an indispensable formal element of predicates rather than a merely probable one is dependent on its association with these shifter paradigms (the significance of which for the development of the declarative as a "context-free" model of reality will be dealt with in the following section). But this association should not be looked on as a merely morphological one, as though the evolution of the inflected verb could be described as the attachment to a proto-verbal predicate of proto-adverbial morphemes denoting tense and person. For such an explanation merely begs the essential question of why these morphemes are indeed necessary to the constitution of the declarative, even to the extent that dummy verbs come into existence to bear them. Our answer to this question must be founded on the already-established dominance of the verbal predicate. It is actions, not relations, that are *essentially* located in time and that differ in nature according as they are performed by speaker or hearer.

Thus it would appear that the morphological, paradigmatic elements of the verb merely formalize the verbal nature of predicates, although the passage from the probabilistic dominance we have described to formal dominance must still be explained by an additional element. This element is the linguistic *present* constituted by the declarative. We have already seen the germ of this present in the imperative, which can be said to possess an incipient tense because it refers to a real time outside of linguistic presence *stricto sensu* (i.e., the time of the speech act), although referential time is intended not as independent of this presence but as an extension of it. In contrast, the declarative, even in its most primitive form, provides a model of a present independent of linguistic presence and thus possesses a true tense, even if, as we must assume, the existence of a paradigm of tenses is a later development. The existence of the verb is thus prior to its grammatical inflections, but this is only so because, even before the existence of tense paradigms, the declarative sentence already possesses a tense. Once this has been more clearly established, the emergence of the verb as the general predicative form will follow, because, as we shall show, tense is an essentially verbal category.

Linguistic Present and Linguistic Presence

As a negative-ostensive the nascent declarative would appear to stand in the same dependent relation toward linguistic presence as its positive counterpart. The absence of a hammer "takes place" in the same real time and space as its presence: the presence of communication as established by the speaker of the imperative. But the function of the declarative model is very different, even at this stage, from that of the ostensive. The latter is a re-creation of communal presence focused on a significant new phenomenon; the declarative functions in an already-established linguistic presence to negate the model proposed by the first speaker. The information contained in the declarative thus acts as a bar to the anticipated fulfillment of his request, and in doing so establishes a barrier between the prolonged linguistic presence within which this fulfillment was awaited and the situation at hand. The model of reality presented by the negative ostensive can, of course, be acted on, but the model for such action is not given by linguistic form. If the answer to the original imperative be, for example, that the hammer is "over there," then the first speaker can make use of this information to go and get it. The relation of act to model, however, is now no longer immediate but analytical: The declarative has presented a state-of-affairs, and the realization of the original speaker's desire within this state-of-affairs is neither dependent on the linguistic presence of the speakers nor, indeed, mediated by the utterance at all, because going to get the hammer is in no way implicit in the fact of its being over there. It is the fact that the hammer is over there *now* (rather than yesterday or tomorrow) that makes the appropriative action possible, not the fact that it is *said* now to be over there. The correspondance between the now of the utterance and the now of the being-over-there of the hammer is thus not essential to the declarative model; it is merely a coincidence. If the second speaker had said that the hammer was indeed over there yesterday, his interlocutor might still act (perhaps differently) on this information, and the same would be true if he learned it would be over there tomorrow, in which case he might decide to wait a day or seek another hammer elsewhere. This locative predicate has, of course, evolved beyond the simple negative. But the same considerations apply even in the more primitive case. The original imperative expressed a desire that was to be immediately satisfied through performance. The negative-ostensive reply makes it clear that the original desire cannot be so satisfied and leaves it to the first speaker whether he will redefine his desire in more realistic terms. The negative-ostensive model refers to the *present*, but at the same time it does not establish but rather annuls the relationship between this present and the linguistic presence of the speakers. The imperative was founded on the faith that these two were inseparable, or rather that there was no present but the linguistic presence, prolonged sufficiently into the future to permit the presentification of its referent. The negative ostensive reveals, on the contrary, the illusion of this faith in the magical powers of the communication situation.

Thus the declarative has a tense from the beginning, even if at first it be only the present. For the other tenses too are presents, but presents of the past or future: To say the hammer was there yesterday is to say that, yesterday, it was *present*, yesterday's present being from the context-free perspective of the model just like today's. This present is that of the declarative model as a whole, yet it is within this model specifically an element of the *predicate*. The topic is requested by the first speaker and denied by the second, but whether it exists at all in the world it has a reality in linguistic presence. Its absence or even its nonexistence is what is said about it by the predicate. The topic as such is simply a given of the linguistic model, as the topic-comment sentence makes explicit by setting it off in first position, independent of the grammatical dependencies of the rest of the sentence. Philosophers have been confused by the coordinate subject-predicate form into arguing for and against the "existence" of such things as round squares. In topic-comment form, however, even if we say "round squares, they cannot even be imagined," the topical linguistic "existence" of the round squares is beyond dispute. The present of the declarative, in which the topic becomes an element of a model of reality, is only realized in the predicate. This predicate need not be verbal in nature. But to the extent that it refers to a *present*, it temporalizes the topic, which is at first presented, as we have just seen, atemporally in a non-referential linguistic presence. Thus the topic-predicate form expresses a passage from the atemporal to the temporal. Now insofar as we can distinguish verbals from nominals, the former are names of *actions*, that is, phenomena that can only be realized in time, whereas nominals exist in the significant memory as atemporal images. But this implies that, when the predicate is verbal, the temporality inherent in the verbal-as-such becomes a property of the topic-as-predicated-of, or we might say that the verbal predicate "verbalizes" the topic. The verbal image, which requires a constant element to undergo the temporal process it designates, becomes subordinated to the topic that itself usurps the role of this formerly neutral element. This usurpation may be found in inchoate form in the imperative, where the performing subject of the verbal imperative was obliged to consider himself in this role. As we have observed, however, this analysis is not explicit in the imperative model, where the subject, although addressed, is not included in the model as such. In the declarative model it is, on the contrary, the atemporal topic that is first presented. Thus the temporality of the verbal does not remain its own, but is predicated of the topic. It is this element of predication which transforms the verbal into a verb.

Adjectival and nominal predicates have no verbal with which to "verbalize" the topic because the adjective or nominal cannot be itself an agent of temporalization. In a sentence like "the hammer (is) broken" or "John (is) sick," the words "broken" or "sick" express states, not actions, and the "now" implicit in the declarative is "verbalized," not in these words, but in the copula, even if unexpressed. This can be seen from the contrast implicit in these declaratives in their original context: The hammer is broken, but used to be whole; John is sick, but used to be well. What is true *now* is not "broken" or "sick" but the being-broken of the hammer, the being-sick of John. Thus the copula is at least an implicit, if not yet an explicit verb. The semantic sources of copulatives in verbs like "to stand" (Latin *stare*), "to bear"

(Sanskrit *bhū*), which denote static "activities" and thus *temporalize* stasis, lend support to this analysis.

Thus declarative predicates acquire a verbal form as the result of their expression of a linguistic present. The other chief grammatical categories, governance and person, also inchoate in the imperative, are likewise formalized as specifications of the predicate and thus as functions of the verb. Imperative verbals may be associated with objects, but cannot be said truly to *govern* them because they designate in themselves a desired performance in which the object is presentified. In the declarative the object becomes an element of the predicate, temporalized by its role in the action denoted by the verb. Thus in a sentence like "John takes (took) the hammer," the hammer is not present in the model as an object of the speaker's desire but as the object of John's action. The hearer is not merely permitted but required to analyze it as subordinate to this action because it is this action alone that constitutes the now of the linguistic present. The category of person is similarly formalized in the declarative model. Here we may neglect the third person, rightly classed by Benveniste as merely the nonpersonal, or if we like "zero-personal," member of the paradigm. In the imperative-declarative dialogue the two speakers are already present to each other in linguistic presence; the second speaker maintains this presence by his answer, at the same time annulling the imperative awaiting of his interlocutor. The first-person or second-person topic, upon its temporalization by the predicate, becomes itself situated in the now of the linguistic present, whereas in the imperative the two persons played complementary roles in the (imperative) speaker's awaiting, the latter as beneficiary, his interlocutor as performer of the act. The "shifter" function of the personal pronouns situates the declarative model relatively to the linguistic presence of the two interlocutors, so that the original speaker, hearing (say) "I" as the topic, must imagine the other speaker in the temporal situation designated by the predicate, which at the same time informs him of the impossibility of the other's effecting the performance he has requested. The declarative verb, by temporalizing the "I"-topic, makes its very existence as a topic dependant on this impossibility, and the same holds true for the second-person topic referring to the original speaker. (This shift in focus is not paralleled by "third-person" statements of, e.g., the absence of the hammer, which was the "topic" of the imperative.)

Thus the declarative model specifically presents one or the other speaker as a "real" element of the present (such as was only implicit in the imperative model), and because the verb carries in the predicate the tense of the present, it will tend to become "personalized" as well. This use of shifter pronouns in the declarative designates roles retroactively in the entire imperative-declarative dialogue and implies that the presence to one another of the two participants, although not included in the imperative model, was a prima facie necessity for its "felicitous" realization. Here language reestablishes the symmetry of the ostensive gestures of pointing which were no doubt the most primitive "shifter" forms. "I" and "you" form a paradigm, with the third-person form standing in contrast to both, in the present of the declarative; the asymmetrical speaker-hearer relation is neutralized within the linguistic model of reality. But this is the same neutralization as was effected by the (linguistic) present on the asymmetry of desire in linguistic presence. Artificial languages may be made "context-free" without reference to the linguistic presence in which their messages are conveyed, but in human language this presence can never simply be ignored if the speakers are to fully liberate themselves from the violence of the original crisis.

The Grammaticality of the Declarative

As we have previously stated this is not the place for an attempt at a detailed derivation of the grammatical structures of the declarative, which is the province of linguistics proper. The very fact that, although there is general agreement on the most fundamental "universals" of human language, these features can be expressed in so large a variety of syntactical and morphological structures, indicates that the empirical analysis of these structures, and the creation of theories to explain their evolution and transformation, would contribute but marginally to our understanding of the fundamental properties of linguistic representation. The apparently cyclic nature of the evolution of mature languages, as well as the fact that all such languages permit of more or less perfect translation from one to another, only confirm that the birth of the declarative effectively marks the end of the dialectical evolution of linguistic forms, and that the unending series of reequilibrations which constitute the later history of linguistic change is, however fascinating in itself, no longer a central locus of the history of human representation. It would then appear that the establishment of the grammatical categories of the declarative, the fundamental ones of which never change, marks a moment of separation between the functionality of linguistic form and its systemic coherence. This separation already existed on the phonological and lexical levels from the beginning of language; the function of ostensive or imperative language was indifferent to sounds and words which, however "motivated" they may have been at their origin, doubtless varied and evolved as they still do today. But the reproduction of this separation on the syntactic level is of a very different sort, because syntactic structures, unlike the preceding, are not wholly without relation to the structures of experience of which they are the models. The most significant sign of this separation is the phenomenon of grammatical *correctness*, which has obvious parallels at the phonological and lexical levels, but not at the higher level of discourse, although the appropriateness criteria for the latter are in many situations very strict indeed, and their violation generally far more severely punished than those of language proper.

The peculiar nature of sentence correctness has led to Chomsky's positing of innate mental structures to explain its acquisition by the child. Such "explanations," of course, explain nothing, and are of little more use as hypotheses than Molière's *vertu dormitive*. The ostensible reason for their advancement is that the child constructs a corpus of syntactic rules on the basis of what appear to be quite limited contacts with language, so that one could scarcely imagine that he would be able to induce these rules from the sentences he has heard unless he were in some way "preprogrammed" to construct them. This is a domain in which empirical study is essential, and we have no hypotheses to present concerning the language-learning process, in which, given the adult use of higher along with lower linguistic forms in speaking to the child, ontogeny could only recapitulate phylogeny in intentional structure, not in apparent meaning. (Thus, for example, it may well be that the child's first utterances are all intended as ostensives, but this may not be apparent from the words alone.) But we may at least hazard the observation that what is truly surprising to Chomsky about the child's linguistic development and has led him to seek refuge in "Cartesian" hypotheses, is not so much his ability to learn a language per se, as the fact that this ability can exercise itself with equal proficiency on such a variety of syntactic structures. Were there only a single language in the world, the child's ability to learn it would appear to be dictated by the very meaning of the words (this being indeed the naive view of nonlinguists, who are more likely to be impatient than amazed at their child's language-learning ability). But the large number of languages, and the unending tendency within each toward restructuring, not merely phonetic and lexical, but syntactic as well, offers an incontrovertible demonstration of the nonnecessity of any particular syntactic rule on the level of specificity at which it must be learned to satisfy the speaker's sense of correctness. Thus linguistic universals, such as they may be, are invisible on the "surface" of language and must consequently be located in a "deep structure" that is made to serve as a synchronic substitute for the *Ursprache* of the nineteenth-century philologists. In Chomsky's early work, *Syntactic Structures* (1957), the deep structure consisted of simple (NP-VP) declarative sentences plus abstract "markers" of (possible) transformations into passives, interrogatives, and so on, as well as the "generalized" transformations that produce subordination. In the later *Aspects* model (1965) the "base" contains the entire meaning of the sentence; subordination is accomplished by "a recursive operation in the base," the transformational component having become "solely interpretative."[4] This more rigorous attachment of deep structure to meaning is for Chomsky and his followers a step toward realizing the ideal of a *universal*

base presumably identical in speakers of all languages.[5]
Transformational grammar attempts to bridge the entire gap
between essential function and arbitrary form, in the process
losing sight of the fact that the pure linguistic function "in
itself" is not a linguistic phenomenon, because language is
a priori contextual and can only be considered outside of its
concrete context by making use of its own structures of
de-contextualization. If this is so then it is chimerical to
postulate a mental or neurological "realization" of the
"meaning" of sentences, as though outside of the realm of
scientific discourse sentences had a "meaning" independent
of their use. Whatever the inadequacies of such constructions,
however, their primary (if not always apparent) motivation
will persist so long as the specific rules of grammar appear to
"express" universal relationships by widely divergent means.

In the perspective taken here sentence correctness is a
function of the topic-predicate bond, which tends to be
reinforced through redundancies of morphological agreement
when emphatic, deliberately redundant forms become habitual without losing their redundant character. Transformational grammar is thus justified in deriving all grammatical
structure from the S-P connection, although mistaken in its
assumption that this connection is itself a primitive term, so
that the contextual origin of the declarative, which is preserved in what we are justified in calling its *esthetic*, is
forgotten, and the decontextualizing features of its intentional structure taken as a priori conditions of language in
general. We have spoken briefly of the importance of the
shifter categories of tense and person, which are only established as grammatical paradigms in the declarative and which
are attached specifically to the temporal-verbal element of
the predicate, which they in fact define as a verb. No doubt
the evident dependence of the various forms of subordination, passivization, and so forth on the simple declarative
makes the notion of "transformation" quite appropriate to
describe their construction. The most complex sentences
merely reproduce in different forms the original S-P connection of the simple declarative; transformational grammar
takes this as its primary postulate. But it accepts this original
connection as a given and so to speak "natural" phenome-

non, inexplicable and in fact requiring no explanation, whereas the rules that govern transformations appear as arbitrary creations, explicable at best as possibilities "selected" from a preestablished "linguistic competence" programmed in the human brain. Thus transformational grammar fails to understand that the same "linguistic intuition" that presides over the operation of these rules is already at work in the constitution of the simple S-P form itself. The generative grammarian is right to see in the S-P form the source of all grammatical form but wrong in believing that the fundamental form, in its simplicity, is not itself an "arbitrary" construction with a historical origin in the context of linguistic presence. This error reflects the fact that the declarative sentence represents not an intermediate stage but the culmination of linguistic evolution as a dialectical process. For were this not the case, and were the transformational rules products of a continuous evolution *ab ovo*, they could not be assimilated to mechanical algorithms even with the imperfect success obtained by transformational grammar. If no understanding of intentional structures is needed for a noncontextual explanation of the functioning of these rules, that is because the presiding intentional structure in all cases is that of the declarative (the interrogative for example being only a variant). But, as the proponents of pragmatic linguistics have observed—whatever the inadequacy of their own formulations of intentional structure, reduced in true "pragmatic" fashion purely to the functional—sentences, whether declaratives or not, are utterances intended in a real context, not "pure forms" possessed of an invariant "meaning" expressed in universal terms in "deep structure." The transformationalists see only linguistic form, the pragmaticists, only function, whereas the intentional structures of language are precisely the means whereby linguistic form structures function. The sort of concrete linguistic analysis that would take this fundamental truth into consideration, or better still, make it the foundation of its theoretical apparatus, has yet to be created, although in recent studies of linguistic change, the desire to explain rather than merely describe the phenomena encountered have led their authors *par la force des choses* to postulate in their subjects what may be for all intents and purposes considered as intentional structures.[6]

The Esthetic of the Declarative

The declarative sentence, as a "context-free" model of reality, is the first attempt at an objective understanding of the universe, and thus the direct precursor of scientific discourse, which merely makes explicit and rigorous the decontextualizing elements of this model. But it is also for the very same reason the origin of all *fictions*, which exploit its liberation from its real context in the opposite fashion, as a source not of objectivity, but of the free expression (and catharsis) of desire. There is, however, no simple parallel between the inchoate existence of these two forms. That of the scientific, because it involves only the explicit element of predication, need not be discussed further at this stage, whereas the proto-literary aspect of the declarative concerns its relationship with desire and is therefore an essentially linguistic rather than discursive phenomenon. It is indeed borne out by the evidence of history, if not of common sense, that the intentional simplicity of scientific discourse could only be attained, or even sought after, through the de-temporalization of a preexisting fictional, that is, temporalized form. But temporalization is, as we have seen, characteristic of predication as such, whereas de-temporalization can only operate nontrivially on a *series* of such predications, which is to say, in a discursive context.

Linguistic forms may be said to possess an "esthetic" as soon as their contemplation, whether in the mind or in linguistic presence, functions to arouse desire—that is, by our hypothesis, from the first moment of their existence. The question as to whether indeed the category of the esthetic requires the prior existence of language, or of formal representational structures in general, hinges on one's definition of desire. If this latter be conceived outside the representational context and thus as independent of the genesis of human representation, then mimesis per se may be taken as evidence of desire, and the imitated model, irrespective of its status as an object of representation, may be considered as an object of esthetic contemplation. But such a definition of the esthetic, to say nothing of desire, situates it outside the intersubjective domain no matter how broadly defined, and thus not only attributes "esthetic" sensations to lower animals, but more pertinently, fails to distinguish between the practical and contemplative moments of mimesis. Certainly there is no point in speaking of imitation as in itself an esthetic phenomenon; the esthetic moment must be limited to the contemplation of the object, even though this moment of contemplation may include in imaginary form an entire "scenario" of mimesis. In what we have defined elsewhere[7] as "esthetic mimesis," the subject's original desire in imitating the model is not of a simply practical nature—to perform the same act—but has as its aim the acquisition of the "being" that appears to be expressed in the model's execution of the act, or, more generally, in any manifestation of an *appearance*. This concept of "being" is purposely vague, for its content can range from social prestige to physical well-being (expressed in the wearing of elegant clothes, in an athletic performance, etc.); its function is merely to designate the substantive object of desire which manifests itself in the appearance. Now the subject may indeed attempt to perform the act of his model, which is to say, to acquire the appearance for himself. If he in fact succeeds in acquiring the "being" or substance that manifests itself in the act, his mimetic activity rejoins the domain of the practical, and is not in essence esthetic (although esthetic moments may indeed emerge and be "transcended" in the course of the mimetic process). But the esthetic moment by which esthetic mimesis is defined is a contemplative one in which the nonequivalence between being and act, or substance and appearance, presents itself to the imagination of the subject. The esthetic imagination is not practical (anticipating possible future activity) but *paradoxical*: On the one hand, possession of the appearance appears to include within itself the possession of the being that is expressed by it; but on the other, because the appearance is an expression of this being, the being must be acquired before the appearance, which can therefore no longer be imitated directly. Thus if the subject sees his model engaged in an athletic performance, he may build up his muscles through exercise to the point at which such a performance is within his reach, in which case his mimetic activity is not essentially esthetic. But if he contends himself with imagining himself running or leaping like his model, then his own possession of the athletic "being" of the model remains purely vicarious, dependent on its real-world possession by the latter, and his contemplation of the model's actions remains esthetic.

This definition of the esthetic nowhere refers to language, nor indeed to any formal system of representation, except insofar as such systems lend significance to the "appearances" to be imitated. Nevertheless it is no accident the the desiring subject's contemplative "possession" of the (real or remembered) image of his model bears an obvious resemblance to the speaker's "possession" of the sacred object in the original event through the intermediary of the protolinguistic sign, a form of possession which gives rise to the "ontological faith" expressed in the inappropriate ostensive. For the subject of esthetic mimesis, the image of his model in the act of appearing is a kind of private "representation," the appearance being like an ostensive sign that, because its presentation is in principle the result of the presence of its referent, can be employed (with the same paradoxical consequences) to obtain the presence of this referent in its absence. Hence although the phenomenon of esthetic mimesis in itself is a purely mental one, it can only attain expression with the advent of (ostensive) language, or its equivalent in other media of representation (e.g., cave drawings of animals). Our sole concern here is with the parallel between what we may justifiably call the "intentional structure" of esthetic representation, mental or physical, and that of specific linguistic forms, because these forms alone lend themselves to the constitution of a formal dialectic.[8] Lacking a language in which to express it, the appearance/being relationship of esthetic mimesis, even if we grant that its expression is possible within other (e.g., iconic) systems of representation, would remain simply unanalysable. Yet the means of expression furnished by the ostensive, although adequate to this task, can scarcely be said to constitute an esthetic object in itself. The ostensive word does not specify a particular mode of appearance of its referent, but the appearance of the referent per se; it *stands for* the substance of the referent, just as in esthetic mimesis a particular phenomenal aspect of the model can be said to "stand for" his being as a whole. Hence ostensive language cannot express the content of the mimetic esthetic imagination but only its form. And as we have seen in our discussion of the inappropriate ostensive, what we have called ontological faith in language is precisely the faith that this form, given the conditions of linguistic presence, is sufficient.

A case in point is the magical use of a person's name to "possess" his being, a quasi-universal phenomenon among primitive peoples, which is often prevented by the expedient of maintaining one's "being" in a secret, sacred name revealed only to privileged members of the family group. The name has in itself no "esthetic" value; it is a merely formal attribute. But if its use is thought to suffice to possess the substantial being of its bearer, then contemplation of the name may be taken as a linguistic equivalent to the contemplation of some more palpable manifestation. Esthetic mimesis is ultimately concerned after all not with appearance but with substance, appearance, here as indeed in all varieties of esthetic form, being only a means to an end. It is for this reason that the development of representational form is a necessary condition of the evolution of esthetic form. The inadequacy in our eyes of the esthetic that expresses itself in the evocation of a name in order to "possess" its bearer comes, not from the esthetic impotency of ostensive language, but, on the contrary, from its excessive power. The desiring subject will only contemplate as much of the model's appearance as he needs in order to assure himself that it expresses the latter's being: If a name suffices, he will go no further. Indeed, the concrete appearances that function in the same fashion in extra-linguistic imagination tend to be of a similar fragmentary "anesthetic" character, as is the case in the parallel forms of "possession" through a piece of clothing, a lock of hair, etc., exercised by practitioners of voodoo and similar rites.

Although the most primitive linguistic signs could already be used as expressions of esthetic mimesis, the very significance that attached to these signs precluded the development of an esthetic internal to the linguistic model. But this is merely to reformulate in esthetic terms the dependency of the noncontext-free elementary linguistic forms on linguistic presence which makes them incapable of furnishing objective models of reality. The "excessive power" of the ostensive-imperative in the esthetic sphere is the exact counterpart of its nonobjectivity because the failure to distinguish between desire and reality is in both cases inherited directly from the original event as the birthplace of linguistic presence. The specifically esthetic consequences of the "subjective" or "non-dialogic" nature of the elementary forms are, however, best expressed not in terms of a simple parallel between the esthetic and the objective or "scientific" capacities of language which become evident in the declarative, but through consideration of the esthetic, not merely of the linguistic models themselves, but of the entire communication situation in which they are presented. The pragmatic paradoxes generated by the use of representational forms in specific situations can then be seen as esthetic in nature, and the genesis of first the ostensive and then the imperative "solutions" to these paradoxes as steps in the evolution not merely of the objective representation of reality, but of esthetic expression.

In this perspective because the ostensive, as the first form of this expression, is wholly dependent on the presence of its object, its own "esthetic value"—i.e., its capacity for evoking when contemplated by its hearer the being-for-desire, or simply the significance of this object—is limited to the moment of deferral in which it presents itself as a model. In the developments leading to the constitution of the imperative, this deferral is prolonged in an awaiting in which the word designating the object becomes for the hearer the model of a practical performance. Here for the first time the utterance can function, outside its practical use, as an object of esthetic contemplation; insofar as the imperative remains an "inappropriate ostensive," its utterance, instead of being realized in practice and thereby annulled as an expression of desire, may be merely *contemplated* as a sign of the absent desire-object. But it is not quite accurate to speak of the object of such contemplation—the linguistic expression of esthetic mimesis—as an *imperative* utterance. Rather, the dialectic of the "inappropriate ostensive" may be said to lead to two complementary results, one being the imperative, in which ontological faith in language is made the basis for a *praxis* that resolves the paradox it contains, and the other, the esthetic contemplation of the linguistic sign, in which this paradoxical faith is not tested in practice but made the object of a second-level contemplative praxis wherein the paradox is enacted, without resolution, in the imagination. This can be said to be the birth of esthetic expression as such; but its effectiveness remains dependent on the linguistic presence that gives the sign a potential, albeit unused power over its real referent. Thus "inappropriate ostensive" language can be said to afford linguistic expression to esthetic mimesis, but only to the extent that it takes real beings as its models, for the relation between the substance of the model and its (linguistic) "appearance" or attribute is guaranteed in the real world, and not, as in esthetic representation proper, within the fictional universe of the representation.

With these considerations in mind we may now examine the declarative form, which provides a context-free model of reality, and possesses by the same token a "context-free" esthetic. Here the linguistic object presented for contemplation is not a mere sign attributed to its referent by the speaker under the guarantee furnished by linguistic presence, but an articulated model consisting of topic and predicate, in which the topic name serves to define what may at this point truly be called a *signified*, which the predicate furnishes with a context-free attribute. The declarative begins where the ostensive-imperative ends, with the designation of an object of common desire—guaranteed in its origin specifically by the preceding imperative, and not merely in general terms by linguistic presence—but instead of letting the appearance of the name suffice as that of the object, it makes the latter reappear in a predicate that explicitly constitutes it as inaccessible to the desire of the (imperative) interlocutor. Thus, precisely by the fact that the declarative model is indifferent to the "magical" power of desire as expressed in the imperative, it at the same time obliges the subject of this desire to contemplate its object *esthetically*, as appearing beyond the practical reach of this desire in an "act" that makes it accessible only within the representational confines of the model. In the declarative the referent is expelled from linguistic presence, appearing only in the model where it is temporalized by the predicate. The relation thereby established between speaker, hearer, and object is structurally identical to the "triangular" model of desire put forth by Girard, which it can be said to "express" in the same way that inappropriate-ostensive language was the expression of the relation of subject and model in esthetic mimesis. Thus in the sense in which desire may be defined as a truly *intersubjective* relation, it can only be said to emerge at this stage. But to define desire in so restrictive a manner would lend itself to the same criticism as the choice of grammarians and linguists to define linguistic form on the basis of the declarative sentence: Such definitions foreclose the possibility of a truly genetic analysis.

In Girard's original triangular model of "metaphysical desire," as propounded in *Mensonge romantique et vérité romanesque* (Grasset, 1961), the desiring subject's relation to the object of his desire was depicted as an intersubjective relationship with a mediator who either openly or covertly "designates," by means never rigorously specified, this object to the subject. The vagueness of this designation is analogous to the indeterminate nature of the relationship between the declarative speaker and the predicate attributed to the object. This predicate, as we have seen, is necessarily temporal, and its temporality designates a moment, real or imaginary, of the speaker's own lived experience that is presumably not shared by his interlocutor. But this experience of the object is not presented as such in the declarative model, from which, as we have seen, the speaker is absent; the model is merely understood to be founded on temporal experience as the source of its predicate. Thus, as opposed to the model of esthetic mimesis, where the mimetic object is desirable only as a (real) attribute of the person being imitated, the triangular model makes the subject's desire dependent on its presence in what might be called the experiential field that surrounds the mediator. In what Girard calls "internal" mediation the mediator may well be invisible to the subject, or even an anonymous *on* of social judgment. Here the field is less the domain of an overtly privileged model than that of social experience in general, and the specific value of individual objects of desire depends not on their real status as attributes but on their representational status as topics of which value is predicated. Triangular desire is thus both more objective and more subjective than esthetic mimesis. On the one hand, it depends on the "objective" form of predication, but on the other, because the source of this predication—that is, the mediator—is absent from the declarative model, the valorization of the object is cut off from any objective test of reliability, such as was always in principle possible in the case of attributes connected to the mediator by real-world associations.

The term "metaphysical" applied by Girard to this model may be taken as a structural criticism of metaphysics in general, in which, as we have already observed, the subject-object relation is posited as primary, when in effect it is merely the mask for an intersubjective relation. Triangular, in contrast to mimetic-esthetic desire, takes a quasi-objective interest in the predicated attributes of the object, and thus becomes, as "Western" metaphysics did in fact become, the source of a natural-scientific concern with phenomena. The triangular theory de-mystifies this objectifying attitude from the perspective of human science, but this de-mystification does not affect the validity of this attitude in the natural-scientific domain. Metaphysical desire is richer than esthetic mimesis because the formal separation it effects between the two elements of the subject's desire (the two sides of the triangle that pass through the vertex of the desiring subject) allows for the full development of both: Thus the objectal relation can become an objective scientific interest, whereas in the intersubjective one, the other becomes a transcendental mediator who usurps the functions of the sacred. Girard is thus not unjustified in assimilating metaphysical desire to a de-ritualized idolatry, which in its more advanced or decadent forms makes all men potentially gods for one another ("des dieux les uns pour les autres"). But the positive or progressive element in this "idolatry," which the institutional perspective of Girard altogether neglects, is the return of the source of human value from the sacred to the profane, which is precisely the mechanism of the universal system of exchange toward which modern (post-) industrial society may be said to be advancing.

The declarative sentence, taken as an objective model of reality, is the foundation of metaphysics. Predication, its distinguishing feature, is both the source of its objectivity (as it situates the topic outside linguistic presence), and at the same time the expression of the mediating role of the (declarative) speaker between his hearer (the speaker of the original imperative) and the object of his desire (the topic). When this role is grasped explicitly by the hearer, the esthetic presence of the declarative is dissolved, and the intersubjective situation becomes that of the dialogic schema discussed in the preceding chapter (p. 135). But in the esthetic contemplation of the declarative model, the speaker does not appear; instead there is only predication "in itself." The predicate is simply alleged as true of the topic, whereas the speaker-mediator, who intends this predicate specifically in order to justify his frustration of the hearer's desire, is absent from the model. Thus it is not the predicate but its predication of the topic which reveals to the detached observer what it hides from its desiring hearer: the presence of a second subject as mediator of his desire.

We can now understand more concretely the position of the declarative in the dialectic of desire. The first (imperative) speaker of the imperative-declarative dialogue already desires the object, because he pronounces its name in order to acquire it. The declarative response transforms this esthetic-mimetic desire into its "triangular" form by providing a mediator for the subject in the person of the second speaker, and a predicative attribute independent of linguistic presence. The subject's original desire was founded on the "magical" power of language to presentify its referent; now this presentification is made purely imaginary, and at the same time, defined for him by another. The second speaker acts as an unavowed mimetic rival, maintaining the desire-object in its inaccessible position in the declarative model through his act of predication, although at the same time never revealing his own agency within his utterance. In practical terms this utterance carriers information that may be of use to the first subject in realizing his desire. But insofar as the utterance itself becomes, within linguistic presence, an object of contemplation, the declarative expresses the absolute inaccessibility of its topic within this presence. Thus to realize the desire, linguistic presence must be *abolished* rather than, as in the imperative, fulfilled. Worldly desire thus now appears as incompatible with linguistic presence, which generates an imaginary, or more precisely, a *fictional* universe. The prolongation of the linguistic presence of the declarative thus leads in the opposite direction from that of the imperative, because the hearer remains thereby immersed in a fictional world in which his desire is incapable of concrete fulfillment. The fiction of the declarative sentence can only prolong itself in fictional discourse, which is to say, in literature.

What, it may be asked, is the function, within a formal theory of representation, of an esthetic analysis of linguistic structures? The great weakness of all esthetics of literature is that they begin with an anesthetic notion of language proper and are then obliged, in order to understand its literary use, to posit a "literary language" defined by some mysterious difference from "ordinary" language. The indefensibility of this position is apparent even from the limited perspective of pragmatic linguistics.[9] But it is not enough to speak vaguely of the "esthetic elements" in language without making clear the structural relation between language and the esthetic. Thus the question should be turned on its head: Language is from the beginning an esthetic phenomenon as much as a communicative one, the two functions being only fully separable at the discursive level. Even the ostensive, which in linguistic presence merely designates its referent and thus can operate as an esthetic expression only during the quasi-instantaneous time of deferral, functions esthetically in significant memory, and lacking this function, its inappropriate use as an imperative—but also, as we have seen, as an expression of "esthetic mimesis"—would be inexplicable.

The marginality of the esthetic, as exhibited in such diverse phenomena as the bohemian life of artists and the estrangement of esthetics from the mainstream of philosophical analysis, merely perpetuates its original and never-quite-forgotten connection with the sacred. No doubt the dependence on "arbitrary" linguistic representation by the ideologies of the modern system of exchange which have effectively displaced, if not replaced, the traditional forms of the sacred, accounts for the resistance of linguistics to esthetic considerations. Certainly this resistance is not to be found in the realm of iconic representation, where the very words "picture" or "image" denote overtly esthetic phenomena. No student of painting or sculpture considers the pictorial or plastic components of artworks as in themselves devoid of esthetic interest, apprehended by means of a formal "competence" to which the esthetic is simply irrelevant. If we are, however, ready to accept such an anomalous situation in the case of language, the only possible explanation is that modern society is characterized, not merely by the exponential growth of the "digital" forms of communication that are modeled on language but by a belief that the arbitrary nature of the linguistic sign guarantees the purely mechanical operation of these forms. This faith is in fact the faith of metaphysics, become no longer an auxiliary but a substitute for that of religion. As we shall see in the following chapter this faith rests on a misinterpretation of the "arbitrariness" of the linguistic sign to which only an evenemential hypothesis of the origin of language can give a concrete anthropological foundation.

The revelation of the internal contradictions of this metaphysical faith, long relegated to the "marginal" domain of esthetics, has since Nietzsche become a staple of "continental" philosophy, of which Derrida is the latest and most radical exponent. American philosophers have safely ignored this trend because its often-complacent nihilism offers little challenge to their own analyses, which are at least "constructive" whether or not they are anything else. Thus they not unjustifiably dismiss "continental" philosophers as tainted with estheticism. Even when both schools concentrate their attention, as both increasingly do, on language, one attempts to de-construct its basis without examining its forms, whereas the other attempts to construct its forms without examining their basis. The present theory, in its attempt to substitute a dialectic for this *dialogue de sourds*, rather than offering a merely "esthetic" criticism of the metaphysical conception of language, offers a criticism of the esthetic basis of this conception which is at the same time a model of its genesis. Only thus, and not through empty "programmatic" declarations, can it be demonstrated that construction and de-construction, in the practices of the rival schools, are in fact equally metaphysical operations.

Chapter **6** Dialogue and Discourse

The speaker of the declarative sentence, as we have seen, presents his utterance but cannot present his presentation, which is nevertheless evident to his interlocutor. The latter may, of course, merely consider the declarative in its practical function as an information-bearing response to the original imperative-interrogative, or, more generally, simply as providing information concerning a topic of interest to him. If this information suffices for practical purposes, the fact that the "objective" declarative model is that of a particular speaker is in itself of no consequence, and the linguistic presence of the interlocutors simply ends with the first exchange. In this case no further contribution is made to the formal dialectic: The declarative is taken at face value as satisfying the needs of the situation. But the hearer may also react in two ways within linguistic presence to the presence of the speaker in his (hearer's) model of the declarative. On the one hand he may consider his interlocutor's predication as in some way inadequate or insufficient, and either request further clarifications or present his version of the temporal phenomenon it describes; in this case he engages in dialogue. Or on the other he may fall subject to the "metaphysical" desire generated by the speaker's role as the predicator absent from the declarative model; in this case he may be said to contemplate the declarative as an esthetic object. The prolongation of linguistic presence in this second case is merely passive on the part of the hearer, but this passivity enthrones the speaker as the "master" of linguistic presence, in which the model he has presented becomes the locus of the hearer's

197

desire. This second instance, where linguistic presence is prolonged, not through the symmetrical activity of both speakers but through the formalization of the original, merely provisional asymmetry of the declarative, is that of *discourse*. It is this latter case that is of greatest interest to the theory of representation, because it alone produces what can truly be called higher intentional structures, although, as we shall see, these structures cannot be constructed within a formal dialectic. We shall therefore devote to discourse the greater portion of our analysis; but due consideration must also be given to the phenomenon of dialogue.

Dialogue

We have already traced the beginnings of dialogue to the imperative-ostensive ("Scalpel!"-"Scalpel") exchange. The negative-ostensive reply to the imperative, which we have hypothesized to be the genesis of the declarative, was an outgrowth of this dialogue, which finds a new position of equilibrium through the conversion of the "doubtful" imperative into a genuine interrogative that no longer requests the presentification of the object but merely information about it. Foreknowledge of the modes in which such information may be presented will lead to its partial anticipation or orientation by the interrogative, such as we find in "wh-questions." And the need for more than one predication concerning a given topic will result in the expansion of the interrogative-declarative dialogue into a series of questions and answers which constitute a "compounding" of the original exchange. The specific modalities of such compound interrogatives need not concern us here, although the fact that the individual declarative sentence does not tend toward indefinite expansion in the dialogic context is not without interest. A predicate is single temporalization of the topic, and the origin of predication, its primary function, is simply to include the topic in a model the temporality of which is not coextensive with linguistic presence. To the degree to which this original function is maintained, we may speak of a "principle of least information," by which the declarative elements of the dialogue tend to be the simplest possible answers that satisfy the specific request of the interrogative. This is what we mean when we say that a sentence should express "a single thought." But because the information required in a given practical context may not be expressible as a "single thought," the functioning of the declarative model must lead to situations in which a single declarative is simply inadequate.

Thus the grammatical refinement of the declarative cannot supply the needs of practical interrogation. But by the same token these needs can be simply met, not by complicating the linguistic form, but by reproducing it each time with different content. Here the crucial point is that the intentional structure of the declarative does not continue to evolve concomitantly with the complexity of the tasks put to it in practical contexts, but remains a fundamental unit of "thought" or information. The topic is, in each successive declarative, wholly absorbed by the temporality of its predicate, yet because this linguistic temporality is independent of the real-time existence of the topic, the same process may be repeated *ad libitum*. This "absorption," by which the topic is rendered for the moment—that of deferral—inaccessible save in the imaginary (linguistic) temporality of the model, defines a mode of functioning of the imagination, which cannot attack an indefinitely large store of information concerning a given topic but requires the topic to be presented to it again and again as an atemporal "thing-in-itself" that falls under the successive temporal domination of a series of predicates. The necessity of formal repetition is in the "compound" dialogue we are discussing manifested by the alternation between the speakers; in discourse it appears within the utterance of a single speaker. A series of interrogative-declarative exchanges is scarcely a "dialectic," yet it exhibits the fundamental characteristic of all higher forms of representation, which is the attachment to a single desire-object of a plurality of moments of desire. Here, of course, the desire is simply for information, and the series of imaginary temporalizations effected by the plurality of declaratives can be said to serve a merely "heuristic" function. Nevertheless, this necessary repetition of the linguistic form constitutes a limitation on the context-free nature of the declarative model, which is shown to guarantee only momentary liberation from linguistic presence. What we might call the "formal rhythm" of all the forms of dialogue and discourse is determined by this limitation, which, seen in a positive light, insures the continual reestablishment of the intersubjective relation between speaker and hearer that underlies the "objective" intentional structure of the declarative, and from which the higher linguistic forms can only escape by constantly reiterating the separation between desire and linguistic presence that is effected in the temporalization of the topic by the predicate.

Dialogue need not of course confine itself to compound interrogation. A complex variety of the latter will follow when a piece of information given in a predicate becomes itself the topical object of further questions. Here the freely "metalinguistic" nature of dialogue becomes manifest: Predication can itself generate objects of desire. The complex, like the compound form of dialogue, is a product of formal repetition, which by the very fact of its compound or paratactic structure lends itself to the constitution of hierarchies of content. What has first appeared as an element of temporality remains in significant memory as atemporal and may itself in turn be retemporalized. The complexity of the content hierarchy thus established is dependent on the simplicity of the declarative form, which has no need to anticipate this hierarchy at any stage but simply creates it *in actu*. But, conversely, the establishment of such hierarchies sequentially in linguistic presence, such that the topic of the final predication could not have been predicted at the beginning of the dialogue, whereas this beginning is later remembered as the foundation of the conclusion, gives rise to the phenomenon of de-temporalization—at first merely "intuitive"—in which the questioner attempts to grasp a posteriori, let us say before a projected repetition of the same or a similar dialogue, the hierarchy as a whole. Once constituted in the irreversibility of linguistic presence, this hierarchy, like the individual predicates, may become an (atemporal) topic of further predication. The second time around the final moment of the dialogue will take on a character of finality; and to the extent that the temporal series of exchanges which constitute the dialogue are not themselves a model of a temporal process, their order may be changed to reflect this finality. This development anticipates within a dialogic context the de-temporalized form of logical scientific discourse. In a true dialogue, where the answer of the second party is in principle never totally predictable, de-temporalization can at best be a general tendency realized in "protocols" of hierarchically related questions.[1] But complex interrogation already provides a practical model for logicoscientific discourse.

Interrogative-declarative dialogue, because it preserves the asymmetry of the original imperative-ostensive exchange without tapping the dialectical possibilities inherent in the intentional structure of the declarative, is an artifically constrained form, dependent for its existence on an asymmetrical extra-linguistic relation between the speakers rather than on the intrinsic limitations of the forms. Thus no historical "stage" is defined by this form, which must from the beginning have been contemporaneous with declarative-declarative and mixed dialogue. We need not attempt to develop the distinctions implied by the last sentence: The dialogue made possible by the declarative is essentially free, like the conversations we engage in every day, this freedom not being, however, incompatible with sequential constraints of varying strength, such that, e.g., interrogatives are normally linked by topic unless an explicit request to change topic is made. The interrogative-declarative dialogue, entirely determined in its form by the simplest and most rigid of such constraints, has served here as a minimal example of dialogue-in-general, the synthetic and proto-discursive elements of which, in particular the "formal rhythm" discussed above, can a fortiori be found in less constrained forms.

We do not propose to consider further the specific sequential constraints of dialogue, which have recently been the object of detailed sociolinguistic analyses. Although any number of *types* of dialogue could be enumerated, there are no *forms* of dialogue as such, and this formal poverty of dialogue is of far greater interest to us than its typological wealth. This poverty should not be taken as a sign that dialogue is more "primitive" than the various forms of discourse. On the contrary, the liberty of dialogue allows it to transcend all formal constraints and thus to remain outside the limitations imposed by the historical process of formal evolution. Were this not the case, the word "dialectic," as applied to both the form taken by this evolution and the ideal form of discourse in which the theoretician aims to describe it, would be an empty slogan. Dialogue, rather than any of the fixed forms of discourse, provides the formal model for the exposition of a theory of representation because it alone permits of an indefinite number of levels of meta-linguistic inclusion; in an ideal model of dialectic each sentence is a predication on the constantly evolving topic constituted by all the preceding sentences. True dialogue, because it takes place in real time, is seldom as productive as its discursive counterpart; but as we all know from our experience with both oral and written discussion, it is far freer. Dialogue is generated according to the simple schema given in chapter 4, in which it is not even necessary to formally distinguish between topic and predicate, the only "constraint" on the hearer of the declarative being to intend the speaker's "objective" model as subordinate to this speaker's own act of linguistic presentification. The intentional structure of the declarative makes it clear that disagreement concerning a predicate will be in principle less fundamental, and consequently less formally constrained in any given type of dialogue than disagreement over the topic, which is indeed often disguised as the former.

It is futile, however, to attempt to establish "dialogic universals" of this sort outside of a given sociological context; constraint "in principle" may often turn out to be no constraint at all. The study of the "pragmatics of human communication," as the title of one significant work has it,[2] must rely not on formal a priori but on the step-by-step analysis of dialogue in its concrete context. The impossibility of a more than statistical generalization of the results thus obtained explains why such analysis has flourished more in the psychiatric context where individuals and their problems are subjected to close scrutiny than in that of linguistics where the notion of relative constraint expressed by "variable rules" has only recently been admitted as a theoretical possibility. Because all *significant* human interaction takes place in dialogue, it is a task of some urgency to discover not only the contextual rules of its operation but the generative properties of its functioning, for example, in "schismogenic" situations (Bateson) or in learning ones. At present our theory of representation can contribute to such study only a general understanding of the relation between desire and linguistic (and other) forms. But the perspective furnished by the formal dialectic should lead the investigation of dialogic phenomena beyond a narrowly empirical search for verifiable local models to the introduction of historical (i.e., dynamic) understanding in situations of increasingly small temporal magnitude—the very possibility of such refinement of the historical dialectic being the result of the universalization of the exchange system both in breadth and in depth that is characteristic of our age. We will develop these considerations in our conclusion.

We may see that dialogue truly has no form because each contribution to it transcends all previous contributions; but a more positive statement of this fact is that each dialogue is itself a new form. Studies of dialogue which concentrate on the discovery of its rules and conventions in a given context must suffer from the inherent limitations of all sociological analyses that, through their regard for the "unbiased" presentation of empirical data, take as their object of study only repeatable events to which the participants attribute no particular significance. In this way representational phenomena may be shown to correlate with measures of social stratification, and so forth, but the significance of the local formal creation that can be found in even the most banal dialogues is most often either ignored entirely or treated as a perturbing element inimical to the collection of uniform data. The ideal situation for these investigations would seem to be a group of people who meet daily in the same narrowly defined context and engage in random variants of the same conversation. A similarly oriented study of a sociologist's career would no doubt favor the case of an individual with a constant output of articles of similar length none of which would indicate any progress over its predecessors.

In those cases where significance is indeed actively sought out for study, the social scientist discovers that no methodol-

ogy is available, because significance is inherently nonquanti-
fiable. Because even the humblest of us learn from our
experiences, and seek in our interactions with others not only
new content but new forms, the social sciences find themselves in the anomalous situation of creating in a deritualized
age an instrument applicable only to the study of ritual. For
if dialogue is not ritual—and a uniquely successful genre of
ritual at that—then it is at least in principle creative of new
form. Because social scientists prefer to study persons of a
lower level of awareness of the regularities of social phenomena than their own, they might, even within the limits of
empiricist methodology, turn their attention to the creative
aspects of dialogue in the limited worlds of their subjects.
But ultimately their study of dialogic phenomena would have
to encompass their own dialogues, not merely in their
"ritual" aspects but as formal creations uncategorizable by
their participants, because it is in these very dialogues that
their own sets of categories would be developed. The theory
would only then attain the goal implicit in human science—
and which in our view should be *explicitly* striven for—of
explaining its own genesis.

Discourse tends to fall into intentional genres determined
by criteria independent of social context and which we may
therefore call "anthropological," whereas dialogue can at best
be classified from without into *types*. But even if we must
content ourselves with a single "genre" of dialogue, the categories of our analysis remain the same: Each dialogue, like
each discourse, may be considered a unique form. This position may appear untenable from the standpoint of a formal
dialectic, but only if we make the error of believing that the
formal dialectic of representation, even on the supralinguistic
level, must progress in linear fashion, from form to form. The
countless "forms" created in dialogues of the past have had
no verifiable specific influence on those of the present, which
nevertheless could not be conceived in the collective absence
of their precursors. But this consequence of our definition of
"form" is far from rendering impossible the pursuit of the
dialectic of representation beyond the linguistic level. It
merely obliges us to renounce any illusions we might have

entertained of an a priori "derivation" of historical reality. The regularities we find in supralinguistic forms may have the rigor of "laws," but they never correspond rigorously to a global intentional structure as they did in the case of linguistic forms. Once supralinguistic forms exist, they each possess their own intentional structure, and generalizations concerning such structures are at best generic and, in the case of dialogue, merely typological. These considerations are at least implicitly accepted in the case of discourse, which has traditionally, at least in its privileged exemplars, been subjected to hermeneutic rather than merely "formal" analysis. We have, however, preferred to advance them in our discussion of dialogue, where typological and not hermeneutic analysis is the only practical possibility, if only to provide a theoretical guarantee of such analysis. The filiation between individual dialogues throughout history is dim indeed, and the attempt to trace its path would be a task not merely hopeless but absurd. But this only means that the study of dialogue is a matter less for anthropology than for sociology, in the broad sense in which it is taken here to designate the study of the empirically observable phenomena of human interaction. Linguistics, insofar as it is the study not of the anthropological foundations of language—by which we refer to the formal dialectic here presented—but of empirically observable linguistic phenomena, falls under the rubric of sociology. And, in effect, when linguists construct the grammar of a language, the raw materials of their study, aside from the texts of culturally significant discourse on which they rely normally only for the languages of the past, are given nowhere else but in dialogue. This is not to say that linguists study dialogue as such, but rather that it is through dialogue that the forms of language are made present to them. In the construction of a synchronic grammar this fact is merely a curiosity because the observed uses of language are abstracted from their lived context and made to exist atemporally; but such is not the case when the object of study is linguistic change. This change is not "given" in dialogue, but it presupposes the historical filiation of the ensemble of dialogues in a given language, the modifications arising in *parole* being spread through innumerable interactions, any one of which may embody, e.g., through the choice of a prestigious phonetic variant or a new lexical item, a particle of formal creation.

Each dialogue may be said to be a new "form"; yet the inaccessibility of these "forms" to theoretical discussion is not merely accidental. Dialogues are never governed by a single intention but by the interaction of two or more; not only are they not predictable in advance, they are not normally even repeatable. Their right to the title of "form" is thus essentially a negative one; each dialogue is a unique new form only because no preexisting form can rigorously be said to apply to it. But as dialogues are only preserved, save in exceptional cases, by fragmentary traces of ideas exchanged and conclusions arrived at, their form never acquires a substantial being; it is maintained only in the guise of the (negative) obligation of the speakers, individual and/or collectively, to say something different on the next occasion. Like the repetitions of the original event, dialogue exists in memory only through its sediments; although each of its instances is unique, these instances are never intended to be retained as unified wholes. Only in discourse can dialogue attain formal substantiality, where the intentions of its different subjects are, in the dramatic genre, subordinated to the single intention of the author-as-subject, or, in the more radical integration of dialectic, absorbed as "moments" of this intention.

In terms of our formal dialectic, dialogue stands in an apparently anomalous position. On the one hand, it is infinitely productive of "higher," supralinguistic forms, transcending all a priori constraints such as eventually limit the viability of the genres of discourse, of which only dialectic escapes such limitation precisely because it shares, in a discursive context, the indefinite freedom of dialogue. On the other, the formal creations of dialogue cannot be said to play a well-defined role in our dialectic. This is not merely because of their normally ephemeral character. The "anomaly" is in fact a necessity: Because the formal freedom of dialogue is given from the outset, it can only "progress" by taking as its content the conclusions of earlier dialogues (as well, of course, as discourses). Thus instead of contributing to the higher-level formal dialectic in which successive discursive forms, bound by generic constraints, can be said to evolve, albeit no longer in the linear fashion of the forms of language, the forms of dialogue follow each other in a multidimensional progression that can only virtually be given historical significance. Cultures may be thought of as in their essence tissues of dialogues because the significance of discourses can only manifest itself through their contribution to ongoing cultural dialogue. But when we come to study the historical evolution and interaction of cultures, the only linguistic monuments available to us are discourses, even in those cases where they are presented in dialogic forms. For constraints on discourse are what define a culture. As these constraints are removed, and the great discursive genres die out, unable to retain discourse within their limits, only dialogue and its discursive counterpart, dialectic, remain. Our conclusion will touch on some of the consequences of this development in our own age.

Discourse

Discourse is the chief vehicle of culture and the most reliable witness of its historical achievements. An even moderately detailed treatment of the major discursive genres and the parameters of their evolution would be impossible here and must be consigned to a future volume. We shall therefore limit ourselves to a cursory overview of the intentional structure of discourse in general and of its chief generic variants.

The extreme complexity and richness of the subject that makes even compendious treatment impossible is not merely an unfortunate contingency. A theory of representation is not an encyclopedia of human science, but at best a general introduction. If each discourse constitutes a form in itself, then no general theory of form can account for the cultural significance of any individual discourse or group of discourses; empirical studies are unavoidable. The pertinence of a general theory to concrete analysis is greatest at the two ends of the historical spectrum: On the one hand, in the domain of the anthropological genesis of representational form, and on the other, in the sociologically accessible field of modernity where the universalization of the system of exchange has led to the decline of cultural discursive constraints and thereby to a simplifying transcendence of formal problems. In contrast, the study of discourse *proprement dit* draws us into the domain of cultural-historical opacity in which the temporal nature of social experience must be lived out, albeit in reduced form, in the discursive—literary or philosophical—model. Because this opacity, which we may characterize more precisely as irreversibility, or resistance to de-temporalization, is reducible only at the cost of the loss of our experience of the discursive forms, our analysis of them cannot be "synthesized" in a general theory. This is not a "problem" solvable by future displays of human ingenuity, but ultimately a cultural choice. One may choose the theory or the discursive-cultural experience, but not both. If in the present work we have taken the first alternative at the expense of the second, it is because the conditions of modernity require that this alternative, whether or not it need be selected once and for all, at the very least be presented. To the extent that any theoretical statement, however provisionally expressed, makes a commitment, we must accept the fact that this present work commits us to the choice of theory over discourse, or more precisely of human science over cultural hermeneutics, as being of greater relevance to our contemporary predicament.

The Intentional Structure of Discourse-in-General

We should not conclude from the foregoing that nothing can be said about discourse in general beyond vapid generalizations. If we are to remain on substantially the same level of generality as in our previous analyses, we must deal with the cultural phenomenon of discourse on the same scale as that, let us say, of imperative language. (For all we know it may be the latter rather than the former phenomenon which has occupied the greater proportion of human chronology.) This means that our analysis, which in principle sacrificed nothing in deriving the form of the imperative, is obliged to sacrifice the specifics of discursive form, about which we know a great deal, in describing the intentional structure of discourse. For this sacrifice to be not merely permissible for "heuristic" reasons, but a functional expression of the choice referred to in the preceding section, the intentional structure of discourse in general must be not a mere generalization but a true structure. Because form is higher than structure, consisting not merely of a set of relations but of an explicit expression, or at least a functional manifestation of them,[3] it may be surprising to encounter in our discussion of discourse a structure that determines the limits of what is properly a formal creation. This "inversion" is precisely the source of the cultural inventiveness of discourse: The intentional structure is no longer, as was the case in the course of intralinguistic formal evolution, simply coexistent with the form conceived as a significant model of reality, for it now merely functions to permit the relevant means of expression, that is, language, to create its own reality, or more precisely, to create a fictional model the relation of which to reality is analogous rather than referential. The discursive prolongation of linguistic presence is a "merely structural" phenomenon that permits the creation of significant form, or in other terms, the generation of desire by the form.

Discourse is, as we have seen, an outgrowth of the esthetic rather than the practical function of the declarative. The speaker of the declarative, insofar as his utterance is not merely understood as conveying practical information, but contemplated "for itself" by the hearer, assumes, within the triangle of desire established by his act of predication, the function of mediator of the hearer's desire for the topical object. Predication is temporalization, and in the linguistic time established by the predicate the object appears within a model that can already be called fictional, because, regardless of its referential nature, it can only be understood within an imaginary universe independent of linguistic presence. The declarative sentence does not, however, establish its own topic, nor, once the topic is given, can it be truly said to guarantee the hearer's desire for it. Rather, this desire, given at the outset, is merely prolonged during the time of linguistic deferral. Insofar as the sentence becomes an object of contemplation, of course, this is not strictly the case because this contemplation may be prolonged at will, but this prolongation is merely a repetition of linguistic time, not an extension of it. Once the hearer's dependence on the speaker is established, however, further predication extending the original deferral and at the same time the temporality of the original declarative model becomes at least conceivable, and a narrative concerning the topic can come into being. But the mere possibility is not in itself a sufficient cause of genesis. The speaker must be both motivated to prolong his utterance and capable of conceiving this prolongation, and neither of these conditions is met in the communication-situation of the declarative as we have defined it, where the topic is predetermined as a real object or action of presumed practical interest to the original (imperative) speaker.

Our understanding of the intentional structure of discourse will then depend on the determination of the general context in which it can be assumed to have arisen. This context cannot be said, strictly speaking, to embody a dialectical contradiction of the kind that had given rise to new linguistic forms. Discourse is not the resolution of a paradox engendered by the functioning of language. The asymmetry of the declarative is corrected not by discourse, but by dialogue. Discourse only prolongs it, or we should rather say, institutionalizes it, because this prolonged asymmetry could not be generated by the declarative form. The asymmetry of the imperative was inherent in the use of language at that stage because of its necessary reference to a linguistic presence that still preserved its original function of transforming mimetic rivalry into collective action. But the speaker of the context-free declarative cannot evoke the authority of this presence as an a priori guarantee for discourse, even if we suppose that he would be motivated to do so. The motivation for discourse can only come from the institution that alone preserves this original authority, but without limiting it to the practical function of mobilizing the community to action in significantly urgent crises: We refer, of course, to ritual.

It is commonplace to attribute a ritual origin to "literary" or fictional discourse: The first narratives are universally assumed to be myths, the first poems, liturgical hymns, etc. But it is inevitably clear from the context of such assertions that discourse is being considered as a cultural, i.e., collectively significant phenomenon altogether separate not only from language as such, the genesis of which is (save in the radically "institutional" theory of Girard) assumed to be an unrelated matter, but even from the supralinguistic forms of dialogue and noninstitutional secular discourse. Thus myth may be considered the first example of "literary" fiction, but this is never taken to imply that previous to the ritual origin of myth individuals could not, for example, give narrative accounts of past events. But although we need not assume that the speakers in an extra-ritual interrogative-declarative dialogue were ever somehow obliged to limit each of their utterances to a single sentence, a formal distinction must be made between the dialogic situation, where speaker-hearer asymmetry is provisional, contingent on the satisfaction of the desire for information on a predetermined topic, and the discursive one, where this asymmetry is established once and for all, and where the hearer expects not practical information but esthetic mediation. Before individuals can tell each other stories outside of the ritual context, the asymmetry of the story-telling situation must be well-established; even a series of tales told by different speakers, as in the *Decameron* or in numerous scenes from the *Arabian Nights*, is not a dialogue nor even a simple extension of dialogue. On the contrary, as the elaborate frame-stories of these and other similar works indicate, such story-telling bouts are themselves secular rituals, the origins of which must be traced to ritual proper rather than to ordinary secular dialogue.

The assumption of a ritual origin of discourse stands in contrast to the secular derivation of linguistic forms, and may appear a dangerous concession to the institutional theory of representation. But to consider discourse, although it makes use of the higher linguistic forms and is all but inconceivable without them, as itself the product of a formal dialectic would be to treat it simply as a "higher" form of language indifferent to its content. Such a definition of discourse would hardly be a radical innovation. On the contrary, it is implicit in the "metaphysical" attitude to language which is that of linguistics as well, insofar as it makes no distinction between discourse and dialogue, and in fact defines the former in the terms we have reserved for the latter (thus "discourse analysis" is in reality the study of dialogue). The reduction of discourse to linguistic form is merely an extension of the original reduction of linguistic form to the "natural" form of the simple declarative. But whereas the declarative, as the guarantee of all grammatical relations, can be made the basis of linguistic form with no falsification of grammatical data (the "only" loss being the historical dialectic of form and desire), the reduction of discourse to language, by putting all of culture on a "natural" basis, renders impossible the elaboration of any notion of cultural significance that is both concrete and collective. Thus either the content of "discourse" is taken from the specific interests of individuals, or when, as in the case of myth, this is manifestly impossible, the content is simply treated as the arbitrary raw material of "structures."

To affirm the institutional nature of discourse, its origin in organized ritual, is to recognize its distinction from the everyday use of language in dialogue. The progress of linguistic form has reflected at each stage a lowering of the threshold of significance, leading to the liberation of the intentional model from the constraint of linguistic presence. The genesis of discourse implies the reversal of the direction of this progress, not through regression to more primitive linguistic forms, but through the "recuperation" of the formal progress by the locus of collective significance. Discourse is, in other words, the result of the interaction of ritual with linguistic form. From this perspective a human society with language, but without discourse, would be unthinkable. Once a linguistic form exists, its use in ritual will generate ritual discourse. Or, conversely, did discourse not develop, the rituals of such a community would cease to guarantee the peace of linguistic presence and the mimetic rivalry generated in dialogue would lead to the breakdown of order in what Girard has called a "sacrificial crisis."

The Ritual Origin of Discourse

Ritual affirms the authority of the sacred object/being over the social order in general, and over linguistic presence in particular. The asymmetry of the speaker-hearer relation during the time of linguistic deferral is guaranteed by the ritual repetition of the original event in which, as we have hypothesized, the designation of an object of common rivalry becomes the sign of the communal renunciation of this rivalry. The sacred being, the original object of proto-linguistic designation, is also the original object of desire. Now the structures of desire follow the evolution of linguistic form; and the desire for the sacred object is no exception to this evolution. Thus the development of a lexical "word" or name designating this object independently of the original context leads to a desire for the object expressed by this name, as concentrating in itself the "powers" exercised by the community in that context. If this desire be now inter-preted in the terms of our analysis of the esthetic of the elementary linguistic forms, calling the name of the sacred being would be the ritual equivalent of the imperative as manifested in prayer, or, negatively, in the common inter-diction on using sacred names, presumably because such utterances are thought to have a "blasphemous" vocative-imperative effect. The ostensive-imperative esthetic discussed in the preceding chapter applies in exemplary fashion to the sacred being, accessible only through its name-as-attribute, and thus, if our analysis is correct, inconceivable except within the structure of this esthetic. That is to say, in ostensive-imperative language the sacred being is necessarily the object of an esthetic mimesis in which the utterance of its name is both equivalent to possession of the powers of the being and at the same time an impossibility because the name is the unalienable property of this being, utterable only when it is re-presented in the ritual context.

Thus ritual constitutes a resolution of the paradox inher-ent in esthetic mimesis. But this resolution cannot be a particularity of one stage of linguistic development. Just as to each stage of the dialectic of linguistic forms there corre-sponds an esthetic in which these forms are contemplated as expressions of the desire of the contemplating subject, so can each stage of this esthetic be presumed to correspond to a stage in religious expression, with the sacred object taking the place of the object of individual desire. The evolution of linguistic form cannot in our hypothesis be accomplished within the domain of ritual because ritual language conveys no information, and hence can lead to no unpredictible consequences. (Thus, for example, the development of the declarative from the negative-ostensive could not arise in ritual where the threshold of significance being maximal, the inability to perform a ritual act could hardly be "explained away" by a declarative.) But the results of this evolution affect language in general and must therefore be felt in the sacred context as well as the secular.

These observations permit us a more precise understanding of the "cathartic" function of ritual. The representional esthetic at each stage of formal evolution finds its ideal object in the sacred, because it is by its very nature only knowable by its attributes of "powers" which are evoked from the very beginning through the use of a representional sign. But, at the same time, the sacred object is not merely ideally "esthetic"; in ritual the paradoxical relation between being and appearance, substance and attribute is transcended by the communal actualization of sacred powers. The ritual reproduction of the original event concentrates in the sacred object the power of nonviolent presence, which we may presume to have extended itself over the preceding crisis, so that in ritual the entire event may be reproduced in peaceful form under the guarantee provided by the sacralized original victim. Now this reproduction is itself "cathartic" in effect: Two participants may, for example, mimic a fight sequence as a dance, making prescribed aggressive gestures without either one being injured or losing control of his actions, so that the aggressive symmetry of the original crisis is transformed into a cooperative harmony.

We owe to Girard (from whom this example is taken) the insight that ritual catharsis is not an a posteriori incorporation of potentially perturbing elements into the order of ritual, as a rationalistic view of its functioning would hold, but rather a reproduction in communal presence of an *original* collective aggression. But the importance of this insight should not blind us to the limitations of the institutional theory in which it finds its place. This conception of catharsis, although refusing the rationalization that would understand ritual as ridding the community a posteriori of its aggressive "impulses," limits its scope to the violence of the original crisis, which is to say, to a mimetic violence anterior to the existence of representation and desire. But these phenomena exist not only in the secular domain but in the sacred as well, and it would be surprising indeed if they did not interact with the original reproductive functioning of ritual.

To the extent that the sacred object exists at all in the significant memory of the members of the community, it exists as *represented*, and insofar as it is only accessible through representation, it becomes an *esthetic* object. Its manifestation in ritual as a guarantee of communal presence thus cannot but take on new functions as the extra-ritual content of this presence evolves from the simple nonviolent designation of the original event to imaginary models progressively more independent of the perceivable state of affairs. When representation was limited to the designation of the sole sacred object, this object was itself present to the members of the community, whose individual desire for it could only come into being a posteriori. But already at the stage of ostensive language, the sacred name existed in significant memory outside of ritual, and at that of the "inappropriate ostensive," the utterance of this name would be imagined to command the presence of the sacred object. The ritual manifestation of the powers of the sacred would thus permit the discharge not only of the "impulses" of prerepresentational mimetic rivalry but of those generated by esthetic mimesis as well. The communal presence of ritual, in actualizing the merely virtual power of the sacred name, would transform the individual desire invested in esthetic mimesis into an agent of communal solidarity in precisely the same way as the ritual reproduction of the original conflict transformed the appropriative impulses of mimetic rivalry into the cooperative activity of the dance. Thus in modern Protestantism, where the already attenuated symbolic violence of the Eucharist has been all but eliminated, the collective singing of hymns of praise maintains its cathartic function, no longer even tenuously linked to the mimetic violence of the original event, but preserving, in its communal evocation of the power of the sacred being, its relationship to the expression of esthetic mimesis through the "inappropriate ostensive." Despite the immense advance over primitive religion realized by the extension of the ritual presence guaranteed by the sacred victim from the immediate community of his murderers to humanity in general, the fact remains that in the collective singing and prayer of even a tiny fragment of this virtual community the collective presence of the congregation suffices to make manifest the power of the divinity to compel this presence, and thus functions to "purge" its individual members of the desire bound up in their personal "esthetic" representation of God as accessible through his name and the images attached to it.[4] A theory of ritual catharsis that fails to account for such phenomena cannot explain the evident continuity between primitive and modern religion in this regard. Because the institutional theory of representation relies wholly on ritual to provide the forms of cultural significance, it is unable to explain the evolution of the representative functions of ritual itself, which it can at best attribute to a progressive revelation, itself beyond explanation, of the true character of the sacred.

The emergence of the declarative, like that of ostensive-imperative language, can be assumed to have made a significant contribution to the cathartic function of ritual. It will be recalled that, in its origin, the declarative model expressed the nonavailability of its object in linguistic presence. The nascent declarative form thus lends itself admirably to a "negative theology" in which the only predicates attributable to the sacred are modalities of absence. If prayer involves an imperative use of the sacred name, then a "theology" of this sort, expressing the inaccessibility of the sacred object, would appear to annul the waiting implicit in this imperative. But in ritual this contradiction does not hold any more than that between the presence demanded by the ostensive and the absence required by the imperative. In the secular world this last contradiction is either annulled by the hearer's performance or experienced contemplatively as the paradox of esthetic mimesis; in the domain of ritual the "performance" of the sacred name resolves the contradiction by actualizing the power of its divine referent. Similarly, the ritual use of the declarative, even when its predicate overtly expresses the inaccessibility of its sacred topic, functions as a negative form of ostensive: To collectively predicate the sacred object's absence is at the same time to evoke its presence in what is merely a new form of prayer. Outside of the ritual context, "negative theology" is paradoxical to the point of affectation, defining its object by its undefinability, knowing it only as unknowable, etc. But the assertion of such predicates in ritual provides a catharsis of the desire attached to the sacred being because, as in the case of the ostensive-imperative, the communal presence of ritual is itself a manifestation of the sacred power invested in the object. And here again, examples of such predicates can readily be found in the Judeo-Christian (not to speak of the Hindu-Buddhist) liturgy. "Negative theology" is the extreme form that might be taken by predication on the topic of the sacred; but from the predicates of simple absence or inaccessibility to those which describe in terms at least imaginarily positive (such as all-powerful, eternal, etc.) the transcendent powers attributed to the sacred being, there is no break in continuity. The very *thought* of the sacred object in declarative language will inspire such predicates, just as this thought inspired the evocations of elementary language. Even "negative theology" is already a form of theology, that is, an attempt to possess the sacred within the context-free model provided by the *logos*, or in other terms, to assert its *truth*. But outside of ritual this truth can at best be experienced esthetically because the object is not merely contingently but essentially absent from linguistic presence.

At the beginning of this discussion we defined as necessary but not sufficient precondition for discourse, as opposed to dialogue, the hearer's desire for the prolongation of linguistic presence wherein, lacking the practical means for the appropriation of the referential object, he wishes to prolong his esthetic contemplation of it. In the ritual context this precondition is certainly met, because the sacred being can evidently not be "appropriated" either directly through the functioning of the imperative or on the basis of practical information supplied in the declarative. But an additional condition is also present that is sufficient to motivate the creation of discourse: The linguistic presence of the sacred object is accompanied by the actualization of its powers, so that the prolongation of linguistic presence is at the same time a prolongation of the communal catharsis of the desire generated by its esthetic contemplation. It might be objected that the prolongation of linguistic presence is not in itself a sufficient condition of discourse because discourse is not simply defined by this prolongation. Yet throughout our discussion we have insisted on the impossibility of an a priori formal definition; discourse is not a product of the formal dialectic but a supralinguistic phenomenon each example of which is a unique form. The discursive intention, unlike the intentionality of linguistic forms, has no preestablished model in which to express itself, because it constructs its model from preexisting linguistic forms that are not modified but merely repeated an indefinite number of times. Thus the emergence of discourse cannot depend on any formal innovation. The crucial distinction between a discourse and a mere series of sentences can only be defined institutionally: It is expected that the desire generated within the discourse will be transcended within it. This is the "closure" of discourse, but this "definition" would be of little use were we not able to specify its original institutional context as that of ritual, where the catharsis or transcendence of desire is implicit in its expression. Here the prolongation of linguistic presence is guaranteed by its association with the original communal presence from which it was derived: The motivation on the part of both speaker and hearer (to the extent that these can be distinguished) may be presumed to exist. What must be established is rather the phenomenon of closure, the internalization of catharsis in the discursive intention, which renders it functionally independent of its original ritual context and permits its adaptation to secular situations.

If predication concerning the divinity remains limited by the predicates of "negative theology," a "discourse" consisting of a series of such predications would be no more independent of the ritual context than a liturgical series of sacred names. Predication, however, unlike mere naming, is a temporalizing activity; the imaginary model constructed by the predicate includes its topic in a fictive temporality independent of that of linguistic presence. Now the practice of ritual, as here understood, is itself temporal because it reproduces an event taking place in real time, and this temporality is oriented toward the final catharsis accomplished in the sacrifice, the entire reproduction being conceived as falling under the direction of the sacred object. But at the same time, this oriented temporality is also that of the genesis of the sacred in the sacralization of this object; and sacralization, in the original event, is nothing other than rendering inaccessible to appropriation by the members of the community. The "theological" predicates, in other words, may be made to apply directly to the *conclusion* of the original event, where the sacred object is indeed inaccessible but at the same time all-powerful, etc., this sacred status corresponding to the end of the process of catharsis in which the acts of mimetic rivalry, including the killing of the sacrificial victim, are carried to a nonviolent conclusion. But if in the original event the powers of the sacred object to compel nonviolence were in fact created through the unpremeditated act of the collectivity as a whole in designating the remains of their victim, in the ritual reproduction of this event, even if the victim is specifically identified with the sacred object as an "incarnation" of it, the sacred power is not conceived as created anew ex nihilo, but as present from the beginning and presiding throughout over its recreation by the community. The sacralization of the original victim, his acquisition of sacred power coincident with his transcendent inaccessibility to appropriation by the others, cannot be conceived as the result of the original murder, because the entire sacralizing process of the original event is now reproduced as nonviolent, that is, under the aegis of the sacred. Thus, at every moment of the ritual, nonviolent communal presence is guaranteed by the presence of the sacred object; at the same time the ritual as a whole leads to the final catharsis in which the participants reproduce the peace-bringing conclusion of the preliminary crisis. *The ritual is structured like a discourse.* But this structure, in the absence of appropriate linguistic expression, cannot be thought by the participants themselves; it consists in a series of acts dictated by collective memory, as realized in previous repetitions.

The predications of "negative theology" correspond, on the one hand, to the situation of the sacred object in general; but on the other, they express the final catharsis in which the power of this object has manifested itself in communal harmony. The preceding stage of the ritual portrays, not this harmony but the collective murder in which the original victim, represented by a sacrificial substitute, is set upon by his fellows, charged with having himself instigated the general crisis. At this point the victim is the object of the desire of each participant in the ritual, yet he is at the same time inaccessible to them as individuals because he (or it) is the property of the sacred being to whom he is sacrificed. Insofar as the ritual reproduces the original event, the members each desire to appropriate the remains of the victim; insofar as this reproduction is performed within a communal presence guaranteed by the preexistence of the sacred being, the victim is a priori inaccessible to this desire. But this inaccessibility is not of the same nature as that of the sacred object. The latter possesses a transcendent status, independent of its role in ritual, of which it is in fact the guarantee; thus absence from the real context of linguistic presence may be truly predicated of it. In contrast, the ritual victim acquires its significance only from its ritual role. Its inaccessibility to desire is a function of this role, in which it is treated as the cause of communal strife and therefore the worthy object of what Girard calls "la violence unanime." Now if the elements of this role be expressed in declarative language, these attributions will be made in the form of predicates; the inaccessibility of the victim will not be expressed thematically, as may be that of the sacred object as such, but formally, by the mere fact of its topical position in a declarative. For the declarative model, as we have seen, whatever its practical usefulness to the hearer in his quest for the topical object, requires him to first situate the object in a "context-free" present separated from the immediacy of linguistic presence. The sacrificial victim as a real being is not indeed inaccessible at all, but in its ritual role it is designated as inaccessible to appropriation by the members of the community, just as was the original victim in the first instance of communal presence. This role is not, however, a static one, but one of becoming; the "guilty" victim of the murder is in the final catharsis the representative of the sacred being whose transcendent status may be directly predicated of it. The space between these two predications, however diversely they may be expressed, is the original space of self-substantive discourse.

In discourse the becoming of ritual is translated into language, in a process that is a first at least potentially extrinsic *understanding* of ritual, and consequently a first step toward de-ritualization, which is nothing other than the usurpation of the functions of ritual by discourse. At the moment we have just described, the ritual is unchanged; all that has happened is that a series of two or more predicates have been applied, in temporal sequence, to the same topic. The enormous cultural significance of this development, second only in importance to the birth of language in the original event, must be made clear.

The speaker of the original discourse has not been defined as distinguishable from the community qua collective subject of ritual. There is no need to dwell on the question of how such utterances may have originated, because they merely express in declarative form what was doubtless already expressed in elementary language by successive "names" of the sacred object. Not that we should mechanically assume that the existence of the declarative form will cause speakers to "translate" their earlier ostensive utterances into the declarative. To designate the victim is to express only the significance of its presence; to call it by a sacred name is to invoke the presence in it of the (absent) sacred object; but to predicate of it guilt or holiness is to include it in a temporalized model that expresses both its real presence and its absence from the immediate context of desire. In their origin such predications, including those of the final catharsis, may be imagined to be merely auxiliary elements of ritual action. But their esthetic functioning makes them potential objects of contemplation in themselves, as so to speak a linguistic realization of the acts being performed, so that the temporal progression of the entire ritual may be accompanied by a series of predications having for topic the original victim-become-sacred-being and applied in the ritual performance to its sacrificial representative. Both in content and in form this process will vary from one ritual to the next; its only necessary features, which are those constitutive of the intentional structure of discourse in general, are these: There must be at least two different predications of the same topic, in a chronological order parallel to the historical order of the reenacted event and therefore capable of serving as a model of it; and the first predicate must arouse a desire concerning the topic which is fulfilled or "purged" in the second. This second condition defines what we have called the "closure" of discourse: its self-sufficient generation and "purgation" of desire. In the ritual context as such this closure does not yet exist because the conclusion is dependent on the fulfillment provided by the sacrifice: The series of predicates remains a reflection of the temporal process of ritual. But once the discursive model has come into being it will tend to develop from a mere auxiliary of ritual into an independent form separable from it and subject to further elaboration. It suffices for this that the declarative be contemplated in itself within the linguistic presence provided by the ritual. The discursive model will then function esthetically in parallel to the progress of the ritual, not merely commenting on it but providing its own internal catharsis as a supplement to it, so that it may be (as many myths are in religious practice) incorporated within it as a quasi-independent element, subject to being taken up independently by a speaker outside the ritual context, if only for the purpose of teaching it to new participants. The final sacralization is, within ritual, the moment of catharsis which the discursive model at first merely reflects, but the predication that reflects the ritual catharsis at the same time effects an independent catharsis within the discursive model. Thus discourse can evolve without conflict with ritual, acting merely as a supplement to it, while preparing its own eventual independence.

The key to the genesis of self-substantive discourse is the fact that the temporalized predicates of the declarative express within linguistic time, and hence in principle independently of the temporality of the ritual, the succession of presents through which the sacrificial victim represents the career of the original victim, of whom it is now known in advance, as it was not in the original event, that he will "become" in the end the sacred being without whom the reproduction could not exist. Ritual is already a fiction, and the expression of this fiction in discourse merely doubles in language what was already not only performed in deed but planned from the beginning in memory. This virtual presence of the end in the beginning is a constitutive feature of discourse; the two predicates of our minimal formulation are not the result of two but of a single intention, so that when the first is expressed, the second is already virtually present to the speaker. In the collective situation of ritual the speaker or *subject* of this intention is identical to the community as a whole; but as soon as discourse becomes partially independent of the ritual situation, even to the extent of being assigned to a single specialized speaker or group of speakers, the fundamental asymmetry of discursive speaker and hearer, or subject and other, becomes explicit. It should, however, be noted that the explicit separation of speaker and hearer is no more necessary to the esthetic functioning of discourse than of ritual. For, in effect, even when the community as a whole is both subject and other of ritual, its temporal progression toward catharsis is guaranteed not by the ritual enactment, but by the preexisting authority of the sacred object/being. In effect, the collective subject of ritual, *and the subject of discourse as well*, are merely acting out a role dictated by the sacred being. This is the crucial point in our characterization of discourse as an essentially institutional phenomenon. The subject of discourse finds the guarantee of his asymmetric position in the a priori existence of the sacred. In his role as speaker he occupies the place of the sacred being in ritual, mediating the desire of the participants for the sacrificial victim, so that instead of attempting to appropriate it for themselves they must await their portion as a gift of the being to whom it has been consecrated.

The "triangular" esthetic of discourse reflects the divinely ordered fiction of ritual. But even when discourse has become independent of ritual, the role of the subject retains the primordial asymmetry inherited from its institutional origin. Discourse has evolved in many directions, and in its de-temporalized logicoscientific varieties its subject claims to guarantee his role entirely through the truths explicitly affirmed within it. But his assumption of this role is necessarily anterior to the guarantee he provides, and would therefore be unthinkable without the prior existence of discourse as an institution inherited from ritual. This is not, however, to claim that discourse must itself remain blind to the nature of these origins, as though it were unable to survive in the absence of a sacred guarantee of its authority. The discourse of the natural sciences offers its own internal guarantees of coherence, the temporal sequence of its manifestation in linguistic presence becoming a model, not of a fictional temporality available to the subject only by virtue of a ultimately sacred status, but of a de-temporalized, logical series. This a posteriori guarantee being sufficient, the question of an a priori guarantee does not arise, which is not, however, to say that such a guarantee does not exist, or that it could simply be dispensed with. But in the "critical" discourse of human science as we conceive it, founded on a theory of representation which is required to justify its own status as a form of discourse purporting to explain the origins of discourse-in-general, the problem of the a priori guarantee is indeed a crucial one; and were we obliged to evoke in justification of it the powers of the sacred, our theory could make little claim to scientific status. But in our hypothesis these powers are ultimately derived from the community, having become present to itself in the original event; and this communal presence is the only "institutional" guarantee absolutely required by discourse. In the modern era the postulation of the virtual existence of a communal presence detached from any explicit form of sacralization is not only a prerequisite of discourse but the sole means of understanding our everyday experience of the social exchange-system within which we live.

The Esthetic of Discourse-in-General

Discourse, born in ritual, becomes independent of it and eventually, we may assume, of sacred subject-matter in general. But once outside the ritual context, the guarantee provided by this context of the "absolute" effectiveness of the final catharsis is lost; in its place is only the closure of the discourse. Closure is, however, not defined by any "objective" criteria independent of the particular discourse to which it applies; it is measured only a posteriori by the latter's success in effecting the catharsis of the desire generated within it. Thus nonritual discourse, even including myth, is not definable within any limits or constraints specifiable in advance. It can only be understood as an institutional, not a formal structure, so that any criteria of "well-formedness" that we may wish to apply to it can only be historical in origin; and this means that the discursive intention, although its preexisting products may fall within the categories defined by these criteria, cannot in principle be bound by them. There are norms of discourse but no grammar; sentences are correct or incorrect, but discourses are merely effective or ineffective, even though the production of an ineffective discourse at a given moment may be severely stigmatized. The norms of discourse, like its origin, are institutional, whereas the norms of linguistic forms are, within the margin defined by optional redundancies, variant forms, etc., defined by the intentional structure of the forms. Thus beyond narrow limits of tolerance, an ill-formed sentence simply is not a sentence and cannot function as one, whatever its speaker's intention, whereas the discursive intention as such provides at least an a priori guarantee of discursive status. In the "serious" practical, ritual, and even esthetic uses of discourse, the purely formal nature of this guarantee is seldom put to the test because the institution of discourse cannot function without certain norms of effectiveness, broadly or narrowly defined according to the situation. But the liberty of the discursive intention with respect to its content may always be asserted in indefinably radical departures from these norms, such as occur in particular in the esthetic realm. A poet may call anything he pleases a poem, even a passage copied from the telephone directory. Such trivial demonstrations of the purely formal nature of the discursive intention, inherently unconstrained even by the "sincere" desire of the subject to produce a genuine effect, are generally intended rather to produce that of scandal. But this scandal is a sign of the institutional rather

than formal basis, not merely of the current norms to which
the various genres of discourse are subject, but of the existence of discourse in general. And far from being confined to
such extreme cases, scandal is at least implicit in the effect of
all creative innovation in discursive form. Quite unlike linguistic forms, which realize their intention simply by
adhering to the norms defined by this intention, discourse
can only realize its intention of closure, which is also an
intention of effectiveness, by violating more or less radically
the preestablished norms that define the expectation of its
audience. Each instance of discourse is, as we have said, a
separate form; and we now see that this designation is not
merely an arbitrary postulation of our theory, but a description of the manner in which discourse necessarily functions
in a worldly context.

The inherent freedom of the subject of discourse does not,
however, prevent us from formulating in general terms (the
degree of generality of which will, of course, have to be more
precisely defined) the norms within which the intentional
structure of discourse has tended to operate under the
partially de-ritualized conditions of what we may call "traditional" society. In this intermediate state between the
primitive and the modern, the norms that divide discourses
into fairly well-defined "genres" are determined, not, as in
language proper, by the formal needs of communication, but
by the historical derivation of discourse from ritual. Ultimately, the theoretical significance of these norms is founded
on the empirical evidence of their functioning, as is the case
for the phenomena of "traditional society" in general, which
in the realm of the human sciences are accessible only to the
mixed or intermediary methodology of what may simply be
called "history," which seeks, without ever being able to
achieve it, the rigor that is at least theoretically possible in
both anthropology on the one hand and sociology on the
other. Any definition of the limits of "traditional society"
can, however, only be, like those of discourse, a virtual or
"intentional" one. From the standpoint of "metaphysics," in
which anthropology and sociology can in principle attain the
perfect rigor of detemporalized models, all of the real
history of mankind can be included within these limits[5] :

De-ritualization begins at the first moment of history, and is never wholly complete. But, in the perspective presented here, because de-ritualization is itself a quantitative phenomenon proceeding by stages, our intentional models of discourse, derived as they are from the ritual reproduction of the original event, permit the extension of the domain of the anthropological indefinitely forward under the empirical guarantee of history, until it rejoins the "sociological" domain of modernity. This is possible because the separation between history and its origin, or between traditional and "primitive" society, is not an ever-widening chasm in which discourse evolves increasingly far from its ritual source, only becoming a genuine cultural expression from the moment at which this origin is in some undefined sense "forgotten." Rather the evolution of discourse is circular, so that the liberation of modernity, precisely when it leads to the most radical departures from the traditional norms, consists in the conscious or unconscious rediscovery of the original ritual sources of these norms.

Ritual, like the discourse directly derived from it, is *diegetic*: Its chronology reproduces a real chronology, so that its temporal direction and, less precisely, the temporal distance between any two moments of the ritual model correspond to a similar direction and distance in the referent. The time of ritual is that of an event, in which the community as a whole participates. In discourse, however, in its minimal state at least, the model is composed of two or more predicates attached in temporal sequence to the sacred victim, representing two or more moments in the transformation undergone in the course of this event. Thus the minimal state of discourse is inherently more schematic than the ritual from which it is derived, and which even in its most primitive state involved not merely the becoming of the victim-divinity but the collective action of the participants in the sacrifice. These actions may, of course, be included in the discursive model, as may any significant facts of the situation, but they are not necessary to it, whereas they are the very heart of ritual. For discourse expresses the esthetic of ritual, not its practice, in which the community realizes the desire generated within this esthetic as the will of the sacred being. The role performed by the sacrificial victim is that of the original victim, but in ritual this role is a passive one that can be played just as well by an animal or even a plant, whereas in discourse it is the active role of a god or hero. This is not merely an empirical observation; it is already evident from our description of the "minimal discourse." Ritual and discourse, which can at this stage appropriately be called myth, give divergent roles to the central figure because the first must realize in the physical world a catharsis which in the second is wholly representational. Thus in ritual the mimetic rivalry of the community is acted out upon the sacrificial victim in the nonviolent presence of the sacred object, whereas in mythic discourse the "triangular" desire aroused by predication is transcended in the final sacralization.

Discourse in its origin is not a rival, but a supplement to ritual; nevertheless, its explicit expression of the esthetic element of ritual tends to promote contemplation as opposed to the active participation of the latter. This is not, of course, the action of an external "influence," but an evolution of ritual itself, discourse being merely an instrument of the self-understanding of its participants. Thus as the god/hero's story is made to supplement and only very gradually to supplant the sacrificial act, the participants are not being seduced by discourse from their communal undertaking. Rather, they are being given through its agency a more satisfactory understanding of the meaning of their act, and for this reason a more satisfactory catharsis. Once the sacrificial victim is not a mere ad hoc equivalent of its model, but a chosen representative, the predicates that attach to it no longer truly have it as their topic, but the original victim, whose "story" in fact provides the axis along which the temporality of ritual progresses. The becoming-explicit of the "story" in discourse constitutes a first reflection on this temporality, separated in its discursive model from the communal (and linguistic) presence of the ritual activity. But once it acquires an independent existence, mythic discourse will tend to detach itself from the temporality of ritual, which it never really describes, because even in the minimal case its model gives the active role to the victim-divinity rather than to the community that, both in the original event and in the practice, if not the "ideology" of ritual, is the agent of both its immolation and its consecration. This "ideology," before the advent of true discourse, or even of the ostensive-imperative evocations of the divinity mentioned above, was simply the fearful sentiment of the presence of the sacred object, the "powers" of which (for us) are merely those of communal presence. In discourse this "ideology" becomes a myth, that is, a falsification, but at the same time it is at least an attempt at understanding what was previously consigned to the silence of the ineffable.

The theoretical opposition between the respective partisans of ritual and myth is founded on the ambiguity of this development. In a gesture of great significance for the "institutional" anthropology to which our own theory owes so much, Girard has defended the cause of ritual against Lévi-Strauss's championing of myth as a privileged locus, not indeed of truth but of "structure." Ritual is more significant because more primordial than myth, which derives from it, falsifies it and indeed "structuralizes" it. By hiding the moment of violence in which the sacred is constituted, myth produces a rationalized version of the original event which tends to reduce it to a set of exchanges among sacred roles or beings, and therefore not only makes possible but is analogous to Lévi-Strauss's own combinatorial analysis, within which a given myth is shown to be equivalent to another under a specified series of transformations. The strength of the institutional theory in this crucial debate is in its defense of the primordiality of ritual, which it rightly situates between the origin and the myths that purport to explain it; its weakness is, however, also apparent. For its rejection of the discourse of myth is at the same time an affirmation of the explicative power of its own discourse as applied to the very same ritual object, so that in condemning the passage from ritual to myth it condemns the historical progression that led to its own emergence. This is not a mere idiosyncrasy of Girard but a demonstration of the imperfectly critical nature (in the Kantian sense) of the institutional theory. For if discourse is merely a derivative of ritual, instead of the product, as it has been presented here, of the interaction between the formal evolution of language and the institutional phenomenon of ritual, its historical growth must be seen as a departure from or "forgetting" of ritual, and thereby of the origin, rather than as the circular movement of its understanding.[6]

From the formal perspective, myth's attribution to divine agency of the origin of nonviolent communal presence and the benefits that accrue from it, although it certainly expresses a "forgetting" of the original human violence that is preserved in ritual, is nevertheless a progressive rather than regressive development. For it is an error to consider the "ideology" of ritual as less false, and consequently as somehow truer, simply because it is unexpressed. In the first place, it *is* expressed by the very designation of the original victim which is subsequently lexicalized as the first element of language. The institutional theory fails to grasp the strict contemporaneity of the origin of language and ritual, conceiving of the former as simply a byproduct of the latter, as though the "powers" of the sacred object could be attributed to it without the mediating agency of representation. Thus is locates the falsity of ritual not in its "ideology" but in the substitution of a sacrificial victim for the original victim, a substitution that is itself already a "forgetting" of the original event, as the progression from human to animal and other "symbolic" substitutes makes clear.[7] Yet these substitutions are also the sign of a growing moral consciousness that is an at least implicit repudiation of the violence of the origin. The basic contradiction of the institutional theory at this essential juncture is that the "forgetting" of original violence is on the one hand the (bad) falsification of myth, but on the other the (good) progression toward nonviolence.[8] The formal theory avoids this contradiction, or at the very least relocates it within the domain of historical contingency. Discourse is the product of a higher level of representational evolution that the designation of the original sacred object in what was at the same time the first "ideological" expression. Its supplementing relation to ritual is at the very least an opening to nonviolence through the substitution of esthetic contemplation for sacrificial participation, although the course of history has shown that it may also provide an ideological defense of accrued violence, both in and out of the ritual context. But no theory that is itself unavoidably a discursive communication can coherently refuse to postulate the ultimate access of discourse to the truth of human representation, which is at the same time the truth of its own origin.

We will gain a better understanding of the "ideological" function of pararitual or mythical discourse if we examine more closely the diegetic model it derives from ritual. The correspondence between the internal temporality of the discursive model and that of its referent (that is, the time of the *énonciation* and that of the *énoncé*) is not in itself a sufficient characterization of discursive intentionality, which in addition seeks to produce a final catharsis analogous to that of ritual. The merely naturalistic description of this catharsis as the generation and annulment (satisfaction or transcendence) of desire, which is the basis for the various recent attempts at a formal narratology, fails to understand either desire or its place in the esthetic relation. As we have seen, the topical "hero" of discourse, in the minimal case described above, passes from the status of declarative topic per se, the object of communal desire whose "presence" in the discursive model makes him inaccessible within linguistic presence, to that of a sacred being of whom inaccessibility is directly predicated, but who at the same time becomes present to the community through his nonviolent "super-vision" of the entire ritual process culminating in the sacrifice. Thus the sacred being exists on two levels in discourse: as the "hero" who undergoes sacralization and as the guarantor of the whole process whose power is revealed in its successful completion. In this second role it is not the sacrificial victim but the speaker, collective or individual, who substitutes for the sacred being. The final catharsis is a transfiguration in which the "hero" acquires within the discursive model the transcendental quality of inaccessibility to desire which the model itself originally possessed in relation to the real world of linguistic presence, this originary transcendence characteristic of the "fictive" discursive model having been, so to speak, entrusted to the speaker by the transcendent being whose story is being told.

It is thus not sufficient to speak of the annulment of the desire generated in the model; the catharsis of discourse is only accomplished in the model because at the end of the story the hero is just as inaccessible in the fictional world of the model as in the real world of linguistic presence. In order to better define precisely in what this inaccessibility consists, we should recall that the original predication concerning the "hero," as represented in ritual by the sacrificial victim, charges him with the instigation of the original communal crisis, which is to say, with being *through his own desire* at the origin of mimetic rivalry, e.g., by bringing disease or bad luck on the on the community as a whole. Hence in the conclusion his acquisition of transcendent status is in effect a liberation from desire. From the guilty rival of the other members of the community, the hero-victim becomes their divine benefactor whose inaccessibility to their own desires merely reflects the sacred status that places him above desire. In the original event sacralization followed on inaccessibility to appropriation; in discourse, as in ritual, this process is reversed. But whereas in ritual sacrifice the victim, after playing the role of its now sacralized original model, is divided up among the participants under the auspices of this model, in discourse the original identity of victim and model is preserved. In the ritual catharsis the transcendent sacred object presides over his own dismemberment and ingestion, whereas in that of discourse, his becoming transcendent itself provides the catharsis, any "tragic" punishment he may suffer being secondary to the termination of his role as mimetic rival to the other members of the community.

The Genres of Discourse

The foregoing discussion has considered the origin of discourse in the ritual context as limited to its narrative form or genre, in which the speaker is distinct from the subject of the action. But the dramatic and lyric genres, which, as we shall see, exhaust the primary possibilities of temporalized discourse (although they may be recombined in any variety of ways), are also derived from ritual. The primacy of the narrative genre is due to the fact that it is the first genre the esthetic effect of which can become, within the ritual context, separable from the catharsis performed by the ritual. The discursive space once created, it can no longer be filled by ritual action because it exists purely within linguistic representation. This is not, as we shall see, the case for the other genres.

The *lyric* genre has already, in a sense, been touched on in our discussion of the ostensive-imperative esthetic. The evocation of the sacred object by the participants in ritual is already a preliminary form of the lyric. For us to be able to speak of discourse proper, this evocation must acquire esthetic closure. Such may be the case in the series of the "names" of the divinity to which we have alluded. But this example makes clear the problematic nature of lyric discourse within a ritual context—a problem that also extends to the dramatic. The evocations of the participants may indeed form a series, but only the presence of the sacred object can be said to provide satisfaction to the desire expressed in these evocations. Thus each separate naming receives its own catharsis in the manifestation of the "powers" of the divinity, the ostensive-imperative (or "inappropriate-ostensive") esthetic not permitting of the construction of a context-free model.

A preliminary analysis of the *dramatic* element of ritual leads to the same conclusion. The separate roles of the participants in the reproduction of the original crisis and its conclusion, which on the evidence of even the most primitive rituals known to ethnographers are often quite highly individualized, may be accompanied by some form of linguistic expression. But even in the case of the mature dramatic forms familiar to us, the words of the participants are pronounced in a context of action, and it is this action that provides the catharsis of their expressed desires. The classification of drama as "discourse" is thus always partly unsatisfactory, although in a nonritual context its status as a *fiction* is unquestionable. But in ritual the acts of the participants, although reproductive of those of the original event, can never be unambiguously defined as "fictional"—that is, as purely representative—because the communal presence in which they take place cannot be partitioned into a space or "scene" of representation and a space of esthetic contemplation. Even when nonparticipating spectators are present, the ritual performance never, save in the most degraded cases, is simply given for their esthetic pleasure.

It thus appears from this preliminary discussion that the narrative genre provides the only formally differentiable example of discourse within ritual. But we need not remain on the level of formal distinctions. Discourse, as we have throughout affirmed, is not a form but an institutional phenomenon. The apparently ambivalent status of the narrative genre as, on the one hand, the prototypical or "unmarked" variety of discourse from which the detemporalized discourse of philosophy and science is directly descended, and on the other, merely one of three fundamental genres of temporalized discourse manifesting itself in the literatures of different societies, is an artifact of the preliminary stage of our theoretical exposition. The fact that, in the present form at least of our theory, this ambivalence must unavoidably be introduced if only to be eliminated in the subsequent discussion is nevertheless worthy of a passing comment. The genres of discourse, unlike the forms of language, are not the product of a (proto-)historical dialectic. But in the rationalistic vision of culture characteristic of metaphysics and, insofar as they do not prudently avoid the question of genesis, the social sciences as well, narrative discourse, bypassing the other genres, becomes the dialectical successor of the declarative. In the de-ritualized context of modern society, narrative theoretical discourse alone can be said to survive as a living genre, so that the elimination of the other genres from consideration would appear to permit the construction of a dialectic in which the highest form is chronologically last and provides the means for understanding the others. Were this indeed the case, all empirical-historical considerations stemming from the institutional aspect of culture could be eliminated. But this theoretical utopia is, appearances to the contrary, incompatible with an authentic formal theory of representation. Without the

nondialectical, or more accurately, para-dialectical evolution
of discourse, the ultimate convergence of the variety of the
world's cultures into a single exchange-system, and their at
least potential description by means of a single theory, would
be inconceivable. The formal simplicity of linguistic forms
and their universal presence, with only superficial variations,
in all human societies is not a sufficient foundation for this
ultimate theoretical and practical unity, for the significant
content expressed within these forms has not yet been
included in the historical process. Only through discourse can
this content, organized in structures of desire, eventually
attain expression. But the process whereby this is accomplished is not reducible to a formal dialectic, because it is
subject in each specific case to the a posteriori criterion of
esthetic effect from which alone the logical criteria of
detemporalized (scientific) discourse could evolve. The existence of the lyric and dramatic genres should remind us that
the esthetic closure of discourse is determined not by formal
criteria but by those of desire. In discourse the genesis of
desire is never the exclusive property of linguistic form,
because the topics therein presented, even when purely fictional, can generate no interest in the audience unless they
correspond in some way to its preexistent preoccupations.
Only in the discourse of theory, where the world of these
preoccupations is itself taken as the object of analysis, can
the creation of a fully self-subsistent model be even
attempted; but the complete closure of theory is inconceivable lacking the closure of the world.

The esthetic closure of discourse is institutional, not
formal; yet the existence of discursive genres need not lack a
theoretical basis. The key to the theory of genres lies in what
we may call their "pseudo-formalization," that is, their
reduction *in esse* to their historical origins within the process
of ritual, it being always understood that in practice they
may depart indefinitely from these formal essences, or
combine with each other in various ways. The activity of
literary criticism, which may be distinguished from hermeneutics by its necessary preoccupation with generic essences
(hermeneutics is indifferent to these, because it seeks beyond
ritual the traces of the origin), can then be seen as that

analysis by which a specific literary text is made to reveal the
latent possibilities of its genre, the ultimate saturability of
generic essences being, if not an explicit postulate of criticism
(the rhetorical posture of which most often implies, or even
affirms the opposite), nevertheless its theoretical precondition.[9] These pseudo-formal essences themselves may be
defined as discursive analogues of the ritual process, conceived not as a (re-)sacralizing, but as an esthetic operation,
which is to say, not insofar as it reproduces the original
event, but insofar as it *represents* it. (We are here concerned
only with linguistic means of representation, but the evolution of the other arts may likewise be referred, and must be if
a "criticism" of their productions is to be attempted, to
pseudo-formal essences of a similar kind.) The three genres
can then be seen to correspond in esse to the three esthetics
expressed or expressible in ritual, which realizes them (or
effects their "closure") on three levels of catharsis.

1. The dramatic genre corresponds to the level of mimetic
   rivalry, the linguistic expression of which is only
   secondary, and the catharsis of which is realized in the
   sacrifice. This is the "zero degree" of the esthetic; but
   the absence of formal evolution, or more properly the
   regression to the original designation of the "sacred"
   object, may be taken as the sign of the greatest esthetic
   potential.

2. The lyric genre corresponds to the level of esthetic
   mimesis, expressible as we have seen in elementary
   (ostensive-imperative) language, as may indeed be
   employed in the liturgical evocation of the sacred
   object, the presence of which in ritual effectuates
   its catharsis.

3. The narrative or "epic" genre corresponds to the level
   of "triangular" desire, as expressed in the declarative,
   the possible emergence of which in the ritual context
   has already been discussed at some length.

It is immediately evident from this schematic representation why the narrative genre is the "unmarked" prototype of
discourse-in-general. The triangular esthetic of the declarative
is not "natural" to ritual because it operates by means of
linguistic models formally separated from the communal

presence realized in ritual. The alliance between discourse and ritual is from the beginning an uneasy one, and, whatever its success, the first can never be merely absorbed into the second. This assertion is in a sense tautological, as we have defined the genesis of discourse as corresponding to the emergence of a catharsis internal to the model that, in the minimal case, consists of two temporally distinct predications on the sacred hero/god as topic. But the fact remains that only the repeated declarative form lends itself to this condition, which cannot be imposed on the proto-lyric or proto-dramatic elements within ritual. And that this definition is no mere arbitrary construct is evident from the existence of the narrative form both in association and in opposition with ritual.

The order of appearance of the three genres in our scheme is the inverse of their historical emergence as literary forms, at least if the Greek model may be taken as canonical. But not only should this inversion not surprise us, it provides us with a model of the circularity of the history of discourse as a whole, at the same time revealing the limits of the purely literary phase of this history. The genre that expresses the most "primitive" esthetic is the last to emerge as a discursive phenomenon detached from ritual for the simple reason that its esthetic is the one most completely fulfilled by ritual. The existence of drama is then rightly taken as an infallible sign of socially traumatic deritualization, or "sacrificial crisis." Narrative discourse, or myth, is the first to differentiate itself from ritual, but the two coexist peacefully in their different domains. The rise of the lyric signifies not in the first place the rise of "individualistic" desire incompatible with communal ritual, as the literary historians are wont to affirm, confusing cause and effect in a typically ad hoc manner (the content of a given literary form always being supposed to provide the "impulse" for that form's existence), but rather the inadequacy of the communal presence of ritual to satisfy the mimetic esthetic of the "inappropriate ostensive" by evoking in its participants a sense of the presence of the divinity. In drama the original ritual catharsis is itself called into question. If the pseudo-formal essence of drama requires not words, but acts, it is then all the more significant that in dramatic discourse these acts are explained and discussed in words. Dialogue, with its indefinitely meta-representational potential, is substituted for the original symmetry of conflict, with the result that the ultimate return to the original resolution—the "sacrifice" of the tragic hero—exemplifies the inevitable circularity of supra-linguistic constructions that belies their formal freedom.[16]

The further elaboration of the historical consequences of this schema belongs to the domain of literary history proper; here it will suffice merely to indicate in what manner the pseudo-formal essences we have described may be converted into intentional structures. In ritual, of course, the problem of intentionality is never posed; once it arises, as in proto-narrative discourse, we have left the domain of ritual *proprement dit*. In contrast, discourse cannot exist without a controlling Subject, who outside the ritual context can no longer simply be identified with the sacred being. It is indeed by the specific relation between this Subject and the other participant "subjects" or "protagonists" of discourse that the genres are most commonly, and simply, distinguished: In the narrative form, the Subject speaks about the hero; in the lyric, the two are identical; and in drama, the Subject lets the hero and his "doubles" fight it out among themselves. We should note that even this informal characterization reveals that the three genres exhaust the possible relations between Subject and protagonists: Literary discourse is construed as the utterance of the former, the latter, or both together. These relations from a saturated schema that may be placed in correspondence with the schema of pseudoformal essences given above.

1. In the dramatic genre the Subject stands above the mimetic rivalry of the characters, only assuring the final (sacrificial) resolution. Thus the Subject maintains the transcendental role of the sacred being, which guarantees the ritual process from without, whereas the characters incarnate the community in crisis. The linguistic element in drama expresses only individual desire, cut off from the silent Subject who guarantees the closure of the whole. But whatever the linguistic

forms used, the esthetic of drama remains that of
mimetic conflict, resolved, as in the original event,
through the designation and elimination of the perturbing element—either the (tragic) protagonist himself or a
(comic) contingent feature shared by one or more characters in their roles as desiring subjects. This esthetic is
prelinguistic or more precisely proto-linguistic; yet
because it depends on designation to put an end to the
conflict, it is a true form of *representation*, distinct
from the ritual *reproduction* of the original event in
which the sacrificial victim is designated in advance. Of
course the Subject/author "knows" in advance the outcome of the conflict, and the spectators as well may be
given to expect it, but the crucial point is that the
designation takes place in the course of the dramatic
representation; that is, it emerges as the necessary and
"rational" resolution of the mimetic conflict, the ratio-
nality of this resolution constituting a "forgetting" of
the arbitrary violence of the original event. Designation
is the representative principle of drama, and ultimately
it is only of secondary interest whether the "victim" be
a unique protagonist or merely an excessive element of
desire. The drama ends with an establishment of universal order from which desire as such has been eliminated.
But there is no well-defined representational form for
the expression of this elimination, which in extreme
cases (such as the "theater of the absurd") may be
realized only in its absence, the nonresolution of the
dramatic conflict indicating a failure of designation, or
in the classic case of *Waiting for Godot*, its fixation on
an absent, and thus already inaccessible being. In terms
of what we may call the "institutional form" of drama
all that is required is a scene of representation, the
progression from conflict to resolution being the
responsibility of the playwright, and thus a historical
contingency out of the reach of the deductions of a
formal dialectic. It is for literary criticism to reestablish
the link between the historical forms of drama and
their ritual origin. The freedom of the work to stray

from its ritual model is entire; but its esthetic requires it to return to this model, not in conscious imitation, but because the resolution of mimetic conflict, in ritual or in drama, can only be accomplished when the community as a whole designates within it some desiring element, essential or contingent, to be removed from the symmetry of rivalry, and thereby from the potentially infinite contestation of dialogue. This designation accomplished, all, and not merely the "victim," rejoin the silence of the Subject.

2. In the lyric genre speech still represents individual desire, as in drama, but this desire is now expressed as that of the Subject, identified not with the sacred being, but rather with one of his supplicants. The esthetic of the lyric is that of the ostensive-imperative appeal to the divinity, utterance of his name-as-attribute being expected to produce his presence. But within the lyric this presence can only be expressed through the expression of still another attribute (or "name"). The lyric is often addressed directly to the object of the Subject's desire, but this is a secondary feature. Within the lyric esthetic the question of *address* is in fact undecidable because the ostensive-imperative evocation, even of a name, is no more "addressed" to its designee than a nominal imperative like "Hammer!" The evocation in linguistic presence is presumed to produce its referent; and in the imaginary universe of discourse, it is precisely this "production" that occurs. But the lyric catharsis is not provided by an actual presence, not even, as in ritual, by the manifestation of the sacred powers of the object which place it out of the reach of individual desire. The language of desire must accomplish this catharsis on its own; the "subjective" language of lyric, unlike that of drama, is not opposed by that of a symmetrically situated other, but must generate its own transcendence in the being of the evoked object. Thus the final silence of the lyric is the "purgation" of esthetic mimesis: The object of desire, evoked by its attributes, reveals its being as

consisting precisely in its otherness, present only by its necessary absence from the realm of worldly desire, the rivalries of which are thereby annulled. The rhythm of lyrical language is derived from the rhythm of ritual, which serves to accentuate the symmetry of the participants' gestures and their integration in an overall nonviolent order. If the lyric more than the other genres retains this rhythm, it is because the expression of subjective desire can only thus provide a guarantee of its harmonious integration into the communal order. Modern poetry has demonstrated that the rhythmic element is merely a conventional, or more properly, institutional feature of the lyric, a survival in fact from its ritual origin; whether or not the lyric can successfully stray so far from its origin is of course an open question. Indeed, free verse parallels in historical time the rise of ethnology and the beginnings of modern society's search for its own origins in ritual.

3. In the narrative form the Subject speaks, but only in the "objective" model of the declarative. Here it is the "topical" protagonist who inhabits the temporal world of desire, and the final catharsis is achieved by a transcendence of desire which liberates him from timebound predicates. As in the lyric, language generates its own transcendence, but narrative language performs this task through the intermediary of the fictional model that it constructs in the "context-free" form of the declarative. The protagonist-"victim" of narrative, unlike that of drama, is unproblematically designated from the outset because the narrative catharsis corresponds to a sacralization fully separable from designation. The "triangular" esthetic of the narrative, which unlike the other genres implicates the hearer/reader as the addressee of the (declarative) narration, makes it the privileged locus for the thematics of metaphysical desire, the desires of the novelistic hero being assimilated to those of the reader, so that his final liberation from the world of desire is at the same time his and the reader's accession to the "objective" position of the

Subject. It is thus no accident that the narrative form provided Girard with his original model of metaphysical desire.

The pseudo-formal essences from which the three genres were derived correspond to the esthetics of the three linguistic forms in their associations with ritual. We may summarize them by saying that drama represents ritual as a whole; lyric takes the viewpoint of a participant; and narrative, that of an observer who retells it as the story of the victim. In each case the discursive genre reformulates the ritual catharsis as a purely esthetic one. Drama, the most radical of the three, finds its catharsis in designation, and thus regresses from ritual to its source in the original event; the lyric catharsis is achieved in the purely verbal presence of the evoked object as inaccessible to desire; that of the narrative, in the passage of its hero from the plane of mimetic rivalry to that of transcendence. The three genres exhaust both the possible relations between language and desire and the possible esthetics of language, the two formulations being in effect equivalent. We may thus, as "spectators" of the dialectic of linguistic forms, recount its stages in order as examples of the three discursive genres: first the "drama" of mimetic rivalry leading to the designation of the sacred object as the first ostensive; then the inappropriate "lyrical" use of the ostensive creating the imperative; and finally the "narrative" negative-ostensive form as the origin of the declarative. But although in each case the esthetic function of the linguistic form was anterior to its use as a means of communication, the emergence of the explicitly "esthetic" forms of discourse is inconceivable without the preexisting context of ritual in which the prolongation of communal presence, as a value in itself, depends on the inclusion within it of a variety of moments linked together by the collective intention of the whole. And the reproductive unity of ritual, which prefigures the representative unity of discourse, is itself merely a reflection of the functional unity of the event that it reenacts. Without the original instance of noninstinctual attention that, in the hypothesis here presented, was the first moment of human culture, neither ritual nor discourse could have acquired the space, both communal and mental, necessary to their existence.

Temporalization and De-temporalization

Discourse, as it emerged from ritual, was temporalized, as was ritual; its own duration followed the irreversible progress of the rite, which itself followed that of the original event. In each successive case we may presume the rigor of the temporal order to have been intensified: Ritual reproduction brings order to the chaos of the original event, and discourse reduces to a linear linguistic series the collective plurality of ritual. But the central feature of irreversible temporality is already present in the original event: the passage from the violence of mimetic rivalry to the peace of communal presence. The irreversibility of this passage is the key to its significance: Peace is not a mere interlude between battles but a new quasi-permanent acquisition founded on the collective renouncement of appropriative designs on the remains of the "sacred" victim. This before/after dichotomy once established, the other elements of ritual were ordered in terms of their (positive or negative) distance from it, and this same ordering would tend to be reproduced in discourse. The diegetic character of discourse, is, however, different from that of ritual, somewhat in the same way that a digital device differs from an analog one. Although each action of ritual may be conceived as the object of a separate reproductive intention, and although the historical continuity leading from the "sedimentary" series of "original events" to ritual proper and its subsequent evolution must have stretched over many generations, the overall intention of ritual manifests itself in time always as an analogy of the original event.[11] The duration of, for example, a dance representing mimetic conflict might vary, but the dance must at least last long enough to permit the universally perceptible establishment of the participants in their ritual roles. In contrast, discourse is composed of separate utterances the duration of which stands in no a priori relation to that of the action or state represented. This is not to speak of its capacity for representing—the "negative ostensive" is a relevant example—states of affairs to which we can assign no diegetic or referential time whatever. In the practical use of language, where linguistic presence is merely a means, the time occupied by utterances is limited only by physiological and neurological constraints, such as may, for example, be avoided by the use of electronic devices. Even in dialogue conceived as of value in itself, where the subject matter is of secondary importance, the duration of a particular topic may well be a function of its significance for the speakers, but discussion of this topic, unless someone is indeed "telling a story," will not follow a strict diegetic line. Narrative discourse, however, at least in its origin, represents the several moments of its hero's story in the chronological order of ritual. Its own duration is therefore an at least directional model of that of its fictional referent, punctuated by predications referring to specific stages of the narrative; between these points the duration of the discourse corresponds to no specific duration in the referent. This depiction of narrative discourse refers of course only to the pseudo-formal essence defined above. Fictional discourse has evolved a great variety of techniques (flashbacks, descriptive passages, narrator's observations, etc.) which may interrupt or invert the correspondence between the temporality of discourse and that of its fictional referent, although the question may be raised as to whether it is possible for narrative to do away with diegesis altogether—whether indeed, beyond even the question of esthetic effectiveness, it is truly possible to understand a narrative as nondiegetic.

Narrative discourse derives its temporalization directly from ritual. In contrast, de-temporalized or logical discourse is a historical development, the first clear attempts at which are found in the pre-Socratics, although nondiegetic compendia of moral sayings, to which we may attribute a kind of discursive intentionality, are found in Egypt some 2,000 years earlier. The notion of logical rigor does not appear to be much older than Aristotle. In the most rigorous forms of logical discourse propositions are deduced from a set of postulates and axioms which also define the rules of procedure. The temporal order of the deductions is considered to be heuristic only, corresponding to no referential time whatever, the truth of a deduced proposition being in no way a function of the time of its deduction, but depending solely on that of the original postulates. All scientific discourse tends toward this ideal of logical rigor, the observed facts of the real world being deduced "analytically" from the set of axioms which constitute the original hypothesis, and the discourse of the natural sciences can at least be said to approach this ideal. In contrast, the discourse of the human sciences stands in an ambiguous relation to both temporalized and de-temporalized discourse, a relation that must be clarified in order to make clear the status we are here proposing for our own theory.

Logical discourse is analytic and thus in principle tautological. In mathematical or purely logical systems analyticity is associated with atemporality, but this association is not necessary: A temporal system may be analytic as well, provided that no extraneous elements enter the system in the course of its operation. Scientific experiments verify hypotheses under such conditions, but always in time. In sciences like physics and inorganic chemistry, where the subject matter is presumed to be, at least logically, without any history, the inclusion of the temporal dimension in a deductive system is not problematic, all reactions and combinations being reversible within the system. The study of more complex structures (astronomical, geological, biological) cannot thus postulate a reversible temporality. We should do well to observe that when the history of a structure is not reversible in the small (i.e., in the "life and death" of an individual manifestation of the structure, or even a significant time period in its existence), neither is it reversible in the large (in the evolution of structures and systems, galaxies, forms of life, etc.). Even though local disequilibria are resolved and homeostasis maintained—this is the substance of the definition of a "structure" existing in time—not only do all individual structures eventually fail, to be replaced by others, but they also necessarily evolve into different structures, either more or less stable depending on the circumstances. A "law of evolution" expressed in this general way applies equally well to stars as to living creatures. Logical models of evolutionary processes too are possible, and the work of astronomers and geologists is devoted in large measure to their formulation, although as structures gain in complexity the predictive value of such models, which is to say their analyticity in temporal conditions, is increasingly limited to local developments that repeat earlier observations. Only the exhaustive analysis of a structure into components whose behavior can itself be analyzed in a reversible or "detemporalized" model can permit the application of such a model to the structure, but the aleatory interaction of, in particular, living creatures with their environment, which is thereby drawn into the ecosystem constituted around the creature, make the formulation of a de-temporalized model of the existence of even an exhaustively analyzed being inconceivable.

Whatever the difference in their internal mechanisms, the evolution of the forms of human culture obeys the same general law as that of astronomical or biological structures. The discursive systems by which we seek to formulate this evolution would therefore at first glance appear to obey the same laws. The higher natural sciences can never expect to attain the ideal reversibility of logical-mathematical discourse, and one may even wonder whether physics and chemistry will not ultimately confront the same barrier, because there is no reason to assume a priori that molecular or even subatomic structures are exempt from the temporal irreversibility that affects all higher structures.[12] The discourse of these sciences thus contains an element of diegesis even though locally it tends toward reversibility. This mixed condition is, however, more an artifact of our analysis than a reality of natural-scientific discourse. Scientists have no problems of expression; they know without reflection just how "scientific" they can be, which is always at least a shade more than their immediate predecessors. Much has been written on the "philosophy of science," but there is little evidence that scientific discourse has even indirectly benefited from the efforts of philosophers to, in effect, study scientific discourse as a form—which, as we have seen, it is not. This fact should not surprise us; although the norms of logical discourse proper have been given increasingly rigorous definitions (and we shall not attempt to question here the well-foundedness of this process), these norms merely constitute one pole of a continuum between temporalized and de-temporalized discourse, the other pole of which is occupied by the diegetic narrative "essence" as defined within ritual. Even at its maximum point, however, diegetic discourse is not continuously analogous to referential temporality but provides only a discrete or "digital" model of it. The diegetic reference points provided by an irreversible sequence of predicates are always separable, because even single predicates must occupy a nonreferential duration of linguistic deferral, and these separations may be prolonged indefinitely without the thread of discourse being broken. The discourse of the natural sciences seeks to prolong the de-temporalized intervals between the moments of irreversible diegesis, the ultimate source of which is the before/after dichotomy of the original event, just as the original deferral is the ultimate source of the rigorous de-temporalization of logic.

Insofar as the human sciences deal with the questions outside the realm of human representation, their endeavor is fully comparable to that of the natural sciences, from which their discourses differ only in degree. The physiology of man differs little from that of the chimpanzee; and in boundary areas like form-perception it is for the scientists to tell us whether qualitative differences are present. But in the domain of representation proper, which includes very nearly the entire subject matter of what are normally called the "human" or "social" sciences, the situation is rather different and it becomes increasingly so as the relationship between the scientific discourse and its subject matter grows more intimate. The constitution of a theory of natural-scientific representation is at best a regional exercise, not an indispensable adjunct and certainly not a prerequisite of the natural sciences. But the human sciences can be said to begin with a theory of representation, in the form of philosophy, and we would claim that they must also end with one—the present attempt not pretending to be any more than a beginning of this end. The discourse of human science is beset by two first-order *aporia*. On the one hand, there is the problem of *feedback*, because any conclusions reached by scientists eventually fall into the public domain where they can influence the behavior of the human subjects under observation (thus whole classes of experiments in which the subjects must remain ignorant of the experimenter's intention become increasingly difficult to pursue, at least among educated subjects; or on a more significant level, the conclusions of economists or political scientists directly affect the activities they describe).[13] On the other, there is that of *self-reference*, because in formulating a theory of human behavior in general, the scientist ultimately refers to his own, not merely in his everyday, nonscientific activities, but specifically in his role as a producer of scientific discourse. The theory of human culture must include itself as an object of study.

To the extent that human scientists, ignoring or neglecting this problematic, continue nonetheless to produce verifiable models of human behavior, their naivety should no doubt, like that of their cousins the natural scientists, be protected from the strictures of theoreticians who (like the present writer) are not themselves engaged in experimental study. Certainly reflection on these problems need not in itself be a ban to the further production of human scientific discourse. If indeed these problems can be said to define the modern era, then the historical progress of the era can only be accelerated by their actualization, thereby creating a qualitatively new type of formal evolution by which not merely an era but a whole epoch of human history may be said to be brought into being. But for the same reason that psychological experimenters can no longer be assured of the naivety of their subjects—or that psychoanalysts cannot prevent their patients from learning the secrets of Freudian mythology—we cannot protect the naivety of the experimenters. If they do not learn these paradoxes from us they will simply learn them elsewhere. Whatever its self-constructed theoretical justifications, which in themselves can be expected to have as little effect as those of the philosophers of science, if the theory of representation indeed discusses problems that are at the heart of the human sciences, then the human scientists will be obliged to study this theory, or to reconstruct it for themselves. It would then no longer be necessary to discuss in the abstract the appropriate form of the discourse of the human sciences. But this not (yet) being the case, these sciences are as a whole vulnerable to contestation, and their discourse to criticism.

It is intuitively evident that the problems of feedback and of self-referentiality are two aspects of the same phenomenon. If the discourse of the human sciences has the cultural world as its object, it is at the same time a part of this world, and thus is both included in its object (feedback) and as such included in itself (self-reference). If these sciences can flourish with little regard for such matters, it is because their discourse is or conceives itself as being marginal to more substantive worldly concerns, and thus as both constituting a marginal part of its own object and as exercising only a marginal influence on it. This marginality is itself an apparently objective and verifiable fact. After all, experiments continue to be conducted, and even when their aims are openly avowed, the behavior of their subjects is little changed by them; and certainly social science can find other data than itself. This sociological reasoning presupposes a fundamental difference between the discourse of the human sciences and the religious and ideological discourse which has stood in a central, not a marginal position, in all cultures, and which has always for that very reason devoted particular attention to its own place in that culture. Scientific discourse, unlike religious or political dogma, appears only in fragmented form; its marginality is a function of the limited scope of its reference. Thus in the case of any particular contribution, its effect on the whole of a given society, or its importance as a cultural manifestation of that society, may indeed be negligeable.

But this is not true of human scientific discourse taken as a whole, nor is it true of a theory of representation that poses the general problem of the paradoxical posture of this discourse. Once it is recognized that cultural discourse is central, not marginal to human society, and that whatever its natural-scientific pretentions, the discourse of the human sciences is the successor to the cultural discourse of the past, the marginality of local and even regional studies will no longer serve as a sufficient reason for neglecting the problem of self-inclusion. For this problem will no longer appear as a marginal problem in a marginal study, but as a central problem in a central study. This does not mean that the specificity of the objects of individual studies will be eliminated. But this specificity will itself be explicitly guaranteed by a theory of

representation which defines the modern era of sociological
research as precisely that period in which the social sciences
can exist, that is, in which cultural discourse can renounce its
traditional transcendental guarantees and, despite the apparent paradoxality of its self-inclusion, become scientific. Each
fragment of this discourse may then become a part of the
whole, not through a merely optative claim to future "gen-
eralizability," but through the conscious orientation of its
author toward understanding, beyond the specific phenomenon under study, the general character of the society that
makes such studies possible. In the most trivial cases this
orientation can have but little effect on the methods and
conclusions of the study in question. But we may expect
it to produce incremental modifications at successive levels
of generality, until, at the level of the theory of representation, it will provide the very substance of the discussion
of modern society.

The foregoing discussion, more hypothetical than theoretical, has taken us apparently far afield from our anthropological and formal concerns. Yet it has been made clear from the
outset that the actuality of the human sciences is also that of
the origin of human culture. The theory of representation is
not indeed independent of its object at any point of the
discussion, because its genesis is at the same time its subject
matter. The forms of language, in this perspective, are preliminary stages in the development of a theory of language. But
certainly these forms are not in any sense "theories" in
themselves. Ritual, however, is a reproduction of the original
event, and the mythic discourse that represents rather than
reproduces the subject matter of ritual can already by seen as
an esthetic, temporalized "theory," the de-temporalization of
which is not a sudden but a gradual process that, we may well
assume, will never end. Our hypothesis of origin is more
logical than that of myth, but it cannot but appear mythical
in the future light of more powerful theories. This is, however, no reason for not formulating such theories explicitly,
rather than maintaining, on the tacitly accepted basis of the
unknowability of the origin, the superstition of the inexplicable transcendence of language.

Our claim is that all culturally significant discourse is in essence a theory of the origin of culture. In myth such an intention is evident, but even in myth the representation of the original event fragments into an indefinite number of separate etiologies. Such fragmentation, like the related creation of "Pantheons" where originally local, independent gods are set as governors over interdependent cultural domains, is probably more the result of external than of internal differentiation. If our hypothesis is correct, then the original "religion" was monotheistic. Unlike Judeo-Christian monotheism, however, it could not maintain the universal supremacy of its god to the exclusion of others. The joining together of different communities produced polytheism rather than syncretism because the mythical discourse that constituted the "theology" of the different parties to the alliance was insufficient qua theory of the origin to permit of dialectical integration. Instead of two versions of the same original *form*, the primitive mythologizers saw the origins of two different cultural *contents*. If today the monotheism of the higher religions has all but expelled polytheism, is not the simplest explanation for this that, buttressed by a more powerful discourse in which the reversible notion of justice rather than the irreversible one of ritual propriety is paramount, the monotheistic mythology provided a more powerful theory of the origin?

We need not postulate in man a mysterious desire to know his own beginnings separate from the desire that motivates his worldly interests. The origin of the human is at the same time the origin of representation, and of desire. The original object of desire—the "sacred" power to compel communal presence—has remained the ultimate object of desire throughout history. Every use of language, whatever its more practical functions, in actualizing the latent presence between the interlocutors, offers a temporary satisfaction of this desire. In discourse these practical functions are cut off from linguistic presence and made to depend mediately on it. Each discourse is a "theory of the origin" because, whatever its terms, in arousing and purging desire within its own closure, it not merely reproduces the form of ritual and, through it, of the

original event, but by transferring this activity to a linguistic
model, it permits its hearer to grasp its "sacralized" topic as a
figure of the power of presence which he experiences in his
role as hearer. Were this power not in fact, as our hypothesis
would have it, that of a real origin, it would indeed be
inexplicable, for it exists only as a function of its own self-
revelation. We "identify," it is true, with the hero of a
story, but the origin of this identification is nothing else but
the fact that, qua hero, he compels our presence, and if the
story is successful, purges us of the desire to possess this
compelling power.

All discourse, then, is "theory," and in the historical
progression from temporalized to de-temporalized discourse
this equivalence is gradually thematized. De-temporalization
is at first a purely local phenomenon within temporalized
discourse. Each predicate, although temporalizing its topic, is
itself realized within a de-temporalized interval of linguistic
deferral, and a series of two predicates linked by implication
rather than diegesis is already a de-temporalized discourse in
miniature. The ideal of complete de-temporalization is
approached only in logic and mathematics; but although their
realizations shade into each other, the intentional structures
of the two discursive modes are significantly different. Temporalized discourse retains the nonthematic, esthetic intention of catharsis it originally borrowed from ritual. It thus
almost inevitably takes a biographical form, in which the
passage from desire to transcendence is realized in the life of
a human or "anthropomorphic" hero (the word "anthropomorphic" being a tautology because it is in fact defined
precisely by substitution for a human hero in temporalized
discourse). In contrast, in scientific discourse catharsis is
thematized as the solution to a problem defined in advance;
the topic is not transfigured by the series of predicates but
merely transformed in a series of formally reversible stages.
The notion of *formal reversibility* should be opposed to both
the real-world reversibility of a physical or chemical reaction
and the logical reversibility of a logicomathematical proof, as
being a feature rather of discourse than of its (real or ideal)
referent. It applies to the description of a temporal process in
causal terms, so that the result is made to appear inherent in

the cause, although the referential situation is not fully analyzed into a reversible model. If we say "the egg broke because it fell to the floor," we create a formally reversible linguistic model in which the egg's breaking is wholly included in its fall, although manifestly insufficient information is given to put the egg back together again in the real world. Although the character of the egg is obviously radically changed by its fall, after which it has in fact ceased to exist as a semantic unit, the stages in the egg's existence do not constitute a passage from mimetic conflict to resolution. But to the extent that this sentence appears as a solution to the problem of how the egg broke, it represents nevertheless a catharsis, not of our desire for the egg, but of our desire for an answer to the question ("Why did the egg break?") presumably already present in our mind.

The topic in de-temporalized discourse is not redefined as an object of desire by the predicates of the discourse, because the discursive catharsis does not involve desire for the object at all. One of the consequences of this fact is that de-temporalized discourse can occupy itself with matters quite remote from cultural origins. The cathartic structure of discourse has in effect been liberated from its self-reflective cultural subject matter to construct formally reversible models of any object of potential interest. Outside of the realm of human representation, the reversibility of de-temporalized discourse is limited only by the analyticity of its component parts, which are always themselves at least formally reversible models. Within this domain, however, reversibility becomes problematic. For if we attempt to describe some aspect of this history of representation in causal terms, we must represent in our discourse the reality that was the "cause" of the representation. Thus, for example, in our hypothetical derivation of the imperative, we assume not only a desire for the referent of the ostensive as mediating a desire for power over communal presence, but, in addition, an inappropriate use of this ostensive as an expression of this desire, which is then understood by a hearer, and so forth. The imperative is "explained" by this causal situation. But if we take this explanation as an example of formal reversibility, we fall into the uncomfortable position of the

behaviorist theory of language which views the linguistic
utterance as a response to a specific stimulus in its external or
internal environment: To speak of desire for the object as
having "generated" the imperative expression, is to make
desire a sufficient cause of speech. Thus the intentional
structure of the imperative is not simply equivalent to the
desire we have offered as an explanation, and our explanation
is not indeed formally reversible. Or, if we redefine our terms
so as to eliminate the intentional gap between desire and
utterance, our analysis, applied to our own discourse, would
make it appear as the result of stimuli generated by the
phenomenon we desire to explain. As this example shows,
human language cannot describe its own functioning within a
formally reversible framework. But despite the impossibility
of formal reversibility, we may still consider our derivation of
the imperative a valid one if it associates an intentional
structure with a specific desire, even through the actual
functioning of the structure in utterance can at best be
predicted, but never treated as *caused* by the presence of
desire.

Empirical studies of language use need not consider the
question of intentionality if their sole purpose is to discover
what kind of linguistic "behavior" is elicited in a given
context. They may even include within the experimental
context a variable of "attentiveness" to one's speech (e.g., in
W. Labov's studies of pronunciation) without making any
qualitative distinction between linguistic intentionality as
such and the deliberateness or carelessness with which we
perform any given task. The concept of intentionality functions in linguistics proper only as a safeguard against the
narrowness of the behaviorist ideology. Chomsky's "refutation" of Skinner[14] is exemplary in this regard: What he is
defending is only secondarily a methodology—and a doubtful
one at that—based on "linguistic intuition," but primarily
this intuition itself, that is, the internal sentiment of linguistic intentionality. It is curious that this sentiment can function within the Chomskian methodology only in the passive
role of judging the correctness of "strings," although its most
evident manifestation is simply the feeling of freedom present in speech, or in the use of language generally: Despite

grammatical and phonetic servitudes, the speaker *says what he means*, and does not respond involuntarily to a stimulus.

But try as he may, there is no way for Chomsky, or for anyone else, to integrate this sentiment into the methodology of linguistics, or if the human sciences in general as they are presently constituted. This methodology itself is behavioristic, based on the at least formal emulation of the reversible models of the natural sciences; intentionality poses not a methodological problem, but a central theoretical issue. And as we now see, this issue forces itself on us precisely in the domain of language, which has been throughout that of the present inquiry. Even the limited (and in the eyes of more recent linguists, largely misguided) use made of the notion of linguistic intentionality by the transformational school is thus of considerable significance because it necessitates at the very least an intuitive opposition to behaviorism, an opposition that has been broadened by Chomsky into an ideological critique. The confusions of this critique are themselves highly instructive. On the one hand, the stimulus-response learning model developed through observation of rats in mazes is evidently inadequate to explain the child's acquisition of language; on the other, the innatist "explanation" of this phenomenon furnished by Chomsky is not, despite the strength of his belief, a condemnation of behaviorism at all, but merely the assertion of a regional distinction within it. If, unlike the rat learning mazes, the child possesses a special "language-acquisition device," this simply means that he reacts in more selective ways than the rat to the linguistic stimuli he receives from his environment. (Similar predispositions are found in more fundamental neurological domains like space perception. In fact the entire hierarchy of the learning process postulated by Piaget—in a far more dialectical fashion than Chomsky—is founded on a hierarchy of similar predispositions.) It is noteworthy that the interactive aspect of language learning, and in particular its highly mimetic character, has been neglected not only in Chomsky's speculations but in various empirical studies they have inspired,[15] where, for example, the speech of children is recorded in a nonconversational setting so that the differentiation between the parental linguistic "stimulus" and the

infantile "response" is maximized in what is in effect merely
a minor readjustment of standard behavioral techniques.

Even Chomsky's fondness for seventeenth-century "Cartesian" theories—which are not, as he imagines, antithetical to
behaviorism, but rather its prescientific ancestors—is not
without larger significance. The Port-Royal equivalence
between being as such and the "linguistic-universal" declarative sentence ensures that the preprogrammed language-
learning capability (which is, as we have just seen, perfectly
compatible with behaviorism) does not operate, as one might
otherwise have imagined, on the basis of a hierarchy of
successive integrations, of which the lower levels would correspond to something like what we have called the elementary
linguistic forms, but rather contains from the very beginning
the S-P model of the declarative. This is of particular interest
because all students of infantile speech have been obliged to
remark that from the beginning the child speaks in "sentences," even though these consist at first of single words.
The child learns from the first not an ostensive or declarative
language, but fragments of mature language, but were his
constructions viewed in the light of a theory of the origin of
language, these early sentences might attract more attention
as already-formed intentional structures and less merely as
products of an apprenticeship in grammatical manipulation
with the declarative always in view as the ultimate telos.[16]
What are incertitudes of the child's grammar from the perspective of the declarative are in large measure simply the
indeterminacies inherent in the elementary sentence forms,
which, as we have taken pains to observe, lack a rigorous set
of grammatical categories. (The situation is, of course, complicated by the presence from the beginning of what are in
the parents' language declarative predicates.)

Thus linguistic intentionality, although an unnecessary
concept in (synchronic) linguistics proper, remains a necessary one in even the inadequate Chomskian formulations of
the genesis of language. The failure of this theory to go
beyond a merely intuitive understanding of the centrality of
intention can be attributed to a timid and ambivalent anti-
behaviorism that defines genesis merely in ontogenetic terms,
while bolstering its refusal to entertain phylogenetic consid-

erations with boldly metaphysical notions of the eternal correspondence between the declarative sentence and (divine) thought. Representational intentionality nevertheless finds in these Chomskian speculations the high point of its functionality in the human sciences as they are presently constituted. But in two areas not normally treated as within the province of these sciences, intentionality is indispensable methodologically (and not merely ideologically). One of these is the study of language origins, considered since the rise of scientific linguistics in the nineteenth century as inaccessible to rigorous methods and consequently deserving of only desultory speculation.[17] The other is that of cultural discourse, the analysis of which is left to critics and hermeneutists normally classified not in the "social" sciences, but in the "humanities," as if to imply that the fundamental characteristics of humanity are not an appropriate object for scientific investigation. The reader will note that the origin of language on the one hand and the present-day crisis of cultural discourse on the other define the historical end-points of the present work. The "circularity" of the discursive hermeneutic of discourse is well-known, and prevents this analysis from achieving scientific status. At the other end of the spectrum, the origin of language is accessible to study only through a proto-historical hypothesis like that presented here. In neither case is there hope of attaining even the formal level of reversibility that characterizes the behaviorist social sciences in general. But neither can the theory of representation take as its model the temporalized discourse of myth or literature.

We would claim that this theory can only be expressed in a discourse neither temporalized nor de-temporalized (although in function it is closer to the latter), but *dialectical*. Dialectic is the result of the integration of the indefinitely transcendent or "meta-linguistic" quality of dialogue within a single discourse. The status of its temporalization must therefore remain indeterminate. On the one hand, it begins with a hypothesis that is strictly diegetic, the empirical data for which are derived from the diegetic forms of myth and ritual; on the other it claims not only to be "scientific" but to provide a basis for the human sciences in general.

Dialectic

The term "dialectic" has hitherto been employed in two different senses: as a category of discourse, the one under which this work should itself be classified; and as the historical process by which, according to our hypothesis, the linguistic forms were originally generated. With the creation of the declarative and the concomitant possibility of free dialogue, the transition is made from what we might call, in Hegelian terms, dialectic.in-itself (for-us) and dialectic for-itself. But if the formal dialectic was by definition constructive of new forms, dialogue as such constructs nothing but itself: Each dialogue is a new form, but not necessarily nor even probably one of general human significance. The historic locus of significant linguistic form has rather been found in the realm of discourse, which is capable of being transmitted across generations by word of mouth and eventually through writing. Discourse may, of course, be constructed as dialogue: This is immediately true of the dramatic genre, as well as such works as Plato's. But the notion that a discourse with a single speaker may constitute in itself a dialectic is already implied by the ambiguity of the word διάλεκτος, which refers both to debate and to speech in general. This notion of dialectic was the basis of Hegelian discourse, which Marx attempted to "stand on its feet" as the privileged discursive mode of the human sciences. Engels and his Soviet admirers attempted to show, like the Port-Royal grammarians in the case of the declarative, that this mode reflected the very structure of reality. This latter attempt has been discredited even among Marxists, although it reappears in a new guise in talk about levels of "communication" fostered by the discovery of the operation of the genetic code; Derrida's concept of the "trace," developed in the introductory section of *De la grammatologie*, is not without reminiscences of it, although his later work gives evidence of a sharp regression from the vision of scientific integration hinted at earlier.

From our own standpoint the "dialectics of nature" is at best a misleading slogan, but the dialectics of culture is very much a reality. All human interaction is dialectical, at least in the weak sense of involving a mutual inclusion in intentional models, a phenomenon that first achieves expression with the birth of the declarative, but which is present, as we have seen, from the beginning of representation. Yet culturally significant discourse, although it may contain elements of dialogue, cannot in general be considered as dialectic. The "monolithic" nature of religious dogma is not a mere impression, and even the writings of Marx, although they purport to construct a dialectical model of social evolution, can hardly be called dialectical: Their single-mindedness is in fact well reflected in the societies whose leaders attribute to them, in however distorted a fashion, dogmatic truth.

Dialectics as the self-conscious expression of culture is even now only a vision, although the analysis we shall present in the final chapter will attempt to justify the pertinence of this vision to modern society. But before we can even think of giving substance to such a vision we must first comprehend the dialectical element latent in discourse in general. Cultural discourse speaks, for the most part, with a single voice, but we must learn to give that voice both less and more credit for controlling the whole than we have been accustomed to do. Less, because the voice of the subject, even if identified with the divinity, cannot eliminate from discourse the presence of rival intentionalities; more, because the unmediated inclusion of the latter would too easily absolve the subject of the responsibility he has tended in recent years to flee. If the evolution of linguistic form may be seen as the creation of increasingly explicit means for representing the other's intention in the intentional structure of the utterance, it should indeed come as no surprise to find that the passage of this evolution to the higher plane of supra-linguistic structures preserves and strengthens this inclusion of the other in the speech of the self.

The catharsis of primitive ritual consists of the (re-) creation of nonviolent communal presence through common participation in the sacrifice of a representative of the sacred being, carried out under the latter's supervision. The remains of the victim, man or beast, are divided and incorporated into the body of each member in a concrete revelation of the sacred within the presence it is presumed to have

created. In even the most primitive discourse, catharsis operates in a quite different manner. Rather than involving even
the imaginary physical appropriation of the sacred being, it
consists entirely in an esthetic identification with his attain-
ment of transcendent status. Whereas in ritual the transcendent becomes immanent, expressing its inaccessibility to
desire and at the same time permitting the collective appropriation of it in fleshly form, in discourse only an appearance
is possessed, the reality being revealed as permanently
beyond our reach. But at the same time, by the transformation of physical appropriation into "identification," an intersubjective relation between hearer and protagonist is
established, mediated by the speaker or Subject. It is in this
triangular relation that we should seek the latent dialectic of
discourse.

The first ritual was a reproduction of the original event,
but not truly a representation of it. This ritual incarnates
rather than *expresses* a "theory" of this event, a fact that
only makes it all the more attractive as an object for theorists.
Now if we examine precisely what we might expect ritual to
be a theory of, it is the relation between, on the one hand,
the passage from the chaos of mimetic rivalry to the nonviolence of communal presence, and on the other, the career
of the (original) victim, which comes to a climax precisely
at the critical moment dividing chaos from order. Ritual
defines this moment by an *act* of sacrifice, but does not
explain why the sacrifice brings about this transformation.
The sacrificial victim, selected in advance, progresses through
the stages of the career of his (or its) sacred model, but only
the sacred being can be said to "understand" this sequence
of events, which is another way of saying that this sequence
is simply dictated by a collective desire to reproduce its
originally beneficent results.

The first reduction of ritual to discourse offers, in its very
simplicity, a kind of esthetic "explanation."[18] The passage
from the role of victim to that of divinity is now presented in
a rigorously linear sequence, so that the temporality of the
hero's career is now not simply contained within the communal catharsis, but situated as parallel to it and thus as already

a form of explanation of it by analogy. For this analogy is not an artifact of our theory; it is realized in the separate catharsis of the narrative, in which the final transfiguration of the hero makes him inaccessible to desire.

Now although this process is certainly a "forgetting" of the communal violence still present in ritual sacrifice, it is nevertheless the beginning of an explanation of the origin reproduced in ritual, and thus anything but a regression from it. As the active role of the hero replaces the passive one of the victim, the sacrificial moment as such, which as we have seen is the crucial "transcendental" moment of ritual—that moment the critical effect of which can least be explained because its explanation would expose the sacred object as merely a creature of the community rather than the inverse— will tend to be rationalized. That is to say, it is deprived of its violent, unmotivated character, so that on the one hand it appears as a punishment for the crime of instigating the mimetic rivalry,[19] and on the other, it does not necessarily lead to the violent death of the victim, who must in any case continue to exist as a transcendent being. The distinction between gods and heroes, certainly not a primitive ritual distinction and indeed one that is unknown to many primitive religions, would appear to result from the dichotomy introduced in myth between heroes who attain the status of transcendence only through death (or a comparable act of sacralization by already transcendant gods), and gods who possess this status from the beginning, although they must nevertheless undergo some form of trial and purification in the course of the mythical narrative. But in either case, and this is the crucial point of our argument, it is the "biography" of the hero of the narrative that provides the link between the two stages of the original event as enacted in ritual.

Considered as a fiction, therefore, mythical discourse may simply be said to be diegetic or temporalized; considered as an explanation of the origin of the social order, this temporalization, actively assumed by the hero, becomes a source of understanding. Although the heroes of myth almost inevitably suffer unexpected misfortunes, their adventures are even more inevitably the result of voluntary action on their part. In other words, the irreversible transformation of the collective condition from chaos to order is paralleled in myth by the irreversible action (and passion) of the hero. The mythical explanation of the origin is rooted in this action, with which the hearer is said to "identify." Identification is simply the imaginary possession of an attribute in which the transcendent being of the hero appears to be contained, or rather is presented by the speaker as being contained, for the triangular relation of narrative, unlike the dual one of esthetic mimesis, includes a third party.

This identification with the hero is esthetic, not cognitive, based as it is on represented experience. But that it is truly a dialectical relationship, the existence of hermeneutics as the study of the "original" meaning of cutural texts is only the most overt proof. The heroic narrative, and in substance any narrative, involves the reader in a triangular relation with the hero, whose experience he possesses in imagination, and the subject of author, himself identified with the sacred not as becoming but as being, whose possession of the narrative-as-totality makes him the possessor of the being of the hero. To identify with the hero is also to become aware of one's difference from him, and in particular, one's distance from the central focus he occupies in communal presence. But this identification, the desire for the hero's being and its transcendence, constitutes at the same time a guarantee of the subject's authority to explain the original passage from chaos to order through his story. The esthetic force of the narrative guarantees its truth, which hermeneutics reinterprets at the level of theoretical understanding appropriate to its own time. Hermeneutics only converts into discourse the dialectical element that was already present in the original relation between reader (or hearer) and text; on the basis of his own identification with the hero, the reader is drawn in effect into a dialogue with the Subject, a dialectical rivalry for the possession of the heroic being which, once detached from the temporality of the hero's career, bears precisely the same relation to the sacred as the being of the Subject-narrator.

This dialectic is not a necessary function of the esthetic experience of discourse, but it is precisely in it that temporal-

ized esthetic discourse becomes explicitly a means of understanding, a "theory" of the origin, thereby eventually
providing the motivating force for the detemporalization of
scientific discourse. If it be asked where this dialectical ''reading'' can be found in the primitive experience of a myth, the
answer is simply in its retelling. Each successive version of a
myth is, like the performance of a ritual, a reproduction of
what the speaker has already heard, but if only because
transitions are easily forgotten, each retelling will tend to
rationalize a bit more than the preceding, explaining the
crucial transformation of both society and hero in more
nearly causal terms. Hence the etiological tendency of myth,
by which it moves toward de-temporalization (e.g., from
legendary origins to Hesiod, and from Hesiod to the pre-
Socratics and thence to the rigor of modern natural science).
The ultimate motivation for this evolution is the dialectical
rivalry of the series of speakers and hearers-turned-speakers
over the de-temporalized being of the transfigured hero. The
opposite evolutionary path, toward the secularized temporality of literary fiction, is motivated rather by rivalry over
the worldly existence of the hero as an object for the temporal identification of third parties. Hence, in essence, the
subject of scientific discourse seeks self-sufficiency, that of
literary discourse, mastery over his audience.

Hermeneutic discourse is not mere retelling; it is a retem-
poralization of myth and thus a reflection of discourse on
itself. Unlike what we have defined as literary criticism,
which consists in referring literary works to their pseudo-
formal essences within ritual, hermeneutic discourse constructs on the basis of a cultural text (the selection of which
remains however fideistic rather than being itself founded on
a hypothesis of origin) what is in effect a hypothetical model
of the origin of culture. The social or human sciences have
evolved through the elimination from such models of unexplained ritual elements, in a word, through their de-ritualization. But in comparison with the wholly de-temporalized
models of the natural sciences, the hypotheses of human
science are imperfect, for however far de-ritualization be
carried, the explanation of the crucial moment, which
presents itself to the theoretician diversely as the origin of

language, or of religion, or of the prohibition of incest, etc., cannot be fully de-temporalized, but retains always its irreversible character.

The recognition of this barrier to de-temporalization, and thus to scientificity in the image of the natural sciences, has appeared at various times in different domains, in language earlier than the rest, and, perhaps more significantly, in the already quite rigorous studies of primitive religion carried out by the pre-World War I generation of anthropologists (particularly Durkheim and his school, but also various English thinkers, such as the "Cambridge ritualists," or somewhat earlier, H. Robertson Smith; nor should we omit Freud). This recognition turned the practitioners of these sciences away from the theory of origins toward more historically accessible tasks, so that today only paleontologists retain their interest in the question, but from a perspective that refuses the radical question of *cultural* origin. Now in all these cases, human science has abandoned the original naively dialectical character of hermeneutics, which was determined by the interaction between the hypothetical discourse of the theoretician and its mythical subject,[20] for what we may simply call behaviorism. This approach offers formal if not analytic reversibility and thus permits the formulation of structural models of cultural phenomena, even if these models remain on a combinatorial level, rather than, like those of the physical sciences, constructing their object analytically from simpler elements.

The present work is an attempt to return *en connaissance de cause* to a dialectical theory of representation. The Girardian hypothesis of the original event, which we have here adopted in modified form, is not simply a contemporary version of the hermeneutic models of the past. For the hypotheses constructed by the thinkers of the "heroic" age of anthropology that we may situate roughly between the appearances of Tylor's *Primitive Culture* in 1871 (or even that of *The Origin of Species* in 1859) and Durkheim's *Les Formes élémentaires de la vie religieuse* in 1912 were only imperfectly dialectical. The myths and rituals referred to by these thinkers all spoke of the origin of culture as an event in the career of a god or hero, and, at the same time (more or less explicitly), of a human community. Their hypotheses, however, inevitably rejected the event-nature of this origin, which was itself attributed to a ritual origin (as in the "dying-god" festivals linked to the agricultural cycle), or simply ignored in favor of the unexplained but presumably gradually emerging consciousness of some form of structural dichotomy, be it nature/man for the animists, death/life for the spiritualists, or ideal/real for Durkheim, who refuted the naive claims of the earlier schools without improving on the underlying structure of their hypotheses.

Girard's model is far more profoundly dialectical. By taking seriously the mythical accounts of an evenemential origin analogous to the critical moment of sacrificial ritual, Girard in effect accepts the authors of these accounts as genuine partners in his own discourse. That he speaks openly of a hypothesis where others have been content to expound a "theory" is also of considerable significance. This hypothesis is clearly a *fiction*, not merely a series of general observations about primitive man, because *only a fiction can "explain" a formally irreversible phenomenon*. That the "original event" must be repeated many times before it can produce, in the "sedimentary" form we have described, unambiguous examples of cultural phenomena is not in any sense a refutation either of the hypothesis *in abstracto* or, more particularly, of its fictional representation—*au contraire*.

The theoreticians who limited themselves "prudently" to describing general tendencies, themselves operating in sedimentary fashion, could merely explain the origin of culture by claiming the preexistence of such tendencies, thus involving themselves in infinite regression. But in an openly diegetic hypothesis the birth of culture is described as an event occurring in what we have termed communal presence, and thus as a phenomenon, however many times repeated, present on each occurrence to the consciousness of its participants. The only proof we have of this consciousness, it may be objected, is found in the distorted forms of ritual and myth, and cannot therefore command our credence. But if ritual and myth "explain" the origin as irreversible, and if our own discourse, as we cannot well deny, is directly descended from these very same phenomena, then on what grounds can our own explanation be formulated in formally reversible terms? The evenemential hypothesis thus accepts, not without a certain humility, the fact that both we and the myth-makers are indeed speaking about the same thing, and that although the content of our explanation may differ radically from theirs, the discursive model in which it is expressed functions in essentially the same manner.

The revelation of the arbitrary nature of the original murder constitutes a decisive response, a genuine dialectical victory, over the rationalizations of mythical discourse. Frazer and even Durkheim reject the form of myth, but accept its content, whereas Girard, by accepting the form, is able to refute the content. But if we seek to know why precisely the discovery of the *arbitrary* nature of the original murder is so significant, the Girardian hypothesis can provide only a moral explanation, the power of which ultimately derives from an a priori belief in the natural symmetry of human relations and the consequent instability of asymmetrical ones. That in his most recent work Girard has felt obliged to found explicitly this belief on divine revelation only demonstrates, religious values aside, the inadequacy of the "institutional" theory on this point. For the asymmetrical situation of the original event cannot indeed, in his exposition of the hypothesis, be made to bring about awareness of the fundamental symmetry of the human condition, as first revealed in Judeo-Christian consciousness. Thus the gradual revelation of the "criminal" nature of the original murder and, as a consequence, of the unsatisfactoriness of sacrifice and of all related "scapegoating" phenomena can in Girard's view only acquire its categorical application to human morality through divine agency.

In our modified version of the hypothesis, however, such an explanation, evidently "undialectical" in the extreme, is avoided. The original event is not merely the origin of the "non-instinctive attention" that makes the sacred object the eventual center of ritual, but at the same time the origin of *representation*. By making the original event of culture in effect a representation of itself, the present version of the hypothesis gives a cognitive and not merely transcendental significance to the arbitrary choice of the original victim.

This arbitrariness is the origin of that of the linguistic sign, the first instance of which occurs precisely in the representation of the victim within the original communal presence. The perception of the asymmetry of the original situation, which becomes explicit in myth, where rationalizing explanations for it are proposed, is thus already present *in posse* from the beginning, only awaiting for its actualization the parallel development of secular language.

But in effect even this description of the original situation is too mechanical, or in other words, insufficiently dialectical. For the very possibility of the emergence of secular language depends on the preliminary actualization in the original sign itself of its "arbitrary" nature, which occurs in the separation of linguistic presence into a formal space of designation on the one hand and, on the other, a specific sacred designatum guaranteeing this presence. The entire course of the dialectic of linguistic form, up to and including the supralinguistic forms of discourse, can indeed be understood as a progressive revelation of the arbitrary character of the linguistic sign, and at the same time of the (proto-) dialectical symmetry of man's relation to linguistic presence, the evolution of form being at the same time a revelation of original content. It is because our version of the hypothesis can explain the primordial unity between cognitive arbitrariness and ethical symmetry—mediated by the esthetic desire invested in the sign—that we may claim it to be "more dialectical" than that of Girard, and the "formal theory" more so than the "institutional theory."

In Girard's exposition the arbitrary nature of the original choice of the victim is revealed in two ways: as the result of his hermeneutic extrapolation from texts of myth and descriptions of ritual, and as a divine revelation made in incomplete form to the Old Testament prophets and completed in the life of Christ as recounted in the Gospels. The second source of revelation, as we have already had occasion to remark, is necessary to justify the presence in discourse—that is, Girard's own—of this truth, which the processes of human representation, as derived in the institutional theory from ritual, would not otherwise be capable of expressing, this inability being in the first instance a moral one. Thus the theoretician, in constructing his hypothesis, maintains his dialogue with the creative subjects of ritual and myth up to the point of acknowledging the validity of the event-nature of the origin, and the concomitant necessity that it be understood in diegetic terms, that is, as a *fiction*, but at the same time he claims to differ absolutely from them in understanding the arbitrariness of the victim, the central figure in this fiction.

We must make more precise the notion of the "arbitrary," which the Saussurian doctrine of the signifier merely locates without explanation in a not altogether rigorously defined de-temporalized model of language.[21] The point is obviously not that no motivation was present in the choice of the original victim; the history of the choice in each case, as recoverable in the mythic text, is a per se demonstration of motivation. The mythic hero nearly always possesses a deformity or other real or imagined distinguishing trait of some sort, and even when his choice is left to "fate," the perpetrators of the murder would never have considered their act to be simply arbitrary, an eventuality that would indeed make the formulation of hermeneutic hypotheses superfluous. Absolute arbitrariness is present not in the choice of the victim, but in the meaning attributed to his remains by the "emissary" mechanism. In Girard's exposition, where the sacred object is simply identified with the victim with no intervening act of representation, the two instances of arbitrariness are the same; and the second, which alone is culturally functional, must be measured by the first, which alone is intelligible.

But what is truly arbitrary in the choice of victim is not the criterion used in the choice but the fact that it is made at all—that the appetites of the collectivity, which are not yet truly desires, guided by no anterior *arbitrary* representation of their object, nevertheless, at a certain level of mimetic development (definable only, if at all, through analogies with other species), tend to converge on a single center. It is this convergence that creates the conditions of communal presence and, at the same time, the first "arbitrary" sign, which we have assumed to be nothing more, in fact, than the perfectly "natural" hesitation between appropriation and renouncement which designates the object. At the first moment of communal presence surrounding the object, certainly the notion of arbitrariness is nowhere to be found; but for precisely this reason we cannot yet speak of a true linguistic sign. It is through the process of desire, in which the sign is associated with its object in imagination, that the object acquires its sacred powers, and that at the same time the arbitrariness of the sign is forged. Although the members of the community cannot yet conceive of evoking the object in its absence, a development that must follow the creation of the simple ostensive, they already construe the sign as its name, the possession of which in imagination makes them participants in the object's own power over the community. The name is already an attribute, separable at least in imagination—and thus in significant memory—from its substance, just as the object is separable, at least in imagination, from the communal presence it commands.

Now if the analyst sees only the second relation, that between object and presence, he may say that although *for him* the relation is arbitrary, motivated only by the original "criminal" choice of the victim, for the participants it is fully motivated by the sacred character attributable to his remains. But if he recognizes the inseparable existence of *both* relations, in which the first is in fact prerequisite to the second, he must recognize as well that the very separability of object from presence depends on the separability of the name or sign of the power commanding this presence from this power itself. But the sign is not a thing but a human production, capable of being reproduced by each individual, and in the prolongation of the first moment of nonviolence into the second, in which an act of *representation* may truly be said to take place, this "arbitrary" power conferred by the sign is indeed shared by all the members of the community. The interdictions that will afterward hold them back from appropriating the object for themselves may also make the sign itself "ineffable." But the ineffability of the sacred name outside of specified ritual contexts is the very proof that the sacred power, although in the real world alienated from its true possessors and vouchsafed to what may be no more than a few bones, is, in the imaginary domain, which is already that

of language, the property of each individual capable of reproducing the sign.

Thus, at the first moment in which intentional human
language may be said to exist, its "speakers" already possess,
in the sign, a "theory" of the original event, an understanding
of the original alienation through which alone nonviolent
presence can be maintained. Insofar as the original victim was
chosen "arbitrarily" by all, each member of the community
now possesses within his mind the principle of this unanim-
ity. Thus it is not enough to accept the mythographer's
ritually derived intuition of the fictional nature of our understanding of the original event. We must first accept the
original participant's still more primitive intuition of its
expressibility by means of a sign. We can now see that this
sign is arbitrary, not because of any Saussurian lack of
historical connection with its referent, but because its arbitrary—that is, transcendent—power is ultimately subject to
the arbitrary—that is, *intentional*—choice of the speaker. And
this intentional power is indeed none other than that which
we employ in our explanation. Our complicity in the original
event is not merely a moral but an intellectual one. Thus our
dialogue with our primitive ancestors cannot limit itself to
unmasking their responsibility for the "God-given" transition
from precultural chaos to cultural order, but must uncover
their creation of its first significant gesture, their conferral of
a name on God himself.

The remainder of the formal dialectic outlined in the
preceding chapters can now be more easily understood as the
product of what is from the outset a dialectical relation to
the first users of language. Our use of words is an expression
of the same desire as theirs; if we have reason to believe that
our attempt to conquer the power of communal presence
through the use of arbitrary symbols is somehow closer to
the truth than their own, this reason can only be found in the
evolution undergone by this presence in the historical interval
between the origin of language and the emergence of modern
society. Because dialectic begins, not with the creation of
discourse, which is no doubt the product of a relatively
advanced and differentiated stage of society, but with the
origin of language, we need not be limited in our perspective

on modernity by the frontiers of culturally significant discourse, which are of increasingly less importance in a de-
ritualized world. Discourse has been from the first both a
hermeneutic and an esthetic elaboration of previous discourse, a reproduction of the original liberation from ritual.
To go beyond this relationship to the prediscursive origins of
linguistic representation is finally to liberate theory from its
traditional metaphysic, and at the same time to free human
science from its empiricist-behaviorist dependence on the
discourse of the natural sciences. Certainly Girard's hypothesis, although it remains as we have seen ultimately tied to
the "institutional" context of ritual and the discourse that
has emerged from it, is an incomparably significant step
toward this liberation, albeit one whose internal contradictions are a sign of the necessity of a still more radical
departure.

Metaphysics has ever been the enemy of dialectic. The
metaphysical subject knows its object without desiring it,
commands the presence of his audience without seeking
power, emerges unscathed from the triangle of desire he has
created. All of Girard's work, from his early critiques of
Existentialism and its deluded exaltation of the "free" hero
of romantic desire to his prophetic affirmation of the radical
nonviolence of the Judeo-Christian tradition, can be conceived as a single enterprise of liberation from discursive
metaphysics and the resentful unavowed desire it fosters in
all who fall under its influence. If this enterprise has nevertheless its limitations, which it can surpass only with the aid
of transcendental revelation, it is because this liberation from
metaphysics remains itself bound to discursive expression.
From Cervantes and Dostoevsky to the Evangelists, the guarantees Girard has offered for the conquest of metaphysical
desire and of the mimetic violence it masks are examples of
diegetic discourse untouched by the malaise of a modernity
which, behind its infantile parricidal mythology, expresses an
intuition of the necessary transcendence of the formal—and
not merely the substantial—limits of cultural discourse. This
is not to disparage the power of the liberation from metaphysics revealed in these texts, nor to suggest that our own
text is not itself discursive—albeit in a less constrained sense

than the discourse of present-day social science. For we may at least claim that our dialectic does not accept the exemplarity of any historical form of discourse, that its dialogue is not with these forms but with language, with representation as such.

The paradoxically transcendental relationship between discourse and the language of which it is constituted is the great mystery—esthetically grasped but hidden from cognition—from which metaphysics, the cultural expression of metaphysical desire, has from the beginning drawn its strength. Language is taken as the naive expression of desire, of which it can only be purged in the transcendental catharsis achieved in discourse through the mediation of the Subject. The Subject, proprietor from the outset of the totality of his discourse, is thus already released from desire as the protagonist will be at the conclusion. The circularity of this relationship, which in the European novelistic tradition is the revelation of Proust, is already present, as we have seen, in primitive discourse as it emerges from ritual. But whatever existential guarantees he may offer of his transcendent status, the Subject is no more a god than his reader. The temporality of discourse may prolong itself into an analogy of life experience, but it is never more than an extension of the deferral already present in the first proto-linguistic sign. The pretentions of discourse to transcendence of the limits of language are unfounded; for language from the beginning has understood its own arbitrary nature. It is the revelation of the falsity of these pretentions that spells the end of the esthetic of discourse, and this revelation can only be accomplished through a dialectical theory of representation, a preliminary and perhaps unavoidably primitive form of which we have presented here.

In its transcendence of the temporal esthetic of discourse this theory becomes a basis for a truly historical human science, no longer obliged to seek safety in the "black box" of synchronic structures, but capable of constructing hypothetical models independent of esthetic criteria. For the guarantee of the transcendence of desire—the desire for explanation, which is not something peculiar to science, but the very same desire to possess the power over communal presence that exists from the origin of language—is no longer to be sought in a diegetic catharsis essentially inaccessible to verification other than by esthetic intuition, but in the dialectical genesis of a new form of representation. Thus our hypothetical description of the "original event" need no longer be judged as a fiction, guaranteed by the ritual and mythic representation from which it was hermeneutically derived, but as a *dialectically* reversible model of the genesis of the most primitive possible form of representation. Representation guarantees its own genesis, in a "circular" model that no longer turns on itself without end in the "bad infinity" of the so-called "hermeneutic circle," where text and theory support each other like reflections in parallel mirrors. *The genesis of a form must be recoverable in the intentional structure of that form*—a simple truth, no doubt, but one ever inaccessible to a representational mode in which the Subject, all-powerful and invisible, presumes to possess the atemporal secret of the form which he condescends to reveal in temporal terms to his time-bound reader.

7 A Perspective on Modernity

The dialectic of representational form is inhabited, as we have freely admitted, by the desire to command communal presence. But only in a particular historical context could this desire become a theme of representation. Writers always seek readers, and theoreticians, converts to their theories. Beyond these truisms, however, lies the radical truth that not until the theoretician's desire to communicate his theory becomes itself the ultimate subject matter of the theory can theoretical discourse be said to embody a critical understanding of its own genesis. The first characteristic of modernity is that it is, in the Kantian sense, the age of criticism.

The legitimacy of defining modernity within a dialectic of representation is unlikely to be accepted by the majority of those social scientists who are directly concerned with it, although such a definition is the only basis on which sociology can be integrated with anthropology. The opposition between "primary" and "secondary" historical factors, or between infrastructure and superstructure, has always been expressed in metaphysical terms, as though one's original choice were inspired by divine revelation and the facts organized to fit it. Thus, far from center of the social sciences, humanists have often debated the legitimacy of "literary history"—a concept that if understood as the historical dialectic of discourse would have been truly revolutionary, but which has instead been confined until very recently by the timid modesty of its defenders to suggesting a vague correlation between "history" and literature, viewed as a subcategory of the historical. (Thus transitions between one literary mode and another may be "explained" by sociohistorical phenomena.) The possibility of an independent history of literature without external reference is hopelessly parochial and artificial. It cannot justify its concern with the institution of literature and at the same time avoid all reference to other institutions. But history in general is parochial and artificial, whatever sets of facts it is willing to consider as significant, so long as it is not informed by an overall conception of human becoming, which is to say, so long as it is not a mediation between the anthropology of man-in-general and the sociology of the present. Merely to tell the story of England or of France is to do nothing more than storytelling. The recital of facts only interests us for what it reveals about human society in general and contemporary society in particular. And because most historians have no clear picture of their mediating role, these revelations must be extracted from a text that depends solely on tradition and the historian's intuition as its criteria of significance.[1]

The institutions of linguistic representation, like all cultural institutions in the modern era, are undergoing an increasingly radical process of de-ritualization. The necessity of the noninstitutional, formal dialectic that we propose is made increasingly apparent by the formalism of contemporary literature, its rejection of traditional norms, particularly that of diegesis. The conquest of the literary institution by anti-institutional trends, a phenomenon typical of culture since the Romantic era, has now reached a radicality too profound to be understood by means of a discourse incapable of questioning the limits of this institution. But as literature grows more radically anti-institutional, *antidiscursive* in the sense in which traditional discourse is the expression of metaphysics, it can no longer remain esthetic. At a certain point, antiliterature is no longer literature, just as antimusic is no longer music.

Thus we shall not make such phenomena as the *nouveau roman* the point of departure for our examination of the modern. In effect we need begin with nothing more than the fact that modernity is what makes a critical theory of representation possible. For a critical theory, by explaining its own genesis, makes its own dialectic the "motor of history."

Marxism has its own critical pretentions, and its partisans will not fail to object to the "idealism" of a self-contained dialectic of mere words, the task of dialectics being to change the world, not to explain it, and certainly not to explain it as being itself essentially only a series of inadequate explanations. But representative constraints are no less real than material constraints. Whether modernity is explained better by modes of production-relations or modes of representation cannot be decided by simply affirming that the former "secrete" the latter—nor do we intend to affirm that the latter secrete the former. It is not, however, illegitimate to claim that production-relations "secrete" a consciousness of production-relations, and representations (or more precisely, representation-relations), of representation. Marxism claims to understand the content of these secretions, but cannot quite explain why they fail to operate on so many of the victims of these relations. Marxism has become, as a global phenomenon, more a religion of *ressentiment* than a dialectical theory, an anti-institution so institutionalized that it can no longer dare to examine production-relations as anything but a relationship between rich and poor. The very term "Third World" so popular with Western Marxists is hardly an indication of the nonexploitative nature of "socialist" economies. But the existence of a world market can certainly not be summed up in an allegorical opposition between a global "bourgeoisie" and a global "proletariat." This distinction is no longer a dialectical one; its "resolution" offers no perspective other than a banal averaging-out of distinctions. In contrast, a theory of representation offers the basis for a genuine sociological perspective. For production-relations in fact are increasingly assimilated in modern society to representation-relations, mediated by exchanges of information rather than "labor-power." The sociology of modernity cannot function within the antimetaphysics of "proletarian ideology" at a time when metaphysical discourse is increasingly less relevant to the understanding or even the "ideological" justification of social relations.

How then are we to begin our analysis of these relations, if the traditional discourse which served in the past as their justification has lost its legitimacy? The theory of representation can only explain its own genesis if it can first explain the conditions of communal presence within which it purports not merely to manifest itself but to *operate*. These conditions cannot be summed up in a vague notion of "receptivity." If in the most general sense we may say that, throughout its history, traditional discourse reflected and legitimized the various hierarchical modes of social relations, the enormous differences between which, from the perspective of modernity, become thus only secondary, the replacement of the traditional mode of discourse by dialectics must correspond to the emergence of a radically nonhierarchical mode of such relations. It is our contention that this mode, in which the asymmetry of communication takes the reversible form of dialogue rather than the irreversible one of traditional discourse, is increasingly realized in an ever-expanding system of exchange, the origins of which can be traced to the establishment of the free "bourgeois" market at the center of social relations at the beginning of the industrial era.

Marx had no difficulty in pointing out the fallacy of the liberal theory of the market, in which capitalist and worker alike were "free" to sell their economic goods at a price fixed by the laws of supply and demand. But although "labor power" was surely not a "good" comparable to the products of labor, the inequality of early industrial production-relations was no doubt more a function of preexisting conditions that made workers newcomers to the system of exchange of industrial society than of the necessities of either industrialization or of the market economy. It is noteworthy that the subsistence-level exploitation typical of midnineteenth-century England has nowhere subsisted as a general condition of industrial laborers over more than one or two generations. This transitional state should be contrasted with the millenial poverty of agricultural labor in certain regions. It constitutes rather an economic form of *immigration*, with the geographical form of which it is often associated (this association is particularly striking in the case of turn-of-the-century America), than a structural economic necessity, although the very possibility of so large a number of new entrants into the market system is evidently a function of the introduction of new industrial processes.

The inclusion of the former agricultural-urban proletariat in the industrial labor force was, whatever the hardships it inflicted, the extension of rationalized exchange relations to a fraction of the population who had previously lived under a "patriarchal" system that, as Marx well saw, was doomed by the dialectic of history. The much-decried imperialism of the end of the century, however strongly we may condemn its exploitative features, should be seen in the same light. But the creation of a world market is only the most external characteristic of modernity. To speak of monopolies as putting an end to the "free" market is to focus on the price-fixing mechanism as its central feature, when the most significant aspect of the modern exchange system is rather its mediation of relations between persons.

Even the most superficial observation of the advanced societies of today, where oligopoly and barely disguised price-fixing have long been accepted features of the economy, reveals that the primary area of social relations is not the market for goods and services but the job market in which the members of the society sell their acquired skills in exchange for both money and status. Here even the word "market" is misleading, for (with the exception of a small and diminishing percentage of *rentiers*) the active life of the entire population consists of a continuous presence in the professional arena. The Marxian model of the industrial worker selling his undifferentiated labor-power at an always-falling market price is no longer valid even in the industrial sector. In an ever-increasing proportion, the work-history of the members of advanced societies may better be thought of as a *career* in which the continual acquisition of new skills plays a major part, so that one's market position relative to others varies continuously, one's active life being oriented toward a goal which may be redefined at more than one moment of the process. Thus rather than seeing the modern corporation as a member of vast conspiracy against free competition, we should better understand it as the locus of a continuing competition for higher levels of status and income, while its products are elements of a system of consumption which functions as the mode of expression of social relations.

The notion of "surplus value" has little or no relevance to the salary-scale of a modern corporation or other large institution. The "labor-power" of modern society is indefinitely and increasingly differentiated, with each differential accretion (or diminution) of skills being continually tested in the marketplace. Thus the concept of a self-chosen and open-ended career, perhaps the most significant creation of the industrial era, but passed over in silence by an ideology that understands modern social relations only in dichotomous terms actually more appropriate to the feudal caste-society they replaced (the "capitalist" being for Marx, if not for Schumpeter, essentially an undifferentiated property owner, just as the proletarian is an undifferentiated purveyor of labor-power), has now extended its influence to social levels far removed from the limited sector of the entrepreneurial bourgeoisie in which it originated. This development, and the concomitant emergence of the system of consumption in which it is expressed, may be considered the crucial determinants of social relations in the modern era.

If we would believe the majority of the critics of the "consumer society," the productive lives of its members pale in significance beside their commitment to "leisure" activities and to consumption in general. Even a critic as astute as Jean Baudrillard,[2] to whom we owe the profound insight that the domain of consumption is a *system of signs* and not merely an unstructured locus of "conspicuous" nonproductive activities, has virtually nothing to say about modern man's participation in the universe of production. A reader from another planet would think that human beings were merely consumers of goods produced by mysterious divinities who manipulate them from afar; the "consumer society" always has an aura of 1984. But not only are the consumers also (and, so to speak, incidentally) the producers; their consumption is, in its significant aspect, which coincides with its signifying one, nothing but a reflection of what we shall call their "posture" toward the domain of production. *Posture* is not equivalent to *status*, although it depends on it, as the etymology of the words makes clear: One must have a place to stand before one can strike a pose. The notion of a quasi-independent, alienated antiworld of consumption in which one realizes one's dreams of a freedom inaccessible in the sphere of production is pure myth, and its uncritical perpetuation by critics of the consumer society is proof that they are far more susceptible to the wiles of the advertisers than the supposedly alienated "consumers" they purport to defend. In the ads the buyer of a car or a can of beer is encouraged to identify with high-status figures whose *professional* role is almost always at least implicitly presented, and often focused on. When he in fact purchases these items, however, he is reflecting not their status, but his own, with the crucial qualification that the additional connotations established by advertising, and even more importantly, by the word-of-mouth reputation of the product, its physical form, the symbolism of its name, etc. establish a posture that transcends this status. Each posture, constructed from a considerable variety of consumption decisions, may be considered as a "message" made up of the connotative *signs* that are the products and services purchased. The myths of advertising, insulting as they mostly are even to the average intelligence, are vehicles for establishing these signs, and whether they are "believed" or not (and no one will ever admit to believing them), their presence in the media makes them as objective and unavoidable in their vehicular role as the grammatical "errors" and unsavory neologisms that the reluctant speaker cannot avoid assimilating from his linguistic environment. But it is not without significance that advertising presents itself almost inevitably as *fiction*, that is, as discourse, yet a discourse that presumes openly to forment mimesis rather than "purge" it, and to associate attributes with beings otherwise devoid of them, rather than, like discourse in its traditional function, to demonstrate the inaccessibility and hence the essential separation of being from its "illusory" attributes. If we seek in the modern world a true "anti-discourse," we would perhaps do better to examine the productions of Madison Avenue than those of the Editions de Minuit.

What we have called the "posture" of an individual consists of his global relationship at a given time to the system of production of which he is a part. At any given moment, the totality of "appearances" acquired in the market, from automobiles and houses to breakfast foods, defines a synchronic cut in a continuum of consumer choices, itself never wholly stable, but which, even more significantly, never expresses a merely momentary attitude but an existential commitment to what is often called a "life style." Thus, on the basis of his present status, the consumer may express his orientation toward a future higher status or his rejection of the "rat race," assumed as a mere necessity; he may express solidarity with his ethnic origin or an exotic interest in other cultures, etc. These expressions may be actuated in the privacy of one's home or in public, but they always contain a social component. Our understanding of this component is the basis for further social interaction. This is not to deny that nonconsumptive factors like physical appearance or speech accents also play an important role in social inter- action. These, too, are subject to the influence of consump- tion (via cosmetics or plastic surgery), and it is interesting to note that a not easily modifiable trait like accent, still so important as a sign of class distinction in Europe, is in recently settled areas like California considered merely a nonhierarchical mark of regional origin. Accent is a poor signifier in modern society—acquired in childhood and only imperfectly modifiable after puberty, its inertial component is too great to make it a faithful measure of continuously changing posture. The "cash nexus" of the market place provides, in contrast, a considerable degree of control on the pretentions of posture in relation to status. But the number of products available to persons of even limited incomes is sufficient to permit the composition of a quite detailed "message." Various alternatives (e.g., small foreign cars) are especially appropriate for situations high in status but only moderate in income, of which university teaching may be the classic example.

The separate elements from which the "message" of pos- ture is composed are, from an economic standpoint, objects of consumption. We must now examine their functioning as representations. As visible attributes of their bearer, they express his posture as a "being," and thus become potential objects of esthetic mimesis. Contemplation of individual ele- ments of the message reveals the coherence of the whole, and thus arouses the desire to possess this coherence through the acquisition of these elements in the market. The function of advertising in this regard is crucial. Advertising provides a message of exceptional coherence generally associated with a discourse in which a specific product-attribute is singled out as the key to the whole. It thus serves to reinforce major choices in the system, such as automobiles. But even when the specific choice it promotes is of marginal importance (e.g., detergents, laxatives, etc.), it nevertheless reinforces the sign system as a whole through the coherence of the postures incarnated by its actors. No doubt advertising is never a wholly satisfactory form of discourse. The elements of the consumptive message are attributes, not predicates, and their integration into the predicative mode of diegetic discourse is always artificial. The diegetic form of much advertising, centered on a principal character whose salvation is found in the use of product X, makes use of a temporal catharsis in which the acquisition of the product-attribute is so to speak exaggerated into a predicate. Thus a banal transaction is made into the analogue of a "heroic" act of transcendence of desire—one which must be shown at the same time to be easily within the reach of the consumer.

But these inherent contradictions are not signs of the weakness but of the vigor of advertising discourse. Their presence merely serves to weaken by contamination the traditional structures of discourse-in-general, demonstrating better than any number of theoretical denunciations the manipulative nature of discourse and the unjustified superiority of its Subject. If any trend is visible within advertising itself, it is a gradual regression from narrative to lyric, from declarative to ostensive, a phenomenon most clearly visible in the rise some two decades ago of a simplified "advertising syntax" minimizing the grammatical subordinations of the declarative and resorting to the frequent (one might say maximal) use of ostensives. If the pure lyric form indeed constitutes the limit of this process, it can then be said that the discourse of advertising would coincide maximally with the presentation of posture messages by the consumers; much pictorial advertising, particularly in higher-status publications, already consists merely of photographs of typical users of the product in question. The reinforcement through advertising of the system of signs already in social use would then explicitly reveal its rationalizing function. By giving publicity to new products, advertisers continually both expand the sign system and reduce its redundancy. Competing products attempt to survive by creating significant differences that will divide their respective customers along sociological lines; if the products remain "synonymous," they both risk losing their markets to better defined competitors.

The posture message of each individual member of society provokes esthetic mimesis in those who observe him; and the conditions of their mimetic action are rigorously determined, for the goods that constitute his attributes are all accessible on the market. The "being" behind these attributes is not accessible without a considerable temporal investment, since it is founded, as we have said, on professional status. Yet between similar status levels the more flexible system of postures provides various possibilities of mediation, so that attractive attributes may be annexed to one's being. But the most significant advantage of the posture system over the status system lies rather in the opposite direction—that of differentiation and, so to speak, of *dialogue* rather than mere emulation and its concomitant rivalry and resentment. For posture possesses a diachronic component. The message emitted by an individual is not confined to a statement of his present status; it may also express his future aspirations, and in particular his position regarding the question of status in general. Confronted by a person of higher status and/or income, he need not confine himself to futile sentiments of mimetic attraction or even to marginal activities of emulation. He may simply reject the status values incarnated by the other. The spread of "proletarian" dress, particularly blue jeans, among middle-class youth and thence to the parental generation is due to the spread of a pseudo-egalitarian rejection of the claims of status in general, but such rejection has already acquired a highly nuanced range of expression even within the available styles of blue jeans themselves. The posture system, always in disequilibrium, generates an esthetic equality that offsets without annulling them the inequalities of the status system. This is not to say that each "message" is of equal esthetic value, but that, to the extent that they are of esthetic interest at all, these messages cannot be situated within a simple hierarchy of status. Ultimately each individual posture is unique, and the esthetic value of its message is one of coherence rather than conformity to a predetermined model. At the same time the coherence of the message is not a mere momentary collocation of detail, but the expression of the life history of the individual in his relationship to the system of production. This diachronicity of the message makes it more than a simple image; the ensemble of attributes express truly predicative choices, so that although each presents itself ostensively, the effect of the whole can be expressed only by the temporalized predications of the declarative. In a society in which each individual presents himself to others as in effect an open-ended narrative, social relations can indeed be said to be dialectical: Each narration includes (and rejects) all the others, but is always subject to their influence.

If we have claimed that the most significant creation of the industrial era was the conception of the individual life as a *career*, this is because in thus orienting the individual toward the fulfillment of his worldly mimetic desires within the system of production rather than toward their transcendence, the "bourgeois" exchange system made the decisive advance in its age-long rivalry with religious ritual as the central institution in society. The exchange value of a career in status and income is a compensation for services rendered the society as a whole. But the presence of income and status differences, although satisfying the desires of the few for what is effectively a central position in communal presence, at the same time generates a vast resentment in the many. The social thinkers of the nineteenth century were divided in their interpretation of the balance sheet of such socially generated desires. But whereas the relative rigor of Marxism expressed the cruel realities of the age, only half-mad visionaries like Fourier were able to grasp—in however distorted a fashion—the ultimately unlimited capacity of modern society to offer an outlet for these desires.

Nineteenth-century capitalism was far from the "consumer society" of today, even if the familiar *artiste/bourgeois* opposition of the Romantic era already contains the germ of

the crucial distinction between posture and status. The art-
ist's posture was an original creation, copied only marginally
by the newly significant student class; its signs were the
products of handicraft, not of industrial production. In
today's world copies of Théophile Gautier's red vest would
be found in every department store. The emergence of a
system of product signs is the mark of a society in which the
old caste distinctions, perpetuated in early industrial society
in the sharp dichotomy between bourgeois and proletarian,
have been effaced. But at the same time, the association of a
signifying function with each consumer product is only one
aspect of the gradual rise to dominance of the communicative
function within the production process. This evolution is far
from consummated; all indications are rather that it is today
only in its earliest stages. But even at its present level,
information-processing has begun to dominate the application of energy to matter as the most important economic
activity. Such consequences of this development as the rise of
the "new middle class" or the usurpation of the capitalist's
corporate role by technically trained "experts" have been
widely discussed, for the most part in rather sinister terms.
But the direction of this evolution is already sufficiently clear
so that we may look beyond the present to a hypothetical
future of modern society—a hypothesis of the future being as
necessary to a general theory of representation as a hypothesis of the past, the ultimate destiny of representation being
the fulfillment of the possibilities inherent in its origin.

   Much has been made of the scarcity of economic goods,
although once the economy has passed the subsistence level,
scarcity is more a function of the exchange system than the
inverse. Scarcity exists relatively to desire; it is a function of
the nonidentity of real objects and their representations. To
the extent, then, that representations become themselves
significant factors in the economy, the domain of application
of the notion of scarcity must decline. If the productive
process is increasingly dominated by the production of information, then the hierarchical social relations founded on the
relative scarcity of objects of desire, measured in one-dimen-
sionally quantitative terms, must themselves be replaced by a
set of relations which reflect the indefinitely multi-dimen-

sional nature of representation. The postures described above are only available because the means exist to express them in the virtual presence of the community. But the expressivity of consumer products which makes them the vehicles for such postures is itself a function of supplementary signifying activities the cost of which relative to that of the basic product may be considered a measure of the relative importance of social communication as opposed to the "objective" functionality or "use-value" of the product-as-object. By "signifying activities" we refer, of course, to those related to the design and stylization of the product, but also to those of advertising and market research through which the product is assured a place in the sign system of consumption. And in this second category we should note that advertising costs are only secondarily those of the production of the message, but primarily a subsidy to the "media" that present it in association with cultural messages serving to reinforce its connotations. We may distinguish between luxury products, in which design is a function of "quality" and therefore of price, and those products accessible to the middle-income consumer which can enter into the messages of a large variety of status groups (including on occasion the wealthy themselves). The first category of products requires little advertising; its social functioning follows the Veblenian model of "conspicuous consumption" which reflects an essentially hierarchical set of social relations based on the linear criterion of wealth. The second category, on the contrary, involves a greater expenditure on advertising than on design, which is limited to a superficial stylization dictated by market conditions. But today the expansion of the sign system infiltrates even the hierarchical posture expressed by luxury items, so that if sixty years ago the relation between a Rolls-Royce and a Model T Ford was one of simple quantitative superiority, superiority in economic status is now considerably attenuated by horizontal differentiation between "life-styles."

Human and Discursive Temporality

If one asks the man on the street to name the source of religion, his most likely response will be the fear of death.

The fact that the individualized after-life of late medieval Christianity bears little resemblance to the various forms of transtemporal identification with the sacred found in documented primitive religions, and presumably still less to the original form of this identification, does not render this intuition less significant. Death as such is not a communal event, and it is inconceivable that the event celebrated in ritual could derive from the "natural" death of individuals; the attention paid in primitive religion to death in general should rather be seen as a product of its analogy with sacrifice. That death is never "natural" for primitive man is well-known; the disruption in the social order it occasions makes it, like puberty, a focal point of ritual. If modern man considers the disappearance of his individual self as the ultimate irrationality, the attitude toward death incarnated in the original event should be seen not as opposed to but as the primitive source of the modern intuition. This event, in our hypothesis, involves a passage from life to death witnessed by and participated in by the community as a whole. If we consider the body of the victim to be the first object to attract "non-instinctual attention," then rather than death appearing in human consciousness as a feared external force, it is in its first appearance a product of human activity. But the crucial moment of the event is not that of the death of the victim but that of the simultaneous renouncement by the murderers of appropriative aggression toward his remains. At that point the fear of each individual *for his own life* motivates the withdrawal from appropriative action that leads to the first signifying gesture. Representation is from the beginning separated from appropriation, and the representation from its referent, by the fear of death at the hands of one's fellows. We might say that representation is to appropriation as communal presence is to collective violence. Death becomes significant not as the real state of the victim but as an imaginary one for the participants. [3] Representation is thus a choice of life over death because it is first a choice of cooperation over confrontation. At the same time, representation has as its first object the dead victim of such a confrontation. In the ritual reproduction of the original event, the sacrificial victim is the central figure or "hero"; his death marks the end of the period of crisis and the beginning of nonviolent presence. In discourse as it emerges from ritual, the death of the hero, either real or "symbolic," serves as the catharsis, the revelation of his transcendental nature to esthetic contemplation having taken the place of the ritual participation in this nature through physical appropriation.

We have already remarked that the temporality of narrative discourse bears at best an analogous relationship to its referent, and that only as measured between temporally defined predicates. The question as to why such discourse remains effective in establishing an imaginary universe in its reader has not, however, been fully answered until now. The historical element of the answer comes from the original event, as mediated by ritual: Discourse operates within the temporal limits of the original crisis/resolution, which, whether it last a few hours or a few days, is of necessity extremely short in relation to the normal life span of its participants. Above all, the central moment of "non-instinctual attention" could not have been of long duration. The elaboration of ritual is less a prolongation of the critical moment than the addition to it of other episodes. Significance is thus originally a short-term phenomenon, which we may assume to follow more or less the time scheme of a drama, where the speeches of the characters occupy a real time of interaction.

Discursive catharsis, borrowed from the ritual form, is subject to the same limits. When narrative discourse replaces the final division of the sacrificial spoils, then the life and death of the victim-hero will be expressed in the narrative in the short-term temporality borrowed from ritual. As discourse becomes rationalized, and the violent collective component attenuated, the mythic "biography" of the hero, whether terminated by death or a symbolic substitute, remains bounded by these same temporal limits; the hero, as we find him, say, in Homer, has his "story" whose telling occupies a similarly brief period of time. For the hearer of the narrative, the concentration of the significant events of the hero's life span into these limits is a source of esthetic satisfaction. His submission to the desire induced by the "triangular" mediation of the Subject-narrator is dependent on these limits, and consequently on the fictional concentration of lived time that respects them. Death in the fictional context may be feared by the hero and, vicariously, by the hearer, but it is wholly motivated in that it is the source of catharsis. Fear of death is the source of representation, but at the same time it is "purged" by representation, wherein the hero's death corresponds to his acquisition of a transcendent status, beyond the reach of desire, from which he commands communal presence.

The decline of discourse in the modern era may be seen as the diminution of the power of the discursive catharsis to "purge" the fear of death. The career of modern man consists in a series of transcendences of desire taking place in lived time. To the extent that this career continues to hold forth the promise of attaining an ever more commanding position in communal presence, it can be said to function in lived time in the same way as a narrative fiction, the end of which is continually postponed. Evidently the vast majority of human careers do not long maintain such a promise; but neither can it be said that the decline of traditional discourse as the form of significant cultural expression corresponds to the simple disappearance of the esthetic narrative. The success of popular literature, cinema, and above all television with its unending proliferation of "series" of brief narrative-dramatic works demonstrates the vitality of discursive form on a level removed from that of the highest significance, and even those most sensitive to cultural values can scarcely help but "consume" such products. But the crucial difference with traditional culture is that the possibility of catharsis in real time has now been shown to exist. The transfer of significance from ritual to the worldly system of exchange corresponds to the abandonment of fictional for real time. The various "existential" philosophies, with their roots in the Judeo-Christian vision of each life as receiving its proper reward, find their common denominator in the problematic engendered by this abandonment, however much Heidegger's "being for death" may differ from Sartre's definition of transcendence in terms of worldly "projects." In the modern world all signifying phenomena, including in particular the consumptive signs of posture, occur in a *virtual* communal presence rather than the purely fictional one of discourse. Each individual is the bearer of a message virtually present to the entire society, and each such message expresses a diachronic relationship to the system of production which contains its own catharsis, that is, its conditions of fulfillment. But the diachrony of the message is that of life, so that "natural" death becomes its limit. The fear of death does not by any means disappear in the modern world, but it is integrated into the timetable of each individual's projected career, each step of which is meant to occupy a certain period of time determined by his expected life span.

The experience of an individual career in modern society cannot be expressed in a traditional discourse because its course cannot be known from within its own temporal span. The biographical model of the traditional narrative applies only to the dead, not the living. The discursive model that applies to a career still in progress is rather that of dialectic, each moment of which includes and transcends the totality of past moments. But the same is true for the totality of the domain of production, in which, through the agency of individual ambitions, old forms are constantly superseded by new. To the extent that the new forms produced are merely those of physical objects, the process of production may be described diegetically as one of technical progress, but, as we have seen, these objects are bearers of significations, and the process of their production is increasingly determined, not by the physical applications of energy to matter, but by the creation of new information on the basis of old.

The system of exchange as a whole may be represented as a vast and increasingly integrated dialogue in which all the members of society are continuously participating. This dialogue is, of course, an imaginary construct. But the study of social interaction in any specific domain is nothing but the creation of a regional model of this dialogue, reduced to its most significant elements. This characterization might at first appear so general as to be applicable to all societies and not merely to our own. But this is not the case. The dialecticality of any functional model of modern as opposed to traditional society is guaranteed by the ever-accelerating de-ritualization of human interactions wherein each party, rather than following preestablished norms, attempts to transcend his desire in the virtual presence established by the universal system of exchange. Where the totality of the significant actions of each member of society can be said to make up a career in which desire is at each step transcended and redefined through the creation of new representations, the interactions of any group of two or more individuals stand in a dialectical relation, the successes of each inspiring in the others an emulation that is not merely mimetic but creative and open-ended. The same dialecticity is found in consumption as in production—each new "message" is not merely the reflection of a predetermined posture but a redefinition of it in reaction to the messages given out by others. The proto-modern phenomenon of "fashion" is only a rudimentary example of this dialectic, one in which the newness of the message takes precedence over its expressive content. Conversely, the increasing specificity of this content in contemporary society makes each act of consumption which modifies the message express a modification in posture, so that the dialectical pressure toward originality in consumption increasingly becomes a redefinition of the individual's attitude toward the system of production as a whole, and thus of his career within this system.

The system of exchange is nothing but the totality of all significant social interactions, whether or not they actually involve the exchange of goods or services, because they all affect the market by modifying the value of the products available on it. A conversation in which a certain type of product or its content as a posture-sign is even implicitly either praised or ridiculed will have an effect on the demand for that product, and hence on its market value. We may note that this effect is not diminished but enhanced by oligopolistic or monopolistic conditions, large corporations being in a better position than small to diversify their products according to the expressive desires of their consumers. The system of exchange is thus immanent to social interaction, but at the same time it acts as a transcendent control over each specific interaction. This model is in essence that of Adam Smith, in which the "invisible hand" of the market consists merely of the combined effect of all its separate transactions. But its sphere of application in modern society cannot be limited even to the sum total of all product and service markets taken together, because it includes not only acts of buying and selling but the totality of social interactions. The Smithian market is a closed domain in which each act affects the whole and is virtually present to all, although only a few individuals may actually be aware of it. These economic acts are, so to speak, actualized representations, each of which attaches a monetary predicate to a particular product, the type of which is assumed to remain constant throughout the duration of the model. But if we expand this model beyond the strict confines of the market, the representations it includes are no longer limited to the assignment of monetary values.

The totalizing Smithian model is historically the first example of a rigorous construction of transcendence from immanence, and hence of a perfectly de-ritualized system of representation. But it is not dialectical, because it maintains a strict separation between topic and predicate, the first being fixed and the second merely quantitative. Our expanded model, on the contrary, reflects the dialectical relationship of the representations that compose it. The market proper remains the central institution in which the values of both men and their creations are determined, but increasingly the "topics" of evaluation are themselves representations evolved through the interaction of previous representations. Professional activity is increasingly the creation of representations exchanged for money in the marketplace, the individuality of these creations functionally differentiating their creator from others whose professional training may be virtually identical to his. The market value of each individual and each product is measured in money, which makes them commensurable like the goods in the Smithian model, but the interaction of the representations in which professional activity is realized and the representative function of products established makes these values increasingly interdependent with the entire tissue of social communication.

The traditional norms of ritual origin which served to regulate social interactions independently of the market's own mechanism, and which relied on religious ritual and esthetic discourse to purge the desires generated within them, are thus superseded by the regulatory action of the market. All social behavior takes place in virtual presence and is evaluated within it. This evaluation is given "objectively" in terms of market value, and subjectively in terms of the desire generated by each representation in its perceiver—the objective and the subjective values corresponding respectively to the social attributes of status and posture. The free play of subjectivity in posture, which we have described as a liberating, "dialectical" feature of modern social relations, is not simply a means of escape from the objective rigor of an increasingly rationalized and universalized marketplace. The *synchronic* esthetic effect of postures which allows them to interact in a "horizontal" dialogue of life-styles rather than in a vertical status-hierarchy always remains at least implicitly subordinate to their *diachronic* affirmation of their bearers' ultimate place in such a hierarchy, conceived not as an authority-structure but as an ordering of objective social values determined in the marketplace.

Posture, in a word, is a *deferral*, through representation, of the asymmetric relations of the market. By extending to the limits of a lifetime the originally brief period of deferral available through institutionalized forms of sacred and secular representation, the posture-system permits the individual a freedom—not absolute, certainly, but *maximal*—to explore possibilities not yet granted an objective value by the market.

Individual ambitions can thus oppose themselves temporarily to the objective status-system, cutting themselves off from commensurability until such time as their bearers have satisfied the exigencies of their own unique careers. But these careers, once they have been accepted within the market through the integration of their products (i.e., original representations), will be rewarded according to their real importance. This ultimate reward must always be the aim of any significant ambition realizable within the confines of a lifetime. The more marginal the career defined by it, the less directly it can be rewarded at its intermediate stages in the market. But in a universe with no institutionalized transcendent values founded on sacred rites or their discursive substitutes, this very marginality is a sign of ultimate faith in the exchange-system as the objective arbiter of the value of even the most original productions. What Herbert Marcuse condemns as the one-dimensionality of modern society is the all-encompassing, integrative force by which it approximates an immanent ethical realization of the transcendental Hegelian *Weltgeist*. What Marcuse and other "radical" descendants of Hegel lack is the courage to comprehend that it is the hated "bourgeois" market-system that represents the real triumph of dialectic.

The Theory of Representation as a Theory of Modernity

These considerations have taken us far from the formal evolution described in the preceding chapters. The dialectic of modernity, at the opposite end of the historical continuum from that of linguistic form, cannot be rigorously encompassed by a theoretical discourse that can at best contribute an awareness of its general orientation. But the scientific status of our theory of representation is not thereby weakened but strengthened. The de-ritualization of discourse is the source of its truth. Each stage in the dialectic of linguistic forms requires a lowering of the threshold of significance so that at first individual desire and then a model of reality contravening this desire may become acceptable in linguistic presence. With the emergence of the declarative form this phase of the dialectic of representation comes to an end, although the differential significance conferred by ritual in traditional society maintains the a priori dichotomy between profane and sacred representation. The de-ritualization of the modern world in conjunction with the universalization of its exchange system makes all such a priori dichotomies unnecessary, the relative significance of any two representations being hence forth determined by their power to operate on reality. The power of the theory of representation cannot be predetermined, but will emerge, not from its coherence as pure thought, but from its operability, direct or indirect, on the world of human experience.

What we have called the circularity of the historical process should not be taken as a cyclical constraint on its
freedom, but as the necessary form of its transcendence of its
original constraints. If we are only now able to construct a
scientific hypothesis of the origin of culture, it is because the
transcendental functions of culture have been sufficiently
returned to the immanence of social interaction so that the
historical specificity of the original event need no longer
provide for them an institutional guarantee. That is to say,
we may create a hypothetical model of the original event
because its reality is no longer functional. But this hypothesis
does not merely concern the time of origin. If we have
considered ourselves justified in calling it anthropological, it
is because man in general has been defined by the constraints
imposed by his origin. Because these constraints are the
origin of the representations by which he understands his
own behavior, the only possible liberation from them is
through the representation of this process of origination.

The social sciences as presently conceived study the operation of constraints within closed systems; their contribution
to human liberty is available only to those who stand outside
these systems. The paradox of self-inclusion which they face
is the result of their closure: Their theoretical discourse
cannot itself enter the systems whose operation it describes.
The dialectical model we have presented avoids this paradox
by explaining its own genesis from within the system it
represents, the genesis of the model being at the same time
the moment of liberation from it. But what practical effect,
it may be asked, can come from the mere announcement of
this liberation? Or more specifically, how can a hypothesis
concerning the origin of linguistic form be of significance to
modern man?

We have already made the claim that the theory of representation we propose gives for the first time a critical, non-
metaphysical basis to the human sciences, which can only on
this basis be characterized as scientific. But even if this claim
be accepted, one might still inquire as to the significance of
human science as thus conceived. The empirical studies to
which we have frequently alluded may lack an ultimate

epistemological foundation, but they are often of practical use in predicting and controlling behavior, and in any case provide a convenient locus for the accumulation of data, whereas the dialectic we have outlined has no direct method-ological link to empirical reality. Thus even if our theory be ultimately truer to the data than the social sciences as pres-ently constituted, one may still remain unconvinced that this truth, demonstrable only in hermeneutic fashion, is in any way *functional*.

In a society marked by a ritually justified hierarchy there exist cultural discourses that can be said to provide it with a mythical-esthetic basis. The norms of social interaction, fixed in ritual, are justified by myth; at the same time the desires generated by the representation of these norms are tran-scended or "purged" esthetically in literary discourse, which gradually distinguishes itself from myth as the norms become independent from ritual. The history of what we have called traditional society may be analyzed through its significant discourses, which express a given society's own perception of how its origins guarantee its continued existence; and in the context of a general theory of representation, the degree of truth present in each such perception can be ascertained. In modern society, however, there are no cultural discourses to perform this function aside from those of the social sciences themselves, which may become, as has been the case with Marxism, the founding myths of new societies, but which in the Western world remain in the background of a social consciousness generally lacking in a unified ideology. A nation like the United States is not lacking in shared princi-ples of social conduct or in significant documentary expres-sion of them, but there is no discourse or set of discourses which can be referred to by a majority of the members of American society as the basis for its culture. Strictly literary expression is no longer of great cultural significance, and the very notion of literature can no longer be uncritically ac-cepted. The self-consciousness of modern society may find its highest expression in the social sciences, but this self-consciousness is there viewed from without, a subjective attitude discovered through empirical means by a neutral, objective observer. The scientist's own views in such cases are not general statements of social self-consciousness at all, but conclusions concerning the objects of his study. In those cases where the discourse of the social sciences has a true programmatic content, the space in which suggestions are made is marginal to the structures within which they are to operate: An economist's plan for governmental action to reduce inflation or unemployment is meant to have only a marginal effect on the economic laws that regulate the market, so that an increase in the money supply or the discount rate will provoke predictable behavior in its participants. Nor are the (generally pessimistic) analyses of such phenomena as the "consumer society" ever depicted by their authors as themselves products of the society they condemn. Thus there is no privileged set of documents from which hermeneutics can seek to determine the level of self-consciousness of modern society. This should not surprise us, because ultimately even hermeneutics, by the fideistic nature of its conception of the significant, can be said to accept its subject matter from without. The only discourse that can fully express the ideology of the "critical" society of modernity must itself be critical or self-explanatory, that is, must in its very exposition be its own hermeneutic.

The claim of the theory of representation presented in this work to significance as the expression of the self-consciousness of our era may appear circular, because it is based on this theory's own definition of this self-consciousness. Our anthropological dialectic of representation is also a genetic sociology of modernity seen from within, which must guarantee by its present relevance the veracity of its originary hypothesis. The truth of our theory would thus be disconfirmed if it, or others of similar nature, should fail to exercise a profound influence not merely over the discourse of the social sciences in general but over modern society itself.

If we are asked, however, for a demonstration of this influence, we can only reply that the very characteristic which differentiates our own theoretical discourse from that current in the social sciences, that is to say, its dialectical nature, precludes any such a priori demonstration. If modern society is characterized by the essential dialecticality of its fabric of interactions which, because they take place essen-

tially on the plane of representation, are continually creating
new forms by the dialectical transcendence of the old, then
the place of our theory as itself an element in the social
dialectic cannot be known in advance. Because we have no
pretention of standing outside the society in which we function, our theory is an expression of our faith in this society's
capacity to generate and to accept its own truth. Thus
without predicting any specific practical application, we may
at least affirm that if this theory indeed merits a significant
place in the culture it describes, it can only serve to propa-
gate this faith among its audience. The neutrality of the
social sciences has from the beginning been tinged with
pessimism, the view from without always allowing itself the
Romantic luxury of a "tragically" unrealizable superiority to
its object. If this discussion has accomplished nothing else
than the discrediting of this Romantic myth, through which
the ghost of classical metaphysics continues to haunt the
epistemology of human science, its effect will already be
sufficient to guarantee a radical modification of the discourse
by which man attempts to understand himself.

Notes

1. In 1866 the newly founded Société Linguistique de Paris officially excluded from consideration any discussion of the subject.

2. See for example the essays contained in R. W. Westcott, ed., *Language Origins* (Silver Spring, Md.: Linstock Press, 1974).

3. V. our "Pour une esthétique triangulaire," in *Essais d'esthétique paradoxale* (Gallimard, 1977), first published in *Esprit* no. 11 (1973), as well as the forthcoming *Etudes girardiennes* (Grasset).

Chapter 1. Introduction

1. We shall make frequent reference in what follows to the theories expounded in Girard's major anthropological works, *La Violence et le sacré* (Paris: Grasset, 1972) and *Des choses cachées depuis la fondation du monde* (Paris: Grasset, 1978).

2. The definition of religion given by Durkheim makes social unity the result of a primordial separation: "A religion is a solidary system of beliefs and practices relative to things *sacred, that is, separated*, forbidden, *beliefs and practices which unite* in a single moral community, called a Church, all those who adhere to them" (*Les Formes élémentaires de la vie religieuse*, 4th ed., [PUF 1960], p. 65). But Durkheim's account of the origin of this separation itself is as abstractly "supplementary" as Rousseau's theory of the origin of language. Cf. ibid, p. 602-603: "For what defines the sacred is that it is added on (*surajouté*) to the real . . . Upon the real world where profane life takes place [man] *superposes* another which, in a sense, exists only in his thought, but to which he attributes, in relation to the first, a sort of higher dignity. It is thus, in a double sense, an ideal world." (Translation and emphasis ours.)

3. V. the review by G. de Radkowski: "[Girard] nous donne enfin la 'première théorie' réellement athée du religieux et du sacré," *Le Monde*, October 27, 1972.

4. "Le *Logos* de René Girard," in *Etudes girardiennes* (Editions Grasset, forthcoming).

5. These causal factors need not be dealt with here, because in any case the occurrence of quantitative differences is an inevitable result of the existence of a plurality of species. Of course, an anthropology of representation could be extended backward to an ethology or even a biology of mimesis, in which case the origins of mimesis would be dealt with, this time in the perspective of the natural sciences.

6. It is this attention which we shall call *presence*, that is, the presence of the group to itself as mediated by its common object.

7. The emergence of representation from the repetition of events possessing a distinct intentional structure is, as we might expect, paralleled in the emergence of theories of representation: These are always constructed from elements previously consciously intended but not yet wholly representable in the conceptual vocabulary of earlier theories. This parallel is only abstract as applied to incomplete theories; it applies concretely to that founded on the transcendental hypothesis, which can understand all previous theories as so many reproductions of the sacred forms of representation they purported to explain (or explain away), wherein the original object was thus reproduced but never fully *represented*. In this perspective the theories themselves appear as "events," responses to crises and, at least virtually, forms of presence.

8. *Des choses cachées depuis la fondation du monde*, p. 112.

Chapter 2. The Origin of Representation

1. The nature of the passage from appropriation to designation here outlined makes it unnecessary to postulate for it any specific object, such as in particular the body of the "emissary" victim. Thus one can imagine any sort of object so long as it has become the appropriative goal of a collectivity that has reason to fear its own violence. A formal analysis of representation does not require any further presuppositions. This does not, however, imply that we need not heed the specifics of the Girardian hypothesis, which account for the *content* of ritual and myth, nor that we need fear further refinements of this hypothesis. It is sufficient at this point to note that polemic concerning the details of the hypothetical event is no concern of the formal theory; any additional content supplied by the institutional theory beyond the minimum it requires is indifferent to it, because it merely postulates the ultimate independence of the representative form from this content.

2. We use this word here in a nonrigorous sense to denote an object of appropriative interest; the specific notion of desire as distinct from such interest will only be met with later.

3. V. in particular *La Voix et le phénomène* (PUF, 1967) and *De la grammatologie*.

4. We may include "semantic" paradoxes as a subgroup of the logical, the essential feature being not the theoretical level at which they are encountered—for it is a purely external matter, one affected by the conventions of logic, whether the antinomy arise as a result of "semantic" definitions or of those by which one constitutes "logical" operations—but the presence or absence of theory itself from the paradoxical situation.

5. This assertion should not be taken as reflecting a Marxist epistemology. The system of exchange becomes important as itself a machinery for generating and transcending desire only once it begins to generate its own representations, thereby usurping the functions of the sacred, described by Jean Baudrillard as "symbolic exchange." We will return to this question in our concluding chapter.

6. Because this dynamism is fundamental to the subsequent development of the formal theory, it may appear regrettable that a word so marginal as "paradox" must play so large a role in its exposition. Quite evidently, the existence of paradox, at least in this pragmatic sense, is vastly anterior to that of logic. But if we are indeed dealing here with matters "hidden since the foundation of the world," then we should not expect there to be names for them. The Greek παράδοξος means not only unexpected but admirable, miraculous; its etymological meaning of beside or contrary to the δόξα, which is not only expectation but received opinion, makes paradox occupy in Parmenides' system the same position as truth, the alternative to which is precisely the δόξα.

7. The evolution of ritual as such will not preoccupy us here. We may, however, raise the question of the necessity of maintaining the doctrine put forth by Girard of a strict hierarchy of ritual substitution, which he makes the cornerstone of his version of the "institutional" theory—the original event must have a human victim as its sacred object. Our own version of the hypothesis can perfectly well accommodate a nonhuman, or even inanimate "victim," because the essential characteristic of this "victim" is simply that it be subject to *sparagmos* by the participants and that its remains become a potential source of further conflict at a moment when the presence of the whole community arouses the universal fear of such conflict. That collective violence has at least the potential to lead to the murder of humans is indeed an essential element of the crisis, and it expresses itself in the collective fear that puts an end to it. But this fundamental charac-

teristic of human violence has no bearing on the identity of the sacred object. It would seem that Girard's reliance on this doctrine is founded less on its intrinsic indispensability to his theory than on the ease with which it permits him to avoid dealing with the phenomenon of representation in the original event. For if the original victim is human, then *identification* with the victim on the part of the participants in his murder can appear to take the place of *representation* of the "victim"-object as the source of communal presence. But as we have attempted to demonstrate, only the gesture of representation can communicate the "non-instinctive" renouncement of violence among the members of the group, and in any case "identification" is hardly an unambiguous sign of the human, as the widespread identification with "totems" of various sorts clearly demonstrates.

8. The ethical question touched on in the preceding paragraphs cannot be neglected in any formulation of a vision of history. If we have been obliged in the present work to severely limit the scope of such considerations, this does not reflect a desire to minimize their importance as matters for scientific, or more precisely, human-scientific analysis, but rather a conviction that the governing methodology of such analysis must be grounded on an adequately formalized theory of representation. And the primary material from which this theory is to be developed can only be that of language. The facility with which language lends itself to formal analysis provides an obvious heuristic reason for taking this path, but a theory with any pretentions to the name of "science" cannot content itself with heuristic reasons. Rather than attempting at this point to determine the "real" reasons, which should rather emerge from our elaboration of the theory itself, we may simply invert the logical order of the previous statement—something that would be possible within the context of a satisfactory theory, but which at this preliminary stage can only be done as a "wager" in the Pascalian sense—and claim that the greater tractability of language to the enterprise of formalization is itself a proof of its ontological anteriority. The chapters that follow will constitute our attempt to demonstrate the validity of this position.

Chapter 3. The Elementary Linguistic Forms

1. The clearness of the distinction between unarticulated signal and articulated word is not put into question by the possibility that a specific enunciation may consist of a mixture of both. The act of speech has a duration that, in the case of articulated words—those that are explicitly mediated by intersubjective presence—is simply "deferred," the duration of the speech act being considered by both parties as irrelevant, because the presence in which it takes place is experienced

outside of real time. But this duration is real nonetheless, and it can always become voluntarily or involuntarily a locus of further speech acts. Thus the fact that an "ouch!" can be prolonged into an unarticulated cry merely demonstrates that intentionality can be modified, or in the narrow sense, be terminated, in the course of the act of communication. The pertinence of the distinction is not eliminated—on the contrary—by its realization within the act.

2. Examples of the dead/living dichotomy are readily available within the domain of linguistics proper: Thus the ending "-en" signifies the plural in "children" and "oxen," but it cannot be applied by analogy to new words, as can the "living" ending "-s."

3. This is by no means to say that no knowledge was conveyed by the sign. We will use the term "information" in the narrow sense of information concerning the real-world referent of representations, because this content corresponds to the intention of the representation constituted as a model of the real world. The structures of desire that are the dynamic factor in the evolution of linguistic forms are not, of course, limited in their operation to this informational element, which conversely is exclusively important in the detemporalized forms of scientific-logical discourse. To the extent that our own discourse pretends to scientific status, our discussion of language would be inconsistent were we not to consider the pure transmission of information as its highest goal. It should however be noted that our notion of information is not reducible to the quantitative measures of "information theory."

4. The reader may consult the provocative volume of Trân Duc Thao, *Recherches sur l'origine du langage et de la conscience* (Paris: Editions Sociales, 1973), pp. 94-103, for a hypothesis concerning the elaboration of the lexicon of an "original" gestural language. This author perceives the primordiality of the gesture of designation as the first linguistic sign. But because, as befits a dialectical materialist, he situates this act in a *practical* context, he cannot satisfactorily found the distinction between instinctive and intentional designation. Lacking the moment of "non-instinctual attention," Trân must fall back on phenomenological solipsism to ground the intentional relation to the object upon the act of *designating the object to oneself* ("le sujet . . . s'indique l'objct à lui-même," p. 18). Thus the most apparently "communal" philosophy of human conduct, because it fears the *absolute* communal power of the sacred, must construct its theory of signification upon the intuitions of the isolated individual. Here as always, the sacred retains its power over those who remain blind to its originary status within the "social" dialectic.

5. The desire to reduce to naught the specifically human, and thereby to assimilate the social to the natural sciences, often thus

makes scientists correspond to the caricatural evolutionists of the Scopes trial. But it is not on the basis of such sacrifices that science can become a worthy substitute for religion. The science we are here proposing prefers to seek man's redemption in his historical future rather than in his "natural" past; sacrifice is thus assimilated to the irreversible work of time.

6. The Greek word σῆμα, which means both tomb and sign, evidently finds its raison d'être in this practice. The sacred tomb appears not so much as the "signified" of the sign as its *being*, the incarnation in the real world of its status in the lexicon of the *langue*, of which the designative "word" is a realization in the *parole*.

7. In our hypothetical scenario this preservation unfortunately occurs post mortem; but the existence of "sacrificial" rituals in which the victim is not killed, and on occasion even honored, indicates that—as we observed in the case of the victim's human rather than animal status—the murder of the sacred victim is not an essential feature of the process. Here again, of course, Girard's exposition groups such phenomena under the rubric of sacrificial substitution. We state again that, although this categorization may well be empirically correct, it is in any case not ontologically necessary. The *possibility* of *this* murder, founded on the reality of other murders in the crisis situation, is the only indispensable element of the hypothesis.

8. It is not without significance that traditional linguistics, as a result of its bias toward the declarative sentence, has never bothered to include the ostensive in its hierarchy of forms, although it undoubtedly exists in all languages. (See esp. chap. 5.)

9. The role of apprenticeship is instrumental not merely on every level of the formal evolution here described, but in the phenomena of linguistic change traditionally discussed by linguists. The child's difficulties with certain sounds, forms or constructions lead to phonetic, morphological or syntactic adaptation, all of which, of course, interact. (For example, the phonetic changes of medieval French led to the confusion of the various endings of the preterit, derived from the Latin conjugations, and thus the young language learners of the cities, fearful of error, abandoned the preterit for the regularity of compound past, whereas in rural areas less concerned with correctness a simplified preterit form was retained. [We owe this example to A. Martinet.]) More significant are the similar effects of intergenerational transmission on the higher forms of representation; the once-familiar organic metaphors of cultural history are both justified and condemned by this phenomenon. Certain forms (we might call them the "romantic" ones) even present themselves explicitly as nonreproducible. No adequate theory of the dialectic of representation can neglect this question.

Hegel's dialectic, which is presented as a pure interaction of ideas within an immortal spirit, can only deal with the generational aspect obliquely in typological portraits (master and slave, unhappy conscience, the "beautiful soul," etc.) which have significantly enough remained its least perishable part.

10. This fact concerning linguistic form per se, irrespective of what in Hjelmslev's terminology would be called the "substance of the expression," would at first glance appear to imply that language at this stage was chiefly if not wholly verbal, because the obvious pointing gesture could scarcely be absent from a gestural ostensive, and would, conversely, only be possible in those cases of the imperative where the desired object is in view of the speaker. But one could just as easily assume that it was precisely such cases that led to the origin of the imperative; its differentiation from the ostensive would proceed in the same fashion in either case.

11. Our discussion of modification and negation (and of "operators," or sentence modifiers in general) has been postponed for heuristic reasons to the following chapter.

12. One would hope, of course, that these ramifications, however considerable, would result in the diminution of the huge volume of analysis currently being produced without the benefit of an overall theory on the basis of which levels of significance might be established. Thus, until quite recently, linguistic publications were filled—and still are, on occasion—with forty- and fifty-page papers concerned with obscure problems of pronominalization of subjects in subordinate clauses, etc. The recent trends of speech-act theory and the study of universals are in this regard most welcome.

13. Such serial utterances are indeed made by children at the "one-word" stage. V. L. Bloom, *Language Development: Form and Function in Emerging Grammars* (Cambridge, Mass.: MIT Press, 1970), p. 10.

14. What is lacking even at this level in the behavioral model is an understanding of the sense of *designation*, which is not at all the same as association. Thus the psychologists, when teaching "language" to their rats, normally let their pupils "associate" by trial and error the word with its meaning, whereas humans teach language by pointing. It is distressing to read of sentences being uttered in the "presence" of their subject matter as though children learned to speak by associating sentences or even words merely with the "presence" of objects rather than being shown unambiguously what is being referred to. Designation is, as we have seen, the origin of human language and, except in artificially created situations, it is not carried out among animals. The same holds true for animal "speech" as for language-learning: The rat in pressing its lever is not merely "associating" this gesture with the

presence of the cat but in fact designating its presence, and thus in effect performing an extra-specific ostensive. It is curious that although the experimenter by his reward system teaches the rat that his gesture *means* cat, rather than simply being "associated with" its presence, his theory postulates that his own language-learning took place by mere association. But how without the benefit of a divine "experimenter" human beings ever learned that words *designate* their objects rather than simply being "associated with" them is never satisfactorily explained, no doubt because the Humean heritage of experimental psychology (and its ignorance of phenomenology) makes it easy to see designation and association as functionally synonymous.

Chapter 4. The Origin of the Higher Linguistic Forms

1. This scene could be made more realistic if we suppose rather that the ostensive remark is learned in advance as a *cue* by the model, who will present herself on hearing the words "This is our summer creation," or something of the sort. Such refinements only add confirmation to our basic point, because an "imperative" cue is scarcely a speech act at all, the real linguistic communication being made to the buyer.

2. The elaborate social forms by which the speaker does indeed "present himself" in certain surroundings, far from disproving this assertion, pay homage to its accuracy, in the same way that the custom of wearing clothes is not a sign that the human body is without power in social contexts, but of the opposite. The polite forms "clothe," in effect, the naked force of the speech act.

3. A *recursive* understanding of the schema, that is, an awareness of its continued applicability to each contribution to the cultural dialogue, including our own, is characteristic not of metaphysics but of what we shall describe below as *dialectic* (see chapter 6). This understanding alone justifies our preceding attribution to language, despite the asymmetric nature of the communication situation, of the capacity for becoming scientific.

4. The "collective imperative" discussed above might appear to invalidate this assertion. Yet without even considering its association with the mob rather than the community, it is never the expression of a prima facie communal need, but of a specific desire which may at best be construed as the result of a *decision* as to the nature of communal need. ("Need" is opposed to desire here not, of course, as natural to cultural but as social to individual: The need of the community is what it requires in order to remain a community. Thus the ostensive may be said to express "needs" since it designates objects of a priori *communal* significance.) When a collective imperative can be said truly to express need rather than desire, and thus to approximate the ostensive as an

immediate expression of significance, this need is always "mass" rather than collective, that is, the sum of the several individual needs (for example, a group of men lost in the desert crying "Water!" are not collectively but individually thirsty). And this is because of the difference in the intentional structures of the two forms. The ostensive is already lexicalized as a collective need, and any vagueness in the lexicalization is made up for by the presence of the significant object; the imperative cannot refer spontaneously to an absent object of collective need unless the individuals involved all experience it individually. These examples are merely illustrative, not probatory, for ultimately it is not the nature of the objects themselves but of the respective intentional structures of the ostensive and the imperative that determines their classification as objects of need or desire.

5. Or in the case where it is precisely a linguistic performance that is requested, this awaiting does not treat it as an independent intentional structure.

6. The cry "man overboard!" is a similar, less ambiguous example.

7. We do not mean to imply here that "thought" is impossible without language; wordless images are no doubt sufficient for an elementary level of manipulation (e.g., Kohler's apes). We are looking forward here to the development of the higher forms of linguistically based thought, rather than backward to the prelinguistic capacities of the proto-human brain. In this regard negation represents precisely the archetype of an operation dependent on the existence of language, because outside of a formal system of representation it is impossible to conceive of a meta-phenomenon such as negation being "presented" or "imagined" as part of the same model as its (negated) content. This point will be developed further in what follows.

8. Thus in a well-known paper ("On Declarative Sentences," in R. Jacobs and P. Rosenbaum, *Readings in English Transformational Grammar* [Waltham, Mass.: Ginn, 1970], pp. 222-272), J. Ross claimed, on the basis of a motley selection of examples, that an abstract equivalent of the words "I say to you that" is contained in the "deep structure" of declarative sentences in general, but simply "deleted" in the "surface phonological realization." We shall again touch on this hypothesis below, in order to extract the kernel of truth that it contains. We only cite it here as an example of the potentially infinite productivity of the notion of "ellipsis."

9. In this context "Don't" acquires a nuance of annoyance and even of irony from the fact that it is, unlike "No," a true imperative, and therefore not as pure an ellipsis as "No." This difference could be expressed formally by noting that "No" represents "No, you shouldn't (close the door)," whereas "Don't" stands for "Don't close the door,"

where the modal of the question is replaced by the auxiliary of the imperative.

10. Much of the preceding discussion applies equally well to other operators than negation. "Do that again!" or even "Again!" is parallel to "Don't (do that)!" and the same can be said for "operators of manner" like "Faster!" In all these cases the content absent from the linguistic model is supplied by the context, to which the operator refers as it were deictically. That the word "that" in these expressions does not suffice for deixis is clear by comparison with the declarative: "John is doing that" requires, if not a previous linguistic model (in which case it is an ellipsis), a deictic gesture toward some present phenomenon, whereas "Do that again" does not.

Chapter 5. The Declarative

1. We retain the term "verbal" to designate substantive verbal forms which function as nouns. These forms, in our hypothesis, were the original ones, those found in ostensive and imperative language. The participles and infinitives that function as verbals in modern languages do not of course necessarily reveal this historical priority in their morphology.

2. V. Charles Li, ed., *Subject and Topic* (New York: Academic Press, 1976), especially "Topic, Pronouns and Grammatical Agreement" by T. Givon (pp. 149-188).

3. We might hazard the "Whorfian" hypothesis that, if Western languages shared the topic-comment form of Chinese, the growth of Western scientific discourse, based as it is on the rigor of the subject-predicate connection, might have been hampered. The corollary to this hypothesis, that Chinese and related languages would be more likely to become the vehicles of a truly historical-temporal human as opposed to natural science, has not, of course, been borne out. But perhaps in the evolution of scientific discourse the detemporalized must precede the temporal, and the second (subject→topic) leg of the cycle holds the key to the understanding of the whole.

4. *Aspects of the Theory of Syntax* (Cambridge, Mass.: MIT Press, 1965), p. 137; *Topics in the Theory of Generative Grammar* (The Hague: Mouton, 1966), p. 65, which continues "all information relevant to the operation of the interpretative syntactic component should be contained in the generalized phrase-marker generated by base rules."

5. The post-*Aspects* evolution of transformational grammar has followed this pattern of "deepening" the deep structure (see for example R. Lees' article "On Very Deep Grammatical Structure" in Jacobs & Rosenbaum, *Readings in English Transformational Grammar*, pp. 134-144). This ideal was expressed by Chomsky in *Aspects*, p. 117:

To say that formal properties of the base will provide the framework for the characterization of universal categories is to assume that much of the structure of the base is common to all languages. This is a way of stating a traditional view, whose origins can again be traced back at least to the *Grammaire générale et raisonnée* (Lancelot et al., 1660). To the extent that relevant evidence is available today, it seems not unlikely that it is true. Insofar as aspects of the base structure are not specific to a particular language, they need not be stated in the grammar of this language. Instead, they are to be stated only in general linguistic theory, *as part of the definition of the notion "human language" itself*. In traditional terms, they pertain to the form of language in general rather than to the form of particular languages, *and thus presumably reflect what the mind brings to the task of language acquisition* rather than what it discovers (or invents) in the course of carrying out this task [emphasis added].

Thus like the Port-Royal grammarians, Chomsky finds the structure of the declarative sentence etched, if not in nature itself, at least in our brains.

    6. This is the case in the Givon article mentioned earlier (v. note 2 above), as well as in all of W. Labov's sociolinguistic analyses, where, however, intentionality is generally restricted to the phonological level (but see his study of story telling in *Language in the Inner City*, [Philadelphia: University of Pennsylvania Press, 1972], ch. 9, pp. 354-376). Many other texts in such collections as Li's *Subject and Topic, Word Order and Word Order Change* (Austin: University of Texas Press, 1975), etc. could also be cited here; but in no case, to our knowledge at least, has an attempt been made to derive the intentional structure of the declarative sentence from more primitive forms.

    7. V. "Pour une esthétique triangulaire," in *Essais d'esthétique paradoxale*.

    8. The cave-painting case illustrates the impossibility of purely formal consideration of nonlinguistic forms; these paintings, whatever their relationship to the individual desire of the painters, almost certainly had a ritual, and therefore *institutional* function. Hence the participation of the appearance of the animal representations in the being of these animals was not simply mediated by an esthetic judgment (in the Kantian sense), but by this communal function, which accorded to them a conventional "symbolic" value. Lacking, as we do, any knowledge of the institutional function of these paintings, we are unable to arrive at an understanding of the intentional structure they express. The same would not be the case for samples of primitive language, if we in fact possessed them.

    9. V. Mary L. Pratt's persuasive arguments in *Toward a Speech-Act Theory of Literary Discourse* (Bloomington: Indiana University Press, 1977). The ease with which the author, although presenting no very noteworthy theories of her own, demolishes the doctrines of the renowned twentieth-century formalists is less reminiscent of the story

of David and Goliath than of that of the emperor's new clothes. Like M. Jourdain, the speaker of "ordinary language" suddenly discovers that he has indeed been speaking "prose" all his life, when he thought he was only conveying information.

Chapter 6. Dialogue and Discourse

1. In a ritual context, where no practical information is transmitted, the hierarchy of the questions may, of course, be established rigorously in advance. But precisely because of the "informationless" nature of ritual, its rigor remains purely formal rather than being a hard-won abstraction from the relations empirically discovered in the interaction of (interrogative) form and (predicative) content. The hierarchies of ritual, in this example as in general, are never truly de-temporalized, because predictability is not a function of correct anticipation of real possibilities but simply of sacralized repetition. Thus ritual dialogue, and the ritual use of language in general, is not a direct precursor of scientific discourse. We shall see presently that this sacred/secular dichotomy does not hold true for temporalized ("literary") discourse.

2. P. Watzlawick, J. Beavan & D. Jackson, *Pragmatics of Human Communication* (New York: Norton, 1967).

3. Thus we may speak of the *forms* of life, which manifest certain structural possibilities (e.g., of DNA, of adaptation to given environmental conditions, etc.), but can hardly be said to "express" them.

4. Here we are not, of course, taking into account the mediating role of Christ, because the functioning of Protestant ritual, in this particular domain at least, is independent of this role.

5. Thus the hermeneutical study of cultural discourse (in a "historical" perspective) goes hand in hand with the construction of the social sciences on the de-temporalized model of the natural sciences. Human time having been expelled a priori from "science," it can only maintain its existence in the *esthetic* pathos of historical discourse.

6. Girard is not indeed insensitive to the circularity of the general evolution of discourse, which alone can explain the pertinence of his own. But because this movement is in fact incompatible with his theoretical presuppositions, he finds himself obliged to explain it as the result of a providential revelation within the Judeo-Christian tradition, culminating in the figure of Christ, whose liberation from original violence and concomitant understanding of the purely human nature of communal presence is affirmed to be explicable only through divine intervention. This is not the place to engage in polemics on this subject; we need merely note that the invocation of providence here to guarantee the closure of the historical evolution of discourse and of culture in general is at the very least a demonstration that the institutional theory is unable to accomplish this task on its own merits.

7. We may reiterate here that the rigor of this progression, which is indispensable to the institutional theory because it holds ritual to be always the primary, if not the only form of representation of the origin, need not be affirmed by the formal theory, where the sacred object is from the beginning representable outside the ritual context. Or in other terms, if the original victim is represented from the beginning by a *word*, then the human or animal identity of his sacrificial substitute does not necessarily reflect any particular degree of information loss with respect to the original event.

8. We are here obliged unavoidably to simplify the terms of the formal-institutional debate; Girard treats this "contradiction" as a bifurcation expressed historically by the opposition between the Greek tradition, which takes the path of myth, and the Judeo-Christian, which incarnates the moral evolution. From the perspective we are here defending, such historical oppositions are irrelevant because the divine "election" of either path of de-ritualization is not a requirement of our theory.

9. Thus criticism unavoidably affirms both the originality and the historical inevitability of its object. The demonstration of this could be conducted on the basis of examples from even its most banal varieties; but this would require another work.

10. *Oedipus Rex* is no doubt the most striking illustration of this phenomenon, although it is everywhere present, notably in the *agon* of Aristophanean comedy.

11. The refinements of ritual in higher religions make this statement only residually true, for example, of the Eucharistic "sacrifice" of the Mass. These rituals are indeed no more temporally analogous to the original event than the various forms of narrative or dramatic discourse. But if we ask what has replaced in these modern rituals the reproductive activity of the more primitive forms, we find that it is discourse itself: the reading and singing of prayers, and particularly, the reading of a sacred narrative. Prediscursive ritual could only consist of actions, and the order of these actions, at least in its major divisions, would have no other model than the original event with which it is in our hypothesis continuous.

12. The "atomic hypothesis" is a metaphysical, not a scientific doctrine, expressing the ultimate knowability of the real world. It is curious that despite the continuing discoveries concerning the infrastructure of the atom, physicists still speak of "elementary particles," as though anything but the present state of their instruments gave them reason to believe them in some absolute sense "elementary."

13. Thus twentieth-century economic doctrines (e.g., Keynesian theory) can be said to differ essentially from their nineteenth-century counterparts precisely by their intentional *applicability* to the market

situation. The prototype of such "applicable" doctrines, in economics and in the social sciences in general, is no doubt to be found in the work of Karl Marx, not that he lacked either precursors or contemporaries with similar "scientific" intentions.

14. "A review of B. F. Skinner's *Verbal Behavior*," in *Language*, 35, 1 (1959), 26-58.

15. This point, like a number of other relevant criticisms of Chomsky's "intuitionist" approach, has been made by W. Labov in *Sociolinguistic Patterns* (Philadelphia: University of Pennsylvania Press, 1972), chapter 8, pp. 183-259, esp. pp. 185-202.

16. The well-known text of D. McNeill, "Developmental Psycholinguistics" (in F. Smith & G. A. Miller, eds., *The Genesis of Language: a Psycholinguistic Approach* [Cambridge, Mass: MIT Press, 1966]) is exemplary of the Chomskian position in its interpretation of pre-declarative utterances.

17. That this situation may be gradually coming to an end is indicated by the recent researches of Gordon Hewes and others, in which the origin of language has been restored to its original status as an *anthropological* problem, although not yet in the context of a formal theory of representation such as is offered here. See especially R. W. Wescott, ed., *Language Origins* (Silver Spring, Md.: Linstock Press, 1974), which contains an article by Hewes ("Language in Early Hominids," pp. 1-34).

18. We are here referring to narration as the first form of discourse unambiguously separable, even if not yet separate, from its ritual context. The "lyric" evocations of the divinity may be said to constitute an even more primitive recognition of the "dialectical" identity of victim and sacred object—that is, in becoming rather than being. But within ritual, a series of evocations, even in different "names," cannot possess an esthetic unity of its own. Indeed, following this line of reasoning one step further, ritual could be construed as a kind of drama, and thus as full-fledged discourse from the beginning. But if we reject this analysis then we should equally well reject the other. Each stage of the introduction of language into ritual can no doubt be said to provide it with a greater explicative potential, as well as with a more dialectical esthetic. But only the last may actually be opposed to ritual itself as an *explanation* of the origin, which is demonstrated by the fact that it is the first stage to produce a discursive form capable of independent development. Of course, in the looser sense in which ritual too may be thought of as an "explanation," because at the very least it understands the necessary presence of the victim, the introduction of the ostensive-imperative form and the naming of more than one stage in the victim's career can be said to present an improvement in understanding. Provided that we do not confuse this development with the

creation of lyric discourse, there is no harm in referring to this proto-discursive stage as preliminary to, if not directly productive of, the explanation of the origin provided by narrative discourse. For we must again insist on the extra-ritual nature of the dialectic of linguistic form, whithout which discourse could not have emerged within ritual.

19. This "rationalization" might seem to be already present in the original event, at least in the version of the hypothesis given by Girard, and it is certainly a feature of many rituals. But in the original event the very notion of a *crime* against the not yet existing community would have been inconceivable; the concentration of aggression on a single victim could just as easily be triggered by an "arbitrary" distinguishing feature, such as a deformity, which makes him particularly vulnerable to attack.

20. Or its ritual one, insofar as, for the theoretician, if not for its participants, ritual could be considered as itself a virtual discourse—as its own myth, or, more precisely, as its own drama.

21. The lack of rigor becomes apparent if we seek to understand in what sense a rigorously synchronic relation between a sign and its signified could be anything but arbitrary. Even if the sign were an iconic representation of its object, this fact is itself diachronic because the object must exist before the picture; without the knowledge of this derivation the signifying relation would be indeed unmotivated. But it is inconceivable, of course, that, say, a hieroglyphic sign for "cow" which consisted of a drawing of a cow *not* be thought of as diachron-ically derived. "Motivated" as opposed to "unmotivated" signs only appear less arbitrary because they carry with them a guarantee of their diachronic relation to their object, which is lost in the latter case. There are many historical examples of stylization in which this loss can itself be diachronically observed, the most obvious being that of the "hieroglyphs" that today constitute the various alphabets of the world.

Chapter 7. A Perspective on Modernity

1. This is not to belittle the considerable advances made by the historians of the last two decades (in particular those of the *Annales* group in France) in the direction of rigor, even if it be the rigor of the social sciences. The replacement of the historical fable by a proto-sociology makes the past relevant to the present, if only through its geographic and demographic continuity. At the same time, these more rigorous methods, even if they succeed in pushing the frontiers of systematic sociology back to the Middle Ages and beyond, will not of themselves elevate history above the narrow empiricism of the soci-ologists, lacking as they generally are in anthropologically grounded hypotheses concerning human society.

2. See especially *Le Système des objets* (Paris: Gallimard, 1968), *La Société de consommation* (Paris: S.G.P.P., 1970).

3. Here again our analysis makes the murder as such a less significant feature of the original event than in Girard's exposition, where it is the death of the victim that by identification puts an end to the mimetic rivalry of the others. But this death cannot be identified with by its perpetrators; the murder serves only to focus their aggressive activities into an as yet unreflective cooperation, and thus creates a time span in which they are as individuals no longer in danger from the others. It is the renewal of this danger that is prevented by the original gesture of representation.